GOODBYE TO THE MEMORANDUM

An in-depth study of the standard
cargo, war, and strikes clauses

by

J. KENNETH GOODACRE, A.C.I.I.

Partner, Goodacre (Marine Claims Services)
Adjuster of Marine Claims to the Home and
Overseas Insurance Co. Ltd., 1958–68
Adviser to the Chartered Insurance Institute, 1975 –85
Chairman, U.K. Society of Average Adjusters, 1981–84

Author of

Marine Insurance Claims

York-Antwerp Rules, 1974
(contrasted with York-Antwerp Rules, 1950)

Collected Papers on Marine Claims

Institute Time Clauses – Hulls
(a comparison between the 1983 Clauses, and
the 1970 Clauses with subsequent amendments)

LONDON
WITHERBY & CO. LTD.
32–36 Aylesbury Street
London EC1R 0ET

III

Published 1988
1st Edition

ISBN 0 948691 41 7

Printed and published by
Witherby & Co. Ltd.
32-36 Aylesbury Street
London EC1R 0ET
TEL 01-251-5341
FAX 01-251-1296

Foreword

The title chosen by Mr. Kenneth Goodacre for this book is symbolic. In a few short years the "Memorandum" could have been forgotten were it not for Mr. Goodacre's work which expertly supplies the link between the old regime of cargo insurance documentation and the new. It is a timely record produced in the same decade in which the London Market has swept away the old policy and clauses, bravely casting itself adrift from much of the substantial body of English law which sometimes aided and sometimes confused their construction. The title is symbolic of this major step taken by the Market and of its enormous achievement in producing the new policy and clauses, which it can claim to have been highly successful, judging from practical experience of their use since they were introduced in 1982.

It was my good fortune to chair the hard-working sub-committee of the Technical & Clauses Committee which drafted the new Institute Cargo Clauses and Mr. Goodacre's book has stimulated memories of the lengthy but absorbing tasks of not only producing a radical revision of the clauses but also inventing new, clearly worded replacements for those essential provisions which were to be lost with the abolition of the S.G. Policy Form. Perhaps it is permissible to conclude from this book, with considerable satisfaction bearing in mind the skill and knowledge of its author, that the results of those labours in general meet with his approval. Mr. Goodacre rightly refers to the influence of the UNCTAD report of November 1978 in helping to bring about the radical change in London Market attitudes but, again rightly in my opinion, he does not over-emphasise the influence of UNCTAD, whose report, although admirably put together, did not in fact tell the Market anything it did not already know. It is not always appreciated that a revision of the Institute Cargo Clauses had by then been set in motion and it had already been perceived that the time was ripe for that revision to be carried out in some depth. Perhaps UNCTAD can be credited with having helped to tip the balance in favour of the abolition of the S.G. Policy Form, but the

Market's new cargo clauses actually presented far more fundamental changes than were recommended by the UNCTAD Secretariat in their report, including the complete abandonment of the time-honoured concepts of "W.A." and "F.P.A.", taking with them into obscurity the Memorandum, the demise of which is celebrated by the title of this book. It must surely be true to say that it is much simpler now for the practitioner to master what Mr. Goodacre aptly calls the "ABC of cargo insurance".

Mr. Goodacre's treatment of his subject, unlike that of many text-book writers, makes his books by comparison eminently readable, and the form which this volume takes, comprising as it does a series of articles, the first fourteen of which were published in the "Post Magazine", gives it an exceptionally easy style so that it can be read comfortably and agreeably from cover to cover. This welcome quality does not in any way detract from the technical merit of the work, and it will be of great value as a uniquely penetrating examination of the new cargo clauses and their associated war and strikes clauses. I am sure, however, that the reader will appreciate the author's obvious appetite for a good story, and will be tempted to explore with him the events which surrounded the arrival in the Thames in January 1878 of "Three-Finger Jack" with "Cleopatra's Needle" in tow. There is an illustration from the Bible of an early general average sacrifice, and the question "When is a riot not a riot?" is dealt with at length, including a most interesting and comprehensive survey of the relevant cases on that subject, the most recent reference being to Mr. Justice Staughton's judgment in the "Andreas Lemos" case in 1982.

This is a thoroughly researched work of particular interest at this time. It is an important chronicle of a major development in cargo insurance and it will be of great value as a work of reference.

Alan J. Birch, A.C.I.I.
Marine Claims Manager,
Sun Alliance Insurance Group.

Author's Preface

In 1984, at the invitation of Miss Jenny Harris, who was editor of the *Post Magazine* at the time, I was prompted to produce some contributions on a number of topical issues. After a while, however, I found myself irresistibly drawn to the subject of the new cargo clauses, which, to my mind, had only been dealt with in a rather limited manner by contemporary writers.

The abandonment of the old standard marine policy — the S.G. Form — was, of course, one of the most momentous events of our times, and those of us who witnessed the transformation to a new system of insuring goods in the London market, could not fail to be impressed by the awesome task, which was finally completed in January, 1982, on publication of the revised clauses. Because of its importance, therefore, I felt it would be a pity if the reasons for the changes, the comments of leading practitioners of the day, and the views and suggestions of U.N.C.T.A.D. (who were instrumental in providing the stimulus for the "revolution") were not fully recorded.

My primary object was, therefore, to produce a series of articles to show how the *Memorandum* operated and why it was dropped; to explain the differences between the "A", "B" and "C" Clauses; and to elaborate on the clauses which had been introduced or radically altered. This was achieved by publication of fourteen articles in the *Post Magazine* between July 1985 and November 1986.

It soon became clear from the questions raised by readers that a more comprehensive guide would be welcome, and I have been inspired to conduct an examination of the more established clauses in a similar journalistic style, and also to engage in a detailed study of the operation of the war and strikes perils in the context of the present formula.

The overall result has, consequently, turned out to be something of a history of the development of the clauses, combined with an analysis of how the existing case law seems to be appropriate to the current wordings.

Newcomers to the market, and future generations, will soon become used to the new, more simplified, system, and yet will still have recourse to the phraseology in old but tested situations in order to understand the meaning and practical application of many of the terms now in use; accordingly, I have made a point of indulging in a review of some of the clauses of the bygone era (such as the *Sue and Labour Clause*, and the *Free of Capture and Seizure Warranty*) which form an important background to present day study. I hope that in this way the book will prove of value both to students and experienced practitioners alike.

In examining certain aspects of the new clauses I am conscious that I may be raising some controversial issues, particularly in areas where the American Courts have decidedly different ideas to our own. Nevertheless, I am fortified by the words of Lord Goff who, in delivering his judgment in the House of Lords in the case of the *Spiliada* [1987] 1 Lloyd's Rep. 18, paid tribute to the writings of certain jurists by saying:

> "They will observe that I have not agreed with them on all points; but even when I have disagreed with them, I have found their work to be of assistance. For jurists are pilgrims with us on the endless road to unattainable perfection; and we have it on the excellent authority of Geoffrey Chaucer that conversations among pilgrims can be most rewarding."

I am, naturally, very grateful to the *Post Magazine* for their permission to reprint the articles which form the first part of this volume.

J. K. Goodacre
London, January 1988.

Contents

Index of Cases Cited

XV

XVII

Chapter 1

GOODBYE TO THE MEMORANDUM (1)

With the adoption of new clauses in 1982, cargo policies no longer contain the famous "Memorandum". In a series of three articles, the author traces the rise and fall of this peculiar "average clause" and here investigates some of its early development.

A landmark was reached in the history of marine insurance in this country when, at a general meeting held at the Royal Exchange on 12th January 1779, a standard policy form was agreed by Lloyd's Underwriters. It was soon adopted by both the Lloyd's and Company markets, becoming known as the "S.G." Form because of the letters which were shown at the top of the form.

The letters are commonly accepted as referring to ship and goods, the form being couched in such language as to make the policy applicable to every marine adventure, thus, when the Marine Insurance Act was passed in 1906, it was shown as a recommended document in the first schedule, together with certain Rules for Construction.

Similar forms of policy had been in existence since the early 17th century, consequently it could be said that there was some benefit in adhering to a form of words which produced some certainty as to the meaning and effect of the contract of insurance, so that it would represent the intention of the parties — a most desirable factor in business transactions. The difficulty of keeping to such a standard wording, however, was that in times of progress and development, the terms employed became antiquated and unsuitable for modern commerce, hence it was necessary to adapt them to suit current requirements. This was usually accomplished by the attachment of additional clauses with the aim of both amending the terms of cover and supplementing the Marine Insurance Act, causing, on occasions, much astonishment and criticism by the Courts.

1

Before standard clauses were issued by the Institute of London Underwriters, the variety of clauses in use was such that the Underwriter might only find he was not properly acquainted with the terms of a particular clause when the policy was presented to him for signature. The first Institute Cargo Clauses, dating from August, 1912, were therefore issued for the purpose of uniformity and to limit the number of clauses which it was possible to append to the policy.

The basic clauses in general use were the Institute Cargo Clauses (for use in policies "With Average") and the Institute Cargo Clauses (F.P.A.). As can be seen from the following, the former consisted of only seven clauses, the first two of which were concerned with the exclusion of war and strikes risks:

INSTITUTE CARGO CLAUSES

(For Use in Policies "With Average")

1. Warranted free of capture, seizure, or detainment, and the consequences thereof or any attempt thereat (piracy excepted), and also from all consequences of hostilities or warlike operations, whether before or after declaration of war.
2. Warranted free of loss or damage caused by strikers locked out workmen or persons taking part in labour disturbances or riots or civil commotions.
3. General Average and Salvage Charges payable according to Foreign Statement or per York-Antwerp Rules if in accordance with the contract of affreightment.
4. Held covered, at a premium to be arranged, in case of deviation or change of voyage or of any omission or error in the description of the interest, vessel, or voyage.
5. Including (subject to the terms of the Policy) all risks covered by this Policy from shippers' or manufacturers' warehouse until on board the vessel, during transhipment if any, and from the vessel whilst on quays wharves or in sheds during the ordinary course of transit until safely deposited in consignees' or other warehouse at destination named in Policy.
6. Including risk of craft, raft, and/or lighter to and from the vessel. Each craft, raft, and/or lighter to be deemed a separate insurance. The Assured are not to be prejudiced by any agreement exempting lightermen from liability.

7. Including all liberties as per contract of affreightment. The Assured are not to be prejudiced by the presence of the negligence clause and/or latent defect clause in the Bills of Lading and/or Charter Party. The seaworthiness of the vessel as between the Assured and the Assurers is hereby admitted.

As can also be observed, the remaining clauses in the set extended the period of cover from warehouse to warehouse, without any time limits (provided the goods were in the ordinary course of transit), and included craft risks, transhipment, and provision to hold the goods covered in the event of deviation or change of voyage. General Average and Salvage Charges were made payable according to Foreign Statement or per York-Antwerp Rules if in accordance with the contract of affreightment. A Bill of Lading Clause contained the statement that the seaworthiness of the vessel as between the Assured and the Assurers was admitted.

The clauses for use in "with average" policies, therefore, did nothing to alter the ordinary marine perils stated in the policy form, which were assumed to be:

Perils of the seas, fire, pirates, rovers, thieves, jettisons, barratry of the master and mariners, and all other perils, losses, and misfortunes ... [i.e. of a similar kind].

However, the application of these perils depended to a great extent on the "Memorandum" at the foot of the policy form reading:

N.B. Corn, Fish, Salt, Fruit, Flour and Seed, are warranted free from Average, unless General, or the Ship be Stranded; Sugar, Tobacco, Hemp, Flax, Hides and Skins, are warranted free from Average, under Five Pounds *per Cent.*; and all other Goods, also the Ship and Freight are warranted free from Average under Three Pounds *per Cent.* unless General, or the Ship be Stranded.

The inclusion of the Memorandum resulted in the following heads of claim being recoverable from the operation of the specified perils:

Total loss (absolute or constructive)
Partial Loss from accidental cause (Particular Average loss) in the case of goods not specified in the Memorandum, if amounting to 3% of the value, or the ship became stranded.
Partial loss from accidental cause if amounting to 5% of the

3

value of a shipment of sugar, tobacco, hemp, flax, hides, and skins, or the ship became stranded.

Partial loss from accidental cause on shipments of corn, fish, salt, fruit, flour and seed, only if the ship became stranded.

Partial loss from voluntary sacrifice at a time when the adventure was in peril (General Average loss).

Particular charges, incurred for the preservation of the subject matter insured.

Contributions to general average and salvage.

Sue and Labour charges incurred in averting or minimising a loss.

It appears to have been the intention, when the Memorandum was first employed, to deduct the stipulated percentages of 3% and 5% from the claim, leaving only the balance to be paid by Underwriters. It is worthwhile stressing, therefore, that these percentages were, for a great number of years, treated as *attainable* franchises, and, once these were reached, the whole claim became payable, not merely the excess. Also these franchises were restricted to Particular Average claims only, i.e. to actual damage suffered by the goods themselves, and it was not permissible to add general average losses, particular charges, or sue and labour charges to such damage for the purpose of making up the specified percentage. In this regard Rule for Construction No. 13 in the Marine Insurance Act of 1906 states:

> The term "average unless general" means a partial loss of the subject-matter insured other than a general average loss, and does not include "particular charges".

Thus, particular charges could not be recovered unless the damage to the goods reached the required percentage, while sue and labour charges were recoverable to the extent that they succeeded in reducing a claim, or extinguished it altogether by bringing the damage below the franchise. General Average and Salvage remained unaffected by the franchise provisions.

It would seem reasonable to suppose that the object of the Memorandum was not only to free Underwriters from trivial claims on some commodities where the expenses of settlement would be disproportionate to the claim, but also to avoid heavy claims on cargoes susceptible to damage during sea transport. However, with regard to the provision that claims would be payable in the event of the ship being stranded, it is doubtful whether this was intended to widen Underwriters' liability for damage other than that caused by the stranding, but the Courts took a different view and it will be found that Rule for Construction No. 14 sums up the position thus;

> Where the ship has stranded, the insurer is liable for the excepted losses, although the loss is not attributable to the stranding, provided that when the stranding takes place the risk has attached and, if the policy be on goods, that the damaged goods are on board.

Thus, once the ship had stranded, the restrictions imposed by the Memorandum did not apply, and all damages by insured perils during the entire voyage became payable, irrespective of percentage of loss, provided the goods were on board at the time of the stranding.

It is interesting to note that this position was originally challenged only five years after the Memorandum was first inserted in Lloyd's policies in May 1749, but after losing the case (*Cantillon v. London Assurance, 1754*), both the London Assurance and the Royal Exchange Assurance removed the words "or the ship be stranded" from their policies. Competition from Lloyd's Underwriters, however, who were prepared to abide by the decision, soon resulted in the position being accepted, and it was not unusual to see the Memorandum extended by the addition of the words "sunk or burnt", "on fire", or even "or the damage be caused by collision".

Naturally, the words caused much discussion on their precise meaning, bearing in mind that they were so important to Underwriters. In the case of the *Glenlivet* [1894], for instance, where a fire which consumed some of the bunker coal did only slight damage to the ship, it was held that, before a vessel could be considered "burnt" it must have been substantially burnt, otherwise it was not sufficient to establish a claim under the Memorandum. Further cases provided guidance on the meaning of "stranding" "sunk" and "collision".

One result of these decisions was that claims could arise on the first group of commodities, i.e. corn, fish, salt, fruit, flour and seed, from perils other than fire, merely because some part of the ship had been substantially burnt, whereas if the cargo itself took fire and burnt without any damage to the ship, particular average from such a cause was not recoverable.

Moreover, with the inclusion of the Craft Clause, making each craft, raft, or lighter a separate insurance, the principle could be

applied to different portions of the cargo. In this way the memorandum percentages could be applied separately to the value of the
cargo in the vessel or craft, and in addition particular average damage
occurring in the craft was recoverable if the ocean vessel had been
stranded, sunk or burnt etc. with all the cargo on board. Alternatively
if the craft was stranded, sunk or burnt, etc. particular average
damage to cargo in that craft could be recovered, even if the damage
had occurred on the ocean vessel.

The separate nature of the craft was also instrumental in making
the total valuation apportionable, so that the assured could recover
for a total loss of an apportionable part. Thus, in a case where part
of the cargo had been discharged into lighters, and a fire destroyed
the ship and the remaining cargo, it was held the assured could claim
for the loss of the cargo in the ship, notwithstanding that the policy
would not pay for any particular average losses. (*General Insurance
Company of Trieste v. Royal Exchange Assurance, 1897*). In this
connection Section 76(1) of the Marine Insurance Act states:

> Where the subject-matter insured is warranted free from
> particular average, the assured cannot recover for a loss of part,
> other than a loss incurred by a general average sacrifice, unless
> the contract contained in the policy be apportionable; but, if
> the contract be apportionable, the assured may recover for a total
> loss of any apportionable part.

Even before the present century began, therefore, a certain amount
of expertise was required in the assessment of cargo claims ...

Chapter 2

GOODBYE TO THE MEMORANDUM (2)

In the second of three articles, the author follows the progress of the "average" clauses in cargo insurance until 1951, when the standard "All Risks" clauses were issued.

When one observes the very few items named in the Memorandum in the "S.G." Form of policy, it is perhaps not surprising that there was a tendency to develop special wordings. Indeed, the poor experience on many goods, apart from those stipulated in the Memorandum, seems to have led to the adoption of a standard Free of Particular Average Clause in July, 1883, which enabled stricter, but cheaper, terms to be agreed. This ran as follows:

> Warranted free from particular average unless the vessel or craft be stranded, sunk, or burnt, each craft or lighter being deemed a separate insurance. Underwriters, notwithstanding this warranty, to pay for any damage or loss caused by collision with any other ship or craft, and any special charges for warehouse, rent,reshipping, or forwarding, for which they would otherwise be liable. Also to pay the insured value of any package or packages which may be totally lost in transhipment. Grounding in the Suez Canal not to be deemed a strand, but underwriters to pay damage or loss which may be proved to have directly resulted therefrom.

The first Institute Cargo Clauses (F.P.A.), issued in August, 1912, were exactly the same as the clauses for use in policies "with average", but had the additional F.P.A. Clause added which read as follows:

> 8. Warranted free from Particular Average unless the vessel or craft be stranded sunk or burnt, but the Assurers are to pay the insured value of any package or packages which may be totally lost in loading transhipment or discharge, also any loss of or damage to the interest insured which may reasonably be attri-

7

buted to fire, collision or contact of the vessel and/or craft and/or conveyance with any external substance (ice included) other than water, or to discharge of cargo at a port of distress, also to pay landing warehousing forwarding and special charges if incurred.

It is interesting to compare this clause with the original F.P.A. Clause of 1883, as it is readily apparent that cargo Underwriters were not so apprehensive about groundings in the Suez Canal at the time when the Institute Clauses came into being. Due to the presence of a separate craft clause in the 1912 clauses, it was not necessary to show this concession in the F.P.A. Clause itself, and the cover was widened to include the loss of packages in loading or discharge, as well as during transhipment. In the later clause, too, there was a departure from the basic principle of proximate cause, and all damage reasonably attributable to fire, collision or contact with any external substance, including ice, was brought within its ambit.

It will be found that this clause remained substantially the same until it was discarded following the issue of completely new clauses on 1st January, 1982, the notable difference being the addition of the peril "explosion" after "fire" following the Bombay catastrophe of 1944, when the *Fort Stikine*, loaded with explosives and spontaneously conbustible cotton, caught fire and blew up, killing 1250 people, and destroying or damaging 15 vessels.

In 1912, however, there was a wide difference between F.P.A. conditions (as evidenced by the above clause), and "with average" conditions, which were still tied to the Memorandum. Thus, to the extent that the F.P.A. clause expressly covered damage *reasonably attributable* to fire, while the W.A. policy only covered fire damage where this was the *proximate cause* of the loss *and* amounted to the required percentage,the assured could acquire some advantage under the F.P.A. Clause. Similarly, the assured could claim for any package lost in loading, transhipment or discharge if the goods were insured under the F.P.A. Clause, but not under the Memorandum unless there was a provision to treat each package as a separate insurance. It appears to have been the practice to allow the loss of such packages, if this loss, added to that during the voyage, amounted to the required 3 or 5 per cent., or the cargo was on board at the time of a stranding. Since packages lost in loading were never effectively on board, a subsequent stranding was of no avail.

Not unexpectedly, therefore, there was a tendency for special conditions to be negotiated.

Reference to an early edition of Witherby's Clauses Book shows that, at the end of the 1st World War, Institute Clauses were already in operation for Corn, Jute and Nitrates on F.P.A. conditions; while 21 sets of clauses on Frozen Meat provided a variety of conditions from Total Loss to W.A. if amounting to 3% on each carcase or package etc., or on each valuation separately, or on the whole, from every cause resulting in a defective condition of the meat, except bone-taint, improper dressing, cooling and freezing.

There was also a diversity of methods of applying franchises. A special *Bobbin Clause* used for shipments of cotton read:

> To pay average separately on each interest, mark or quality, or on every 5 Tons, 20 Packages, or 100 Bobbins of running numbers, but should the interest be picked, only that part which is actually sea-damaged to be sold for account of Underwriters, and the claim to be arranged without reference to series or percentage.

Indian tea might be written:

> To pay average on each 10 chests, 20 half chests, or 40 quarter chests, following landing numbers, but no claim to attach for wet or damp in respect of any package unless the tea therein shall have been in actual contact with sea water or river water.

The percentage franchise on coffee could be applied to "Every 10 hogsheads, tierces or casks. Each 20 barrels and 50 bags running landing numbers." On Egyptian cotton the franchise might be "Each 10 bales running landing numbers, and on pickings without reference to series or percentage." Glass and chinaware would usually be on the terms: "Warranted free from any claim, general average excepted, unless caused by the vessel being stranded, sunk, or burnt, or by collision with another ship or vessel." If a consignment was subject to ordinary leakage, like coconut oil, it would not be unusual to see a clause such as: "1 per cent for ordinary leakage, computed on the original net weight, to be deducted in case of claim. To pay average if damage amounts to 3 per cent on each series of 5 pipes, 10 puncheons, or 20 hogsheads original numbers."

The purpose of applying the franchise to different proportions of consignments of goods, was to stabilise the figure which the claim would need to reach as the size of shipments steadily grew. Without some concession it would have become inevitable for merchants to have borne an increasingly larger share of claims below the stipulated percentage, this being a burden which they found too onerous. Therefore, sub-divisions of the cargo were found which originally produced valuations of about £100.

Of course, grouping of the damaged bags could result in some discrimination against Underwriters, leading to the franchise being overcome too easily. The intention of the application of "running landing numbers" was to ensure that the goods were taken in the order in which they were landed. However, this was not always practical, because there was a tendency to set aside damaged goods and number them last on the out-turn report. This system was, in any event, sometimes beneficial to Underwriters, as damage could be alleviated by the separation of wet or contaminated goods from sound, and in later years the practice fell into disuse.

As the application of the franchise to series of packages was introduced to assist the assured in reaching the required percentage with less difficulty, it was also incumbent on Underwriters not to utilise such series to the detriment of the assured. Therefore, if the claim was recoverable by applying the franchise to the whole parcel, as if no concession had been granted in the way of series, no regard was to be taken of the fact that the damage to a particular group of packages in the series did not attain the stipulated percentage. This was often made clear by the addition of the words "or on the whole" being inserted after the franchise provision for the series.

In due course the Institute Cargo Clauses (W.A.) became the Standard Clauses for the insurance of goods covering particular average, and contained an Average Clause with close similarities to the F.P.A. Clause, so that many of the benefits created by the extension of cover in the latter clause became common to both types of cover. In the early thirties, therefore, the Average Clause read as follows:

> Warranted free from average under the percentage specified in the Policy unless general, or the vessel or craft be stranded, sunk or burnt, but notwithstanding this warranty, the Underwriters are to pay the insured value of any package which may be totally lost in loading, transhipment or discharge, also for any loss of or damage to the interest insured which may reasonably be

attributed to fire, collision or contact of the vessel and/or craft
and/or conveyance with any external substance (ice included)
other than water, or to discharge of cargo at port of distress.
This Clause shall operate during the whole period covered by
the Policy.

The last sentence was added to nullify the result of a case heard
in 1926, in which it was decided that the terms of the Memorandum
did not apply to goods whilst in warehouse at Rosario awaiting export.

The Institute Cargo Clauses (F.P.A.) were identical except that the
F.P.A.Clause commenced "Warranted free from Particular Average
unless the vessel or craft be stranded, sunk, or burnt ..." and, in
addition, agreed "... to pay landing, warehousing, forwarding, and
special charges if incurred for which Underwriters would be liable
under a policy covering Particular Average ..." As can be seen, the
Clause itself differed very little from that issued in 1912, except to
the extent that the charges mentioned could be recovered if incurred
to prevent a partial loss, this concession evidently being aimed at
preventing difficulties in ascertaining whether a claim for a total loss
might have resulted without such expenditure having been insured.

As a result the only practical difference between the W.A. and
F.P.A. Clauses was that the W.A. Clauses paid for particular average
damage to cargo, proximately caused by heavy weather, if the
percentage of loss specified in the policy was reached.

The difference, however, did become more marked as competition
caused Underwriters to grant wider cover on policies containing the
W.A. Clauses. The tendency was to delete the Memorandum franchise by insuring the goods against loss or damage "irrespective of
percentage" and to include various "extraneous risks" which were
aimed at providing indemnity for negligent handling, rather than
casualties occurring during transport. Such risks could consist of
ordinary leakage and breakage, hook and oil damage, short or non-
delivery, chipping or denting. It also became quite customary to insure
against theft and pilferage, freshwater or rainwater, and sweat damage
occasioned by changes in temperature in the ship's hold which might
not always be the result of closing the ventilators in bad weather.

When these additional risks were added to the cover provided it
was recognised by custom in the market that they were insured
"irrespective of percentage" unless some other provision was made.
This was not always appreciated by newcomers to the scene, who

assumed that the memorandum franchise should be applied where the words "irrespective of percentage" did not appear.

Finally, it became the practice to simply cover the goods against "all risks". The brokers' clauses which came into use varied greatly in content and phraseology, so much so that, in 1951, Underwriters produced the Institute Cargo Clauses (All Risks) in which the appropriate clause read:

> This insurance is against all risks of loss or damage to the subject-matter insured but shall in no case be deemed to extend to cover loss damage or expense proximately caused by delay or inherent vice or nature of the subject-matter insured. Claims recoverable hereunder shall be payable irrespective of percentage.

From that point the three basic average clauses in use, i.e. the F.P.A. Clause, the Average Clause, and the All Risks Clause, served the market well for the next thirty years. But already, the storm clouds were gathering ...

Chapter 3

GOODBYE TO THE MEMORANDUM (3)

In the final article of this series the author describes the events leading to the adoption of the new cargo clauses in January, 1982.

It is probably true to say that until the late 1940s and early 1950s, ocean trade, and concurrently marine insurance, were regulated almost exclusively by colonial powers. From then, however, the conduct of marine insurance began to change dramatically, mainly due to a growing tendency for nationally-orientated markets to become more and more interested in accepting risks on an international basis. Whether this was because of competition between markets to increase premium income, the need to spread risks internationally, or simply to meet the requirements of a more widely dispersed clientele, the result was to alter the relatively simple situation in which only a few nationally-orientated marine insurance markets in developed countries were involved.

As a result of the emergence of independent states from former colonial territories, and the growth of indigenous assureds and insurers in these emergent states, the contractual arrangements between the parties tended to become more complex as local markets sought to obtain conditions which were both understandable and adaptable. New generation insurers and assureds could find existing practices and conditions of cover in traditional markets unnecessarily variegated, cumbersome and complicated, since they were tied to ancient forms and procedures which could not be readily assimilated into their own systems, and did not appear to be relevant to their own requirements.

Thus, the increasing degree of internationalisation in marine insurance created a desire in many parts of the world for a measure of harmonisation in the legal regimes, and led, in 1964, to the United Nations Conference on Trade and Development (UNCTAD) adopting a recommendation that competent international organisations should examine the question of formulating uniform clauses for marine, land and air transport insurances. Subsequently marine insurance was treated as a priority subject in the work programme.

It soon became clear that marine insurance policy forms, which were prepared by the insurers, contained many complicated and archaic clauses which were not apparently interpreted uniformly in many countries. Accordingly, attention was thought to be desirable in the simplification and unification of the clauses in use, so that they could be more readily understood, and would carry the same meaning everywhere in appropriate cases.

Unfortunately it was found that the paucity of information concerning the differences existing between national laws, policy conditions and practices governing marine insurance, made it difficult to produce an overall analysis, and to compensate for the absence of literature the secretariat sent questionnaires to all the states which were members of UNCTAD. It is interesting to note that of the substantive replies received, 45 were from developing countries, 17 from developed market-economy countries, and 6 from socialist countries. In addition, missions were undertaken by secretariat members to certain marine insurance markets as well as to maritime centres in developing countries to obtain a broad perspective of the concerns of both the assured and the insurer. The services of an expert in marine insurance from a major international marine insurance market, who could act as consultant and adviser on various technical aspects of the study, were also secured.

Of course, the majority of the responses received were prepared by insurance organisations in the national market, or by governmental departments, and tended to reflect the perspective of insurers. To obtain a more balanced perspective, special efforts were made to elicit the views of assureds regarding their marine insurance policies, and a significant number of shippers and consignees, after stating they were generally satisfied with their insurance arrangements, revealed a widespread and profound lack of understanding of the specific aspects of their marine policy coverages. It was concluded that far too often assureds were dependent on the insurers' recommendation as to the appropriate policy coverage, or at best that of a broker — often situated in a major marine insurance market having very little contact with the country or assured concerned. This indicated the existence of possible inadequacies in the presentation of the terms and conditions in the standard documentation used for the marine insurance contract.

In trying to determine in what form a standard document might be produced, the secretariat was naturally influenced by the predominent nature of the English market with its well established laws, practices and policy conditions. It was recognised that, at the time when marine insurance practices and conditions of cover were crystallising into recognisably modern forms during the last quarter of the 19th century and the beginning of the present century, British merchant fleets dominated world tonnage, and this fact, combined with the United Kingdom's ascendancy in general commerce and finance, made London the international market centre of marine insurance. Consequently, a distinctive feature of marine insurance is the profound impact the English market, as well as the policy forms, clauses and legislative provisions in force, have had on the conduct of marine insurance internationally, particularly involving developing countries. As a result the secretariat was able to concentrate a large part of its investigation on the English marine insurance legal regime, and when a Report was finally issued in November 1978, much of its content consisted of a hard critical look at the sophisticated English system with suggested improvements which could possibly convert it to international use. It was emphasised, however, that no attempt had been made to single out the English system as being worse than any other; the intention was to strengthen it with positive elements from other legal regimes, so as to revise and simplify it in an international forum, thus fostering an even wider application.

Not unexpectedly, perhaps, much criticism was directed at the S.G. policy form. Although it was conceded that the use of the form together with the attachment of the desired Institute Clauses could result in flexibility in the scope of insurance cover, nevertheless this resulted in a set of policy conditions difficult to follow. Rather than logical overall restructuring and reform of a unified document, modernisation had taken place outside the basis of the contract, which required a complicated patchwork of amendments, exceptions and supplementary clauses — all made to a document which was not constructed with the intention that such amendments would be made.

It was appreciated by the secretariat that changes in the S.G. Form had been resisted on the grounds that it had been the subject of such a large amount of litigation over the years that its meaning had become clear, and its supporters feared that any attempted improvements would initiate a flood of litigation to clarify the new wording. In response to these views the secretariat stated: "Although such arguments merit consideration, the immortalisation of an antiquated and obscurely worded document as being immune from any improvement is excessive and unnecessary. In fact, changes in the legal effect of the documents are made all the time by the attachment of Institute Clauses. When drafted carefully, such changes have not been and need not be the clarion call for a flood of new litigation. Thus the unyielding resistance to any change of the S.G. Form is unfounded." It was therefore suggested that the language of the Form should be up-dated and useless verbiage characteristic of such ancient documents should be eliminated.

For instance, what was the point of retaining a space for the name of the Master, since it was now virtually never inserted? And why should the insurers agree that "... this writing or policy of assurance shall be of as much force and effect as the surest writing or policy of assurance heretofore made in Lombard Street, or in the Royal Exchange, or elsewhere in London ..."? In the view of the secretariat, these were merely historical curiosities which could be discarded without altering the legal effect of the document. Another curious feature, to which attention was drawn, was the "Attestation", this clause referring to the receipt of the premium which, in fact, the assurers had often not so received at the time of issuing the policy.

It was also felt that consideration should be given to whether phrases which were superseded by attached Institute Clauses should be eliminated, such as the "touch and stay" clause, permitting the vessel "... to proceed and sail and touch and stay at any port or place whatsoever ...". Such rights were usually governed either by statutory provision or by specific policy wording (see Rule for Construction No.6 of the Marine Insurance Act).

As far as the "Memorandum" was concerned, it was pointed out that, in cargo insurance, the Institute Cargo Clauses "All Risks" paid irrespective of the percentage of loss, thereby rendering the Memorandum ineffective. Furthermore, "F.P.A." conditions contained provisions to be read in substitution of the Memorandum. Only the Institute Cargo Clauses (W.A.) referred to the Memorandum, and for this purpose the relevant parts of the Memorandum could be incorporated into those specific clauses. Therefore, there was no difficulty envisaged in eliminating the Memorandum from the S.G.

Form; actually some countries, utilising variants of the form, had already taken steps in that direction.

The secretariat was also of the opinion that the wording of the Perils Clause, commencing "Touching the adventures and perils which we the assurers are contented to bear and do take upon us in this voyage ...", was so antiquated, and the draftsmanship so inadequate, that it was extremely difficult for individuals to understand, unless they were highly familiar with English law. It was suggested that the concept "perils of the sea" should be clarified to indicate that it embraced only "fortuitous" events, and that the word "thieves", which had been held to refer only to theft with violence, could be shown as "assailing thieves", as in the American version of the clause, in order to avoid the possible misunderstanding of "pilferage" being included. The American version was also found preferable to clarify the phrase "... and of all other perils, losses and misfortunes, that have or shall come to the hurt, detriment, or damage of the said goods ...", this having been reworded to indicate that, according to legal doctrine, only perils "similar" to those previously enumerated were to be included by the phrase, thereby avoiding the uninformed becoming misled.

It was further suggested that perils which no longer applied in a modern context, such as "letters of mart and countermart" or "rovers", could also be eliminated. In this way the terms of the Perils Clause which were considered to be "war risks", but were regularly overridden in the standard English clauses by the *Free of Capture and Seizure Clause*, could also be removed, since the ultimate intent of the clause was never to grant cover for war risks.

However, stress was laid on the complex structure of both the F.P.A. and the W.A. Clauses, as a result of which neither was easily understandable by anyone not too familiar with cargo insurance coverages. It was thought that the Average Clause and the F.P.A. Clause, which were similar in presentation, each suffered from attempting to accomplish too much in one sentence, with no logical breakdown between their distinctive functions. The suggested remedy was to draw a clear distinction between wording which expanded the risks insured against, and wording which affected the indemnity payable for losses caused by insured risks. The absence of such a separation meant that the intent of the clause was not readily discernable, and this, combined with the confusion created by the antiquated S.G. Form, led to the overall presentation of the policy becoming extremely difficult to understand by the average assured.

Concerning the "All Risks" Clauses, the secretariat concluded that the problems of presentation were not so complex as a result of the use of a simplified approach involving a broad grant of coverage for all risks but subject to certain exceptions. Such a method clearly facilitated the task of the assured in determining whether the insurance met his particular needs, and in comparing the cover with other variations. In fact, the secretariat approved this "all risks minus exceptions" approach so much that they went so far as to recommend that it could be employed to structure three levels of cargo insurance from which the assured could choose, depending on the level of the premium.

Nevertheless, despite its simplified format, an "All Risks" version of the clauses could easily mislead an assured into thinking that a wider coverage was granted than was actually the case. Assureds frequently purchase this type of insurance on the assumption that it provides protection against any loss or damage however caused, short of, perhaps, wilful misconduct of the assured or the expressly stated exceptions. Any clauses so entitled should necessarily call attention to the limits of its coverage, since the phrase "risk of loss or damage" is used in a technical sense to exclude normal losses which occur in the shipment of some types of commodities, such as a certain percentage of loss of weight or volume with grains or fluids. The exclusion of this type of loss is based on the concept that a "risk" of loss or damage does not include losses of an inevitable nature, as might be termed normal transit loss or damage.

The Institute Cargo Clauses (All Risks) have, of course, traditionally excluded "loss damage or expense proximately caused by delay or inherent vice or nature of the subject-matter insured." The secretariat, however, thought it would be useful if it were made clear that the exclusion of delay embraced situations where the delay itself was caused by an insured peril, as expressed in Section 55(2)(b) of the Marine Insurance Act, 1906. On the other hand, it was evidently felt that the delay exclusion was incorrectly founded upon the concept of delay as being a distinct "peril" which could cause loss or damage. In fact, delay might be nothing more than a channel through which a peril could operate, and the secretariat concluded that "... if the peril causing the delay is an insured risk in the policy, then any physical damage resulting from the delay is legitimately within the

18

scope of the transport risks from which the cargo owner seeks protection when purchasing his insurance cover." It was in this area that the secretariat felt the standard coverage offered by the Institute Clauses was quite inadequate. Indeed, indemnification was considered to be appropriate in some cases where the assured could suffer from "loss of market" due to delay.

It is to the credit of Underwriters in this country, that when the Report was issued, they were prepared to study the suggestions and criticisms expressed by UNCTAD, and to set up a Working Party to find ways and means to achieve greater clarity, and put an end to much of the mystique created by the system in use. The results are now known the world over, and with the introduction of three new sets of standard conditions in January, 1982, designated with the first three letters of the alphabet, it can now be said that we have entered an era in which practitioners need to know the ABC of cargo insurance.

The traditional S.G. Form, together with its time-honoured Memorandum, were conspicuously absent in the new regime. Thus, Underwriters had succeeded in dealing with the criticisms of these antiquated wordings "at a stroke".

Chapter 4

THE ABC OF THE MARINE CARGO CLAUSES.

Following his articles leading up to the adoption of the new cargo clauses, the author now compares the basic cover provided by the three standard sets.

In dispensing with the S.G. Form, and replacing this with a new Marine Policy Form which does not contain any of the normal conditions of the insurance, but basically sets out the details of the interest insured together with Underwriters' proportions of the risk, the London Market was able, in January 1982, to issue revised sets of clauses aimed at providing simplicity and clarity of the cover available, without having to refer to the policy itself. It was thought that this more direct approach would end much of the mystique which had developed under the old system, and help the layman to understand the provisions more easily, so that disputes and litigation would be reduced.

As with the old system, there are three basic sets of standard clauses, but these are now designated "A" "B" and "C" according to the degree of indemnity provided, and all reference to "with average" and "free of particular average" has disappeared with the "Memorandum", permitting a more logical and readable format.

The Institute Cargo Clauses (C) provide the most limited conditions, cover being granted against major casualties in the following way:

RISKS COVERED
1   This insurance covers, except as provided in Clauses 4, 5, 6 and 7 below,
    1.1   loss of or damage to the subject-matter insured reasonably attributable to
    1.1.1   fire or explosion
    1.1.2   vessel or craft being stranded grounded sunk or capsized

1.1.3   overturning or derailment of land conveyance
1.1.4   collision or contact of vessel craft or conveyance with any external object other than water
1.1.5   discharge of cargo at a port of distress, ·
1.2   loss of or damage to the subject-matter insured caused by
1.2.1   general average sacrifice
1.2.2   jettison.

It must first of all be pointed out that the clause is framed on the basis of named risks less exclusions, and the onus of proof is on the assured to show that an insured peril has operated. Once this has been done there is a *prima facie* claim against the Underwriters, and the burden of proof is then shifted to them if they wish to plead that the claim is not recoverable because of the application of any of the exclusion clauses.

It will be seen, however, that so far as the first five perils are concerned, the assured is relieved from the strict application of the doctrine of proximate cause, and it is only necessary to show that any loss or damage to the goods is reasonably attributable to the perils described. Although the word "proximately" has been omitted from Clause 1.2 before the words "caused by", this has only been carried out in the interests of simplicity, as many foreign assureds are not familiar with the term. Nevertheless, Section 55(2)(a) of the Marine Insurance Act, 1906, will continue to apply, so that an assured will have to demonstrate that a general average sacrifice, or jettison, is the effective cause of loss or damage. This should not be too onerous.

Some speculation arises from the inclusion of "jettison" as well as "general average sacrifice", as the jettison of cargo overboard in time of peril will normally fall to be dealt with as a general average sacrifice if it is carried in accordance with the recognised custom of the trade (Rule 1 of the York-Antwerp Rules, 1974). This will hold good even if the ship and cargo are in the same ownership (S.66(7) of the Marine Insurance Act). Possibly the intention is to preserve the peril from the S.G. Form rather than to give the impression of providing a more extensive cover than actually exists. At any rate UNCTAD feel, on balance, that they would prefer to retain the word for purposes of drawing up their own international clauses.*

Concern has also been expressed by practitioners over the omission of the general words which followed the perils in the S. G. Form,

* But see *Achille Lauro* incident on page 218

21

i.e. "... and all other perils, losses, and misfortunes, that have or shall come to the hurt, detriment, or damage of the said goods ..." Although this could only be construed to include perils similar in kind to those specifically mentioned in the policy (see Rule for Construction No. 12 of the Marine Insurance Act) it was felt that the absence of the words might lead to a diminution of the cover. In drafting up the new clauses, however, Underwriters had taken up the point made by UNCTAD that the words could be misleading to an assured who might believe that he had wider cover than intended. Moreover, on a review of previous cases, it was thought that the words would produce little or no advantage to an assured in the context of the new clauses. In the classic case of *Symington and Co. v. Union Insurance Society of Canton* [1928], for example, where fire broke out on the jetty at Algeciras, and to prevent the fire spreading, part of a consignment of cork was jettisoned into the water, while other parts were saturated with seawater, it was held by Roche, J. in the High Court that the loss was one which might reasonably be attributed to "fire". The Court of Appeal, however, while being fortified by the fact that the policy also covered "jettison" and perils of a similar kind, were clearly sympathetic towards the judgment of Kelly, C.B. in the fire insurance case of *Stanley v. Western Insurance Co.* [1868] to the effect that any loss resulting from an apparently necessary and *bona fide* effort to put out a fire, or to prevent it from spreading, is a proximate consequence of fire and, therefore, within the peril.

Nowadays it is commonly accepted that loss or damage caused by the use of water or other means to extinguish a fire, and any resultant smoke or heat damage caused by the fire, is recoverable from Underwriters, even if such loss or damage is restricted to that proximately caused by fire. It seems clear from the deliberations by UNCTAD, however, that the secretariat is satisfied it can be assumed that all such loss or damage is recoverable under the phrase "reasonably attributable to fire". In fact, it has gone so far as to express the opinion that the words are sufficiently wide to include smoke damage emanating from a distant, even controlled, and otherwise innocuous fire. Consequently it is not anticipated that any difficulty would arise under the new clauses if a similar situation to that encountered in the *Symington* case, arose today.

The Institute Cargo Clauses (B) provide cover against the same perils, but also insure against additional named risks so as to provide an assured with a kind of "middle-of-the-road" set of conditions. The difference between the "B" and "C" Clauses is much wider in comparison with the old "W.A." and "F.P.A." Clauses, this being considered to serve the needs of the assured more satisfactorily. The additional cover can be summarised as follows:

(a) loss or damage reasonably attributable to earthquake, volcanic eruption, or lightning (Clause 1.1.6).

(b) loss or damage caused by washing overboard (Clause 1.2.2).

(c) loss or damage caused by entry of sea, lake, or river water into vessel, craft, hold, conveyance, container, liftvan, or place of storage (Clause 1.2.3).

(d) total loss of any package lost overboard or dropped whilst loading on to, or unloading from, vessel or craft (Clause 1.3).

Significantly there is no longer any reference to "perils of the sea" as such, although many of the stipulated risks are allied to the phrase. However, there is now no mention of heavy weather, with the result that any loss or damage ascribed to the movement of cargo during adverse weather conditions is not recoverable under the "B" or "C" Clauses; similarly, loss of cargo over the ship's side in bad seas can only be the subject of a claim under the "B" Clauses if it is actually *washed* overboard, not if it simply breaks loose. While loss or damage caused by sweat of the hold in consequence of having to close the ventilators, when the weather conditions so require, is no longer recoverable as a "peril of the sea", Underwriters are prepared to consider such claims under the "B" Clauses on the basis that the action was necessarily and reasonably taken to prevent the *entry of seawater* affecting the goods. In this respect they feel the matter is governed by the observations of Lord Wright in *Canada Rice Mills, Ltd. v. Union Marine and General Insurance Co. Ltd.* (1940) who, although dealing with similar circumstances as a "peril of the sea", was also in agreement with the principles laid down in *Stanley v. Western Insurance Company*.

Mention should also perhaps be made that there is no provision for damage caused by rainwater under these restricted conditions, or for any form of theft (whether clandestine, violent, or simply petty pilferage), neither are the risks of barratry and piracy included. "Piracy" has ceased to be one of the perils shown in the War Clauses, and cover for this risk can, therefore, only be obtained under the "A" Clauses.

On the other hand, compared with the old "W.A." and "F.P.A." Clauses, there is a considerable extension of cover provided by the "B" Clauses, inasmuch as the entry of sea, lake, or river water into the means of conveyance or the place of storage can result in claims for flood damage which were not previously contemplated.

Another addition to the cover is derived from Underwriters' willingness to indemnify the assured for loss or damage reasonable attributable to earthquake, volcanic eruption, or lightning. UNCTAD favour the addition of the words "or similar natural calamities" to make the clause more general in its application. This would at least take care of so-called "tidal waves" which occur from disturbances in the bed of the ocean. In Japan, where these waves are termed "tsunami", heights of up to 100 feet have been experienced this century, and it is previously recorded that one such wave reached 210 feet. Their origins can be earthquakes as far out to sea as 125 miles, and since the clauses cover loss or damage *reasonably attributable* to earthquake, claims from this source (which are capable of depositing vessels several hundred feet inland) would obviously qualify for sympathetic consideration, whether or not they should happen to fall within any of the other named perils.

The Institute Cargo Clauses (A) replace the previous "All Risks" Clauses, and therefore cover the goods against all risks of loss or damage. Reference to "All Risks" in the title of the clauses was dropped in favour of. a more mundane designation, so as to avoid giving assureds the impression that the cover granted is wider than it actually is — an important point when bearing in mind current legislation in favour of the consumer, such as the Trade Descriptions Act.

The confusion arises not only from the fact that the clauses contain numerous exclusions, but also because the restrictive nature of the term "risk" is often not fully appreciated. As Lord Sumner said in the case of *Gaunt v. British and Foreign Marine Insurance Co.* [1921]: "There is a limit to 'all risks'. There are risks, and risks insured against. Accordingly, the expression does not cover inherent vice, or mere wear and tear, or British capture. It covers a risk not a certainty; it is something which happens to the subject-matter from without, not the natural behaviour of that subject-matter being what it is in the circumstances under which it is carried."

24

This case serves to illustrate the fundamental difference in the burden of proof required on the part of the assured under the "A" clauses, as compared with the "B" and "C" clauses. A consignment of wool which had been insured from the sheep's back until shipped on board at Punta Arenas, was found to be water damaged on arrival in England. It was established that the damage occurred before shipment, and was quite exceptional, although it was not possible to ascertain how it happened. Apparently the wool was sometimes stored in the open, was frequently carried on deck on the local steamers according to custom, and bad weather had been experienced.

Lord Sterndale said: "I think that where the evidence shows damage quite exceptional, and such as has never in a long experience been known to arise under the normal conditions of such transit, there is evidence of the existence of a casualty or something accidental and of a danger or contingency which might or might not arise, although the particular nature of the casualty was not ascertained. It would, of course, have been competent to the insurers to rebut this *prima facie* case by proving that the loss occurred by something outside the insured perils but no such evidence was given ... These were policies of an unusual kind against all risks and it was sufficient to show that the loss was occasioned by a casualty or something accidental without proving further in what the exact nature of that casualty consisted."

Thus, under an "all risks" cover, an assured is considered to have discharged his burden of proof by showing that the cause of loss is one insured against, although he is unable to point to a specific occurrence, provided it has happened during the currency of the policy. The onus is then shifted to Underwriters to demonstrate, if they can, that the loss is one caught by any of the exceptions detailed in the policy.

Underwriters have taken the opportunity to indicate in the exclusions clauses that it is not their intention to pay for loss or damage which is not fortuitous, and therefore stress they are not liable for inherent vice and delay, wilful misconduct of the assured, and such inevitable losses as ordinary leakage, loss in weight or volume, or ordinary wear and tear. These exclusions, however, merely echo the provisions of Section 55 of the Marine Insurance Act, 1906, and are shown to assist the assured.

New exclusions relate to the insolvency or financial default of the vessel's owners, managers, charterers or operators, and from the use of any weapon of war employing nuclear fission etc.. The growing concern by Underwriters of the use of vessels, or other means of transport, which may not be suitable for the anticipated transit is now reflected in the *Unseaworthiness and Unfitness Exclusion Clause* which relieves them from loss damage or expense arising from the privity of the assured or their servants to carriage by such unsuitable means. Bad packing is also excluded but does not extend to bad stowage where a container or liftvan is stowed by a third party after commencement of the insurance.

In the "B" and "C" Clauses the exclusions are taken a little further by the avoidance of claims for deliberate damage to, or deliberate destruction of the goods by the wrongful act of any person. It is possible to delete this clause by payment of an additional premium and the incorporation of a *Malicious Damage Clause* specially designed for the purpose.*

As the main object of the clauses is to provide cover against *physical* loss or damage, in distinction to economic loss or consequential loss, such as could arise from loss of market occurring from delay, one might wonder why the opportunity was not taken to specify this clearly by insertion of the word "physical". The reason for this seems to lie in the fact that it would be inappropriate to use the word bearing in mind that, in some cases, provision is made to pay for expenses incurred in avoiding a loss. Clause 12, for instance, recognises that a cargo policy not only covers loss or damage to the goods themselves but also frustration of the adventure by a marine peril. In cases where the insured transit is terminated short of destination as a result of the operation of a risk covered by the policy, the Underwriters, in order to avoid a claim for a total loss, will reimburse the assured for extra charges reasonably incurred in unloading, storing and forwarding the goods to the original destination. Again, in Clause 2, a general average contribution may well include expenses incurred during the prolongation of the voyage occasioned by the carrying ship having to enter a port of refuge. In other circumstances Underwriters prefer to rely on the special exclusion clause relating to delay to make it clear that they do not accept liability for loss damage or expense *proximately* caused by delay, even if the delay be caused by a risk insured against.

Generally speaking the new clauses have been well received, although brokers have expressed the view that they would have liked

* see page 88

to have seen fewer exclusions, particularly those relating to insolvency and unseaworthiness. At the end of the day, however, it has to be acknowledged that Underwriters must have the final say in the extent of the cover they are prepared to offer, but they have indicated that cover under either the "B" and "C" clauses can be extended by payment of a suitable additional premium.

The main source of criticism has been the American market where they are anxious to maintain their existing coverage, insisting that the new clauses are more restrictive that those available internationally, and may not be in the best interests of policyholders. Nevertheless, the US market is prepared to write business under the new clauses if pressed to do so, while UK insurers have expressed their willingness to accommodate American assureds by providing coverage under their own domestic clauses where required.

While this might be seen as a certain amount of "back-scratching" at least one thing seems reasonably certain; the new clauses can be grasped quite quickly, and they show just how confusing the old clauses tended to be.

Chapter 5

WHO CAN CLAIM UNDER THE POLICY?

Continuing his analysis of the standard cargo clauses, the author reflects on the disappearance of the "lost or not lost" clause in its old form, and looks at the pitfalls of insurable interest and assignment.

While the disposal of the S.G. Form meant that much of the archaic and antiquated wording, which was so unintelligible to many assureds, could be quietly forgotten — especially the "Memorandum" — it was necessary to carry some of the conditions expressed in the old policy form into the new clauses. Thus it will be found that the new Institute Cargo Clauses have been enlarged to embrace the "lost or not lost" wording, also the provisions relating to the *Sue and Labour Clause* and the *Waiver Clause*, although not in identical terms.

The "lost or not lost" clause has been part of the standard wording in marine policies for some centuries, and appears in a transcript of a policy in the possession of the Bodleian Library, Oxford, dated 15th February, 1613, which covered goods to be shipped in the *Tiger* "from London to Zante, Petrasse, and Saphalonia" on behalf of the London merchants Morris Abbott and Devereaux Wogan. There is much speculation as to whether this is the vessel referred to by Shakespeare in both *Macbeth* and *Twelfth Night*.

In Shakespeare's days, of course, trading conditions were such that insurances were necessarily effected without knowing whether the ship was in safety or not, or whether it had even sailed. Consequently, it appears most likely that the words were first inserted for the benefit of English merchants who required insurance on their ships or cargoes during a homeward voyage, this later being extended to outward voyages as well. Even today, with goods frequently changing hands in the course of a voyage, the buyer is not in a position, at the time of his purchase, to know whether they have already suffered damage in transit. Clearly, therefore, some measure of protection is required for merchants who are ignorant of the true state of affairs when insuring the goods, otherwise business would become quite difficult.

Naturally such protection cannot be provided without the basic consideration of the contract having to be based upon the utmost good faith, but where the assured and the Underwriter are both in an equal state of knowledge, the Courts have been prepared to uphold insurances effected subsequently to a loss. Indeed, in *Mead v Davison* [1835], where an insurance was accepted and the premium paid before a loss, it was held that the clause was binding on the Underwriter, although the policy was not issued until after the loss had occurred, and both parties were aware of it. Later, when the Marine Insurance Act was put in the Statute Book in 1906, the position was regulated by Rule for Construction No. 1 appearing in the First Schedule to the Act, reading:

> Where the subject-matter is insured "lost or not lost", and the loss has occurred before the contract is concluded, the risk attaches unless, at such time the assured was aware of the loss, and the insurer was not.

In *Carter v. Boehm* [1766], Lord Mansfield had occasion to deal with the circumstances in which the insurer might be aware of the safe arrival of a risk presented to him for insurance, although this fact was not known to the assured. In his judgment "The policy would equally be void against the Underwriter if he concealed anything within his own knowledge as, for example, if he insured a ship on a voyage, and he privately knew that she had already arrived, and in such circumstances he would be liable to return the premium paid."

In modern practice, where an assured has regular shipments, these are more conveniently insured on a forward basis under an open cover, so that it is not necessary to negotiate the terms of individual risks. Moreover, since an Underwriter is bound to accept all shipments coming within its scope, the assured is protected in the event that, by some mischance, a declaration is not made until after a known loss has occurred, the value of the goods being determined by the basis shown in the open cover.

While, up to this point, the position may seem to be relatively straight-forward, complications can be introduced by the rules governing assignability and insurable interest.

Originally, the fact that a cargo policy was assignable, so that a buyer of goods could obtain the beneficial rights of payment in the event of loss or damage, was to be found in the language at the beginning of the S.G. Form, where reference was made to "... all and every other person or persons to whom the same doth, may, or shall appertain, in part or in all ..." There is no such equivalent wording in the present Institute Cargo Clauses. but this is not important as the provisions of the Marine Insurance Act are perfectly clear. Section 50(1), for instance, states:

> A marine policy is assignable unless it contains terms expressly prohibiting assignment. It may be assigned either before or after loss.

In practice the policy can be assigned by blank endorsement, but any other customary manner can be employed. (Sec. 50(3)). Once the policy has been properly assigned, the assignee will stand in the shoes of the assignor and be able to sue in his own name. On the other hand he will have no better rights than the assignor, consequently the Underwriter can make any defence against the assignee that he would be entitled to make if the action had been brought in the name of the person for whom the policy was effected (Sec. 50(2)). Thus a breach of good faith on the part of the seller would render the policy voidable, although the buyer was entirely innocent of the breach.

However, it must be emphasised that assignment of the policy is not an incident of the sale, and so the transfer of the property in the goods does not by itself entitle a purchaser to the protection of the policy. If the assignment is to be valid, the assured must assign or agree to assign the policy before he parts with his interest in the goods. In this regard Section 15 of the Marine Insurance Act provides:

> Where the assured assigns or otherwise parts with his interest in the subject-matter insured, he does not thereby transfer to the assignee his rights under the contract of insurance, unless there be an express or implied agreement with the assignee to that effect.

It is further stated in Sec. 51 of the Act, that if the assured fails to agree to assign the policy, either expressly or implicitly, before he has parted with or lost his interest in the goods, any subsequent assignment of the policy is inoperative. It is, therefore, apparent that the contract of sale plays an important part, as this normally determines who is responsible for insuring the goods, and whether it is intended to protect the interests of other parties who will subsequently be concerned in the adventure.

This section of the Act is, perhaps, best illustrated by the case of *North of England Oil Cake Co. v. Archangel Maritime Insurance Co.* [1875], concerning a shipment of linseed which was sold whilst the vessel was on a voyage from Constantinople to London. The terms of sale provided for the interest in the goods to pass to the buyers after such goods were ready for delivery at the port, but whilst discharge was being carried out by public lighters employed by the purchasers, one lighter sank with its cargo. Such a loss was recoverable under the terms of the policy, as the risk in lighters was included, but although the policy was assigned to the buyers after the loss, they were held to be unable to recover because the rights under the policy remained with the sellers. However, since the sellers had already parted with their interest in the goods on delivery into the lighters, the policy was rendered ineffective. An agreement to assign the policy at the time of sale would have kept the policy in operation for the benefit of the assignees; as it was the sellers were not prejudiced by the loss of the linseed, the delivery by them into lighters constituting a fulfilment of the contract which left them with nothing to assign.

The following year, in *Anderson v. Morice* [1876], the Courts had occasion to deliberate over a consignment of rice which it had been intended to ship on the *Sunbeam* from Rangoon to London. The terms of the sale stipulated that the property in the goods would pass to the assured when the whole cargo was on board, but, unfortunately, when the vessel was only partly loaded, she sprang a leak and sank with the rice already shipped. Since the cargo had not been appropriated to the contract by putting it all on board, it was held that the assured had no insurable interest at the time of the loss, and could not acquire any interest subsequent to the loss.

These cases clearly show that before a claim can be admitted under a policy it is necessary to demonstrate that the assured had an interest in the cargo at the time of loss, in other words he stood to be "prejudiced by its loss or by damage thereto" (Sec. 5(2) of the M.I.A.). Effect is given to this basic principle by Section 6 of the Marine Insurance Act, in which the relation to the "lost or not lost" clause is mentioned:

> 6(1) The assured must be interested in the subject-matter insured at the time of loss though he need not be interested

when the insurance is effected: Provided that where the subject-matter is insured "lost or not lost," the assured may recover although he may not have acquired his interest until after the loss, unless at the time of effecting the contract of insurance the assured was aware of the loss, and the insurer was not.

6(2)   Where the assured has no interest at the time of the loss, he cannot acquire interest by any act or election after he is aware of the loss.

The "lost or not lost" provision resulted from the case of *Sutherland v. Pratt* [1843] where the Court was asked whether it was an answer to an action on the policy that the plaintiff did not acquire an interest in the goods until after sea damage had occurred. It was decided it was not, Parke, B. stating that a policy containing such a clause was "clearly a contract of indemnity against all past as well as all future losses sustained by the assured, in respect of the interest insured."

But to what extent can the clause be made retrospective? In the case of any ordinary c.i.f. transaction little difficulty appears to arise. The seller is able to insure the goods from warehouse to warehouse, and, although the transfer of the risk passes to the buyer on shipment, the latter is protected by the "lost or not lost" clause, if the policy has been properly assigned. A relevant case on this subject was that of *Aron and Co. (Inc.) v. Miall* [1928], the buyers in this instance having purchased a quantity of cocoa beans on c.i.f. terms from the West Coast of Africa to Boston, which the sellers had insured from the time of leaving the factory or warehouse in the interior. Before the goods were shipped in an ocean-going steamer they suffered damage by rain and surf, leading to the argument that the buyers were not interested in the cocoa beans before shipment, and consequently were not able to claim for such damage. It was held by Roche, J., and confirmed on appeal, that a policy indorsed in blank and assigned in accordance with the custom of marine insurance in England passed to the assignee all rights held by the assignor in the policy.

In the case of c. and f. contracts, however, some difficulty can be caused by the fact that the insurance is arranged by the buyers, who do not have any insurable interest before shipment. This was particularly evident in *Reinhart Company v. Joshua Hoyle and Sons, Ltd.* [1961], involving a consignment of 50 bales of cotton in transit from the U.S.A. via the Mexican port of Mazatlan to Liverpool. In this case the c. and f. contract, which incorporated the rules of the Liverpool Cotton Association, required the buyers to take out insurance to include the risk of country damage, but the sellers were to reimburse the buyers for any loss not covered by insurance due to the goods arriving in a country-damaged condition, or having damage of a pre-shipment nature. In pursuance of their obligations, therefore, the buyers effected an insurance on "all risks" terms, including country damage, the policy incorporating the usual warehouse to warehouse clause, although being expressed to cover the goods "at and from" the port of shipment. On arrival in Liverpool the cotton was found to be "country damaged", but it could not be ascertained at what point the damage had occurred, only that the goods had not been placed in a warehouse prior to shipment but left on the quay for about a week.

The question before the Court was whether the sellers were liable to pay the buyers a sum representing country damage, the latter contending that their policy did not cover the damage, because the policy did not apply to any damage occurring before arrival at loading port, at which time they had no insurable interest in the goods. The sellers argued that as the goods were insured "lost or not lost", and were covered for country damage it was immaterial whether the damage occurred before the buyers insured or became owners of the goods. Mr. Justice Pearson held that it was the duty of the buyers to ensure that they effected a proper marine insurance, so as to protect the interests of the sellers as well as those of the buyers, and therefore there was no liability on the sellers to indemnify the buyers.

This decision has upheld in the Court of Appeal by a majority decision, insofar as two of the judges agreed that the buyers were under a contractual obligation to effect an appropriate insurance against country damage, and, if they failed to do so, they were in breach of contract. However, there were differences of opinion as to the extent of cover provided by the policy.

In the leading judgment Lord Justice Sellers maintained that, as the bales were damaged before shipment and the risk of country damage was specifically covered, that was a risk insurers had agreed to cover as an extension of the ordinary marine policy. He was of the opinion that it was possible to effect a policy in respect of a loss which might have already occurred, and which happened before the assured acquired an insurable interest, the words "lost or not lost" being apt to cover partial loss. Lord Justice Willmer, on the other hand, did not consider that *Sutherland v. Pratt* was any authority for the proposition that an assured could recover in respect of a loss which had already occurred before the period of risk specified in the policy had commenced, and, as the policy specified a voyage commencing "at and from" a port of shipment, it could not cover country damage. Lord Justice Donovan supported the view that the policy itself insured the cotton when loaded at the port of shipment, and, accordingly, country damage and pre-shipment damage were obviously excluded. In a dissenting judgment, therefore, he concluded that the buyers were not bound to insure against country damage, and consequently they had a valid claim against the sellers.

While this was primarily a case about a dispute under a contract of sale, the incidental reference to the insurance terms did raise the question as to whether the duration of the risk, as described in the policy, was paramount. Such a question was to come up again in the "exotic oils" case, *Fuerst Day Lawson Ltd. v. Orion Insurance Co. Ltd.* [1980].

Here, large consignments of citronella, clove leaf oil, patchouli and cananga, used in the manufacture of soap and perfume, and shipped from Indonesia, were found to be the subject of a large scale fraud, as the drums contained nothing more than water on arrival in Europe, except for a thin film of oil for deception purposes.

Although the policy was on "all risks" terms, and was expressed to cover the goods from warehouse to warehouse, lost or not lost, it was contended by the Underwriters that the substitution could only have happened before the drums had been shipped on board the various vessels, and since the buyers, as cost and freight purchasers, had no insurable interest until shipment, they could rely on *Anderson v. Morice* to decline the claim, despite the "lost or not lost" provision in the policy. The buyers argued that since the passing of the Marine Insurance Act, they could depend on the very wide definition of insurable interest in Sec. 5(2) of that Act, consequently *Anderson v. Morice* was no longer good law, and they could recover under the "lost or not lost" clause, although they might not have acquired their interest until after the loss.

Mr. Justice Mocatta, however, was not persuaded that the buyers had discharged the burden of proof upon them of establishing, on the balance of probabilities, that the oils they had agreed to buy had ever started their transit from the godown or any other warehouse, and the claim failed on that point. He agreed that the arguments by the respective parties on the question of insurable interest, and the merits of the "lost or not lost" clause, raised points of some difficulty, but, as he put it, "... since upon my conclusion of the facts they do not arise for decision, I merely record them and express no view as to which should prevail."

As can be appreciated, the legal position was somewhat obscure at the time when the clauses came up for revision, and Underwriters have taken steps to remedy some of the uncertainty by the introduction of the *Insurable Interest Clause* reading:

    11.1   In order to recover under this insurance the Assured must have an insurable interest in the subject-matter insured at the time of the loss.

    11.2   Subject to 11.1 above, the Assured shall be entitled to recover for insured loss occurring during the period covered by this insurance, notwithstanding that the loss occurred before the contract of insurance was concluded, unless the Assured were aware of the loss and the Underwriters were not.

Thus, it is now clearly stated that the loss must be restricted to the period of cover described in the policy, thereby removing all doubt on the point. Unlike Sec. 6(1) of the Marine Insurance Act, the clause does not expressly provide that the person claiming on the policy need not have an interest at the time when the insurance is effected, but presumably this is to be inferred.

How the best intentions can go sadly awry is illustrated by the more recent case of *Silver Dolphin Products Ltd. v. Parcels and General Assurance Association Ltd.* [1984].

At the beginning of January, 1982, the plaintiffs bought a quantity of soap and scent f.o.b. New York for approximately $50,000. After being packed in a container, the goods were loaded on board the *TFL Jefferson*, which sailed from that port sometime between 8th and 14th January, bound for Felixstowe. Unfortunately, on the 18th January the vessel encountered severe weather, and the container was washed overboard and lost.

In this case the goods were declared under an open cover which had been arranged between the container operators and the defendant Underwriters, but, due to a series of delays, the declaration was not received until 19th January, on which date the certificate was issued.

The voyage was shown to be "from 19-1-82 at sea. Via/To Felixstowe to London W/house", nobody concerned with the effecting of the insurance being aware that the container had been lost.

In accordance with the terms of the open cover, the goods were insured subject to the Institute Cargo Clauses (All Risks) 1.1.63, and cover was to attach from the time the assured became at risk or assumed interest, thence to continue in transit until delivery at final destination. A special condition, relating to goods purchased on f.o.b., f.a.s., or similar terms, stated that such goods were to be at Underwriters' risk from the time they left the suppliers' factory. Despite this condition it was contended that the contract, as contained in the certificate, defined the period of the voyage and the starting point of the insurance, accordingly the goods were not insured until they were at sea on 19th January, this being the "place named in the policy" as referred to in the standard clauses.

In the end, although be found it a difficult decision to reach, Mr. Justice Neil could see no escape from the conclusion that the words used were not merely identifying the vessel and the voyage by reference to a geographical location on a particular date, but were specifying the voyage and also the time from which the cover was to date. As he saw it, the date in the certificate specified the date on which cover under the contract of insurance began, but if the words had been "from New York" there would have been a strong argument for saying that, by reason of the special condition, the cover would have operated from the suppliers' premises.

It is apparent that a good deal of care is required on the part of both the seller and the buyer to recognise their insurance obligations, and to ensure that the requisite cover is maintained, if their respective interests are to be fully protected during the whole of the material time the property is at risk.

Chapter 6

MINIMISING LOSSES (1)

The traditional "sue and labour" clause has disappeared under the new standard cargo conditions, to be replaced by new provisions relating to the duties of the assured. In this article Kenneth Goodacre explains, with the aid of some historical background, how the clause could be of special benefit to an assured. In a subsequent article he will look at the new provisions to see how they compare.

In January 1878, school children had the benefit of a day's holiday to join the crowds in cheering the progress of the tug *Anglia* as she made her way up the Thames from Greenwich to the East India Docks, thence to proceed to Westminster. Known as "Three-Finger Jack" because of the arrangement of her funnels — one forward amidships, and a pair abreast further aft — she probably made a fine sight as her paddle-wheels, 15 feet in diameter, threshed the water.

The main object of the exuberence, however, was the strange cylindrical vessel which she had in tow, for this contained the well-known "Cleopatra's Needle", which was finally erected on 12th September, 1878, on the Victoria Embankment, at a site chosen by the prime minister of the day, Benjamin Disraeli. It was the culmination of a patriotic effort to bring the monelith from Alexandria, which had involved a daring act of seamanship costing six lives, and required salvage services by the steamer *Fitzmaurice*, in the Bay of Biscay. It was these services which were the subject of a Court action to decide the meaning and extent of the *Sue and Labour* Clause in the standard marine policy, and had some influence in the formulation of the Marine Insurance Act.

Although the obelisk was first quarried about 1500 B.C. it was not removed to Alexandria and erected there until about 15 B.C.. It apparently fell and lay neglected, half buried in the sands, for some centuries, until it was discovered by the famous Scottish general, Sir Ralph Abercromby, in 1801.

His presence there was the result of Napoleon's ambition to strike a blow against France's most powerful enemy, England, by opening a route to India, and thus threatening this "jewel in the crown". Napoleon had already put Egypt at his mercy by winning the Battle of the Pyramids in July, 1798, near Cairo, and had ships available for the purpose of landing reinforcements, but his plans were frustrated by Nelson's dramatic victory at Aboukir Bay on lst August 1798, (the "Battle of the Nile") when the French fleet was destroyed. Napoleon returned to France, and it fell to Abercromby to deal with the expeditionary army he had left behind. Landing at Aboukir Bay in 1801 despite a hostile reception by the enemy, his soldiers forced the French to retreat towards Alexandria. Several days of fighting ensued, but although a determined effort was made by the enemy troops, they were defeated with heavy loss, and both Alexandria and Cairo capitulated. Abercromby was severely wounded during the battle, but continued to give orders until he fainted, dying a few days later. It was his wish to have the Needle removed to England to commemorate this victory, and in 1819 it was presented to the British nation, as a worthy memorial of Nelson and Abercromby, by the Viceroy of Egypt.

However, it was obviously no mean task to bring a huge carved monument of granite, 68½ feet high, and weighing about 200 tons, many hundreds of miles across the sea, and nobody was anxious to take up the offer. But it seems that with a growing interest in Egypt consequent on the opening of the Suez Canal in 1869, and the acquisition of the major part of the shares by Disraeli in 1875, attention was again directed at the project.

Sponsorship was forthcoming from one Erasmus Wilson, a London Surgeon, who was prepared to pay £10,000 if the obelisk could be transported to London, and there erected uninjured. Thus, a " no-cure, no pay" agreement was reached with John Dixon, a civil engineer, who was patriotic enough to take the risk, as it was not expected that the £10,000 would more than cover the expenses, much of which would be spent on setting the obelisk on its site. Notable for his construction of several bridges in Britain, and for building the first railway in China, he conceived the idea of building a vessel, to be named the *Cleopatra*, specially designed to transport the Needle. This was, in fact, little more than a cylindrical iron case in which the obelisk could be stowed and in which it would float. The vessel had no other use, and was fit for no other purpose. It was quite subordinate to its cargo, and the cost of its construction was, for all practical purposes nothing more than part of the cost of transporting the obelisk. This work was carried out at the modest price of about £1,000, as the builders did not seek to make a large profit from such a noble cause, and it was then dismantled and taken to Alexandria.

By mid-September 1877 the obelisk was in the casing, ready to be towed to England. It is said that before being launched it fell into a pre-historic tomb, and then, after being towed into the sea by tugs, struck a rock and sank, requiring it to be raised and repaired. In the event, the strange craft, complete with a keel and rudder, also a deck and cabin, to accommodate a crew of six, left Alexandria in the tow of the steamship *Olga* (which had been engaged by Dixon at a cost of £900) on the 21st September, 1877. By this time, Dixon had incurred expenditure of about £4,000, and so he took out insurance for this sum, against "total loss only" of the cylinder and its contents.

Nothing untoward happened until the two vessels reached the Bay of Biscay, when a severe storm was encountered, resulting in the cargo shifting in the *Cleopatra*, and causing her to list heavily. The *Olga* was compelled to cast off so as to avoid danger to both vessels, and a boat was put out to try and take off the crew of the *Cleopatra*. Unfortunately, this boat was carried away by the storm, so it is recorded on the Needle that six men perished in the bold attempt to succour the crew on that day, and lists their names for posterity.

Another attempt the next day proved successful, but then the *Olga* lost sight of the *Cleopatra*, and having vainly endeavoured to find her, gave up the search and carried on to England alone. On the same evening, however, the steamer *Fitzmaurice* came upon the floating obelisk, and succeeded in taking it in tow to Ferrol, where it was refitted and towed from that port to the Thames by the tug *Anglia*.

The Court of Admiralty awarded salvage of £2,000 to the *Fitzmaurice*, based on an estimated value of £25,000 for the property saved. This was paid by John Dixon, who was naturally hopeful that he would be able to recover the outlay under his insurance policies; it was, after all, an expense incurred to prevent a loss which would otherwise have fallen on the Underwriters, the *Cleopatra* and her cargo being in imminent danger of destruction. Possibly he had been advised by his brokers, Barr and Co., that such expenses could be recovered, for reference to the 5th edition of *Arnould* (p.778) would have extracted the opinion that salvage was recoverable from Underwriters "in virtue of an express clause in the policy inserted for such a case, and known as the sue and labour clause", although no authority was quoted to support this proposition. In John Dixon's case, his policies contained the *Sue and Labour Clause* in the familiar style of the S.G. Form as follows:

> And, in case of any loss or misfortune, it shall be lawful for the assured, their factors, servants, and assigns, to sue, labour, and travel for, in, and about the defence, safeguard, and recovery of the said goods and merchandizes, or any part thereof, without prejudice to this insurance, to the charges whereof we the assurers will contribute each one according to the rate and quantity of his sum herein assured.

At the time, however, the *Sue and Labour Clause* was under close consideration by Underwriters, due to the fact that, in another salvage case, the owners of the vessel had elected to repair the vessel at considerable cost, so as to improve her market value, and to claim 100 per cent. of the policy sum. The question in that case (*Aitchison v. Lohre*) was whether the owners could also recover their proportion of the salvage charges under the *Sue and Labour Clause*.

In the Queen's Bench Division it was decided that the salvage, or general average expenditure, described in the case, did not come within that clause, but the Court of Appeal was of a different opinion. Lord Justice Brett said that "the general construction of the clause is that if, by perils insured against, the subject-matter of insurance is brought into such danger that, without unusual or extraordinary labour or expense, a loss will very probably fall on the Underwriters, and if the assured or his agents or servants exert unusual or extraordinary labour, *or if the assured is made liable to unusual or extraordinary expense in or for efforts* to avert a loss, which, if it occurs, will fall on the Underwriters, then each Underwriter will ... pay a sum ..."

It can readily be seen that at this point the Court was in agreement with *Arnould*, and that John Dixon was in with a fair chance. The case of *Dixon v. Whitworth* was argued before Mr. Justice Lindley, who delivered judgment in the assured's favour on 12th May, 1879, by saying: "It is true that the language of the suing and labouring clause does not in terms extend to any services except those rendered by the assured, their factors, servants and assigns: and it is also true that the salvage services in this case were not rendered by Mr. Dixon, nor by any factor, servant or assign of his, unless the salvors are to be regarded as having been his agents by necessity or by ratification. But without discussing how far the salvors can properly be regarded as agents, I take it to be settled that the suing and labouring clause ought to be construed to cover expenditure which the assured necessarily became liable to pay, by way of salvage in respect of preservation from loss which if it had occurred would have fallen on the Underwriters ... in my opinion they are bound by this clause to indemnify the plaintiff, in proportion to the sums they respectively insured, against his loss of the £2,000 awarded for salvage."

Dealing with the fact that John Dixon had only insured in respect of his partial interest in the venture, and whether he was entitled to recover the whole of the £2,000, or only some portion of that sum, he ruled: "This question depends on the true construction and effect of the suing and labouring clause, and, curiously enough, appears never yet to have been decided — at least, in this country. The language of the clause is in favour of the plaintiff, and so in my opinion is its true effect. By it the Underwriters agree to contribute in proportion to the amount subscribed to such charges as the assured shall be put to in preventing a loss which, if not prevented, would fall on the Underwriters. There are no words to the effect that the assured shall only be repaid such proportion of those charges as, on an equitable adjustment between himself and others, would fall on him alone. The agreement is, to contribute (in proportion to the amount subscribed) to the charges of his services. In other words, the Underwriters agree to pay him for his services; each Underwriter agreeing to pay in proportion to the amount for which he insures. Moreover, the early part of the clause authorizes the assured to endeavour to save, not his interest in the thing insured, but the thing itself; and the language of the clause is adapted in cases in which other persons besides himself are interested in that thing. Further, it is now clearly established that this clause is a distinct and independent agreement, which, although occurring in and forming part of the policy, may entitle the assured to recover more than the amount underwritten; see *Lohre v. Aitchison*. Having regard to this principle, and to the language and known object of the clause, I am of the opinion that, whatever services or charges of the assured fairly come within it must be paid for by the Underwriters in proportion to their subscriptions."

Although the *Sue and Labour Clause* did not enable John Dixon to obtain any award for the costs of the Admiralty proceedings, or any of the expenses of re-fitting at Ferrol and towage from that port to London — these not being incurred to avoid a total loss by perils of the sea — at least, he was probably relieved to find the Court was prepared to adopt a favourable attitude towards the salvage charges.

Unfortunately, such pleasure as he might have derived from the decision was not to last very long. Only two months later, when the case of *Aitchison v. Lohre* went to the House of Lords, it was ruled by Lord Blackburn that general average and salvage did not come within either the words or the object of the suing and labouring clause, which was designed to encourage exertion on the part of the assured or their agents themselves, or by persons they had hired for the purpose, not to provide an additional remedy for the recovery, by the assured, of indemnity for a loss which had been assessed by maritime law, in consequence of the peril.

Not surprisingly, therefore, the decision in John Dixon's case was successfully appealed against, the Court finding, on the authority of *Aitchison v. Lohre*, that the Underwriters were not liable to repay the £2,000 awarded as salvage, salvage expenses not being within the *Sue and Labour Clause*, and there being no other provision under which such expenses could be recovered under a policy covering "total loss only". Although it was agreed that the *Cleopatra* was totally lost whilst abandoned, her recovery did away with that total loss, and John Dixon could not recover the expense of saving her from that temporary total loss, although, without the assistance of the salvors there would have been a permanent total loss for which the Underwriters would have been liable.

It must be drawn to attention, nevertheless, that only a part of Mr. Justice Lindley's decision was reversed. The position remained that, without an express provision to the contrary, the expenses recoverable under the *Sue and Labour Clause* could not be reduced in the proportion that the actual value of the subject-matter insured bore to the insured value. In addition, the clause was firmly established to be a supplementary contact entitling an assured to recover any expenses properly incurred pursuant to the clause, even if these were in addition to a total loss — as now evidenced by S.78(1) of the Marine Insurance Act.

Having survived a close encounter with a German bomb during an air-raid in September, 1917, the monument serves to remind us that John Dixon must have been considerably out-of-pocket for all his efforts. Although his name appears on the obelisk as the engineer who erected it on the spot where it stands, it was Erasmus Wilson who was rewarded with a knighthood ...

Chapter 7

MINIMISING LOSSES (2)

Concluding his remarks on the duty of the assured to avert or minimise a loss to his goods, the author illustrates how the courts have applied this burden.

In the previous article it was demonstrated that the *Sue and Labour Clause* occupied a special, but limited, position in the marine insurance contract. In order to show that an expense was recoverable under the clause, the following distinctive features needed to be present:

(1) The loss or misfortune must actually have occurred, or commenced to operate, so that expense was required to avert or diminish a loss covered by the policy.

(2) The expenses must have been incurred by the assured, their factors, servants or assigns.

(3) They had to be incurred solely in connection with one particular interest, i.e. not for the common benefit of the adventure.

It can readily be appreciated that expenses in the nature of general average, or awards to salvors, did not fall within the scope of the clause; in fact S.78(2) of the Marine Insurance Act expressly excludes such charges. However, if a separate contract was undertaken for the sole purpose of saving the cargo, with the salvor becoming the servant of the assured, the costs would naturally qualify as sue and labour charges.

A somewhat unusual application of the clause was upheld in the case of the *Pomeranian* in 1895, which involved a shipment of live cattle insured on terms which included mortality from any cause whatsoever. Due to the vessel having to resort to a port of refuge in order to repair damage to her machinery caused by heavy weather, it became necessary for the captain to purchase extra fodder to prevent the animals starving during the prolonged voyage. In this case the captain was regarded as an agent of the cargo owner in time of necessity.

Possibly the most common use of the clause would be in connection with the reconditioning, at an intermediate port, of goods damaged by an insured peril, so as to prevent further damage, or even a total loss. It must be remembered, however, that Underwriters' liability normally ceases on arrival at destination, and they cannot be called upon to pay for any aggravation of damage to cargo after the expiry of the policy, consequently reconditioning charges at destination will usually be incurred to assess the damage, rather than to avert or diminish a loss which would otherwise fall on them. Such charges are more aptly called "particular charges", which by S.64(2) of the Marine Insurance Act are defined as "expenses incurred by or on behalf of the assured for the safety or preservation of the subject-matter insured, other than general average and salvage charges."

In fact, sue and labour expenses were a special form of particular charges, but occupied a privileged position because of the specific terms of the clause in the policy. No mention is made in the Marine Insurance Act of the measure of indemnity for particular charges, but where they were not recoverable under the *Sue and Labour Clause* it has been the custom to pay such charges when the claim itself was recoverable. In the absence of any supplementary engagement, however, any claim, together with the charges incurred, would be limited to the sum insured.

A similar situation would arise if salvage services, rendered independently of contract, were incurred solely for the benefit of cargo. S.65(1) of the Marine Insurance Act provides that "subject to any express provision in the policy, salvage charges incurred in preventing a loss by perils insured against may be recovered as a loss by those perils", and consequently the limitation of the sum insured would again apply. If the salvage services were rendered for the common benefit, and therefore a general average contribution became payable, this would, in the words of S.66(4) of the Act, be recoverable if the expense was "incurred for the purpose of avoiding, or in connexion with the avoidance of, a peril insured against" and this, too, in the absence of any express stipulation, would be subject to the policy limitation.

Since none of this was readily apparent to an assured not fully conversant with English law and practice, it was not surprising that he might not understand that he could not always recover his full expenditure where successful efforts had been made to prevent a total loss, especially as the Marine Insurance Act imposes a statutory duty on him and his agents, to take reasonable measures to avert or minimise a loss (S.78(4)).

Indicative of this difficulty was the Australian case of *Emperor Goldmining Co.Ltd. v. Switzerland General Insurance Co.Ltd.* (1964) which concerned a cargo of general freight and explosives shipped on an auxiliary ketch bound from Sydney to Fiji. Owing to a leak the ketch was obliged to return to Sydney, and, as part of the cargo was damaged, costs were incurred in unloading, storing and reloading the cargo. The policy covered the cargo on "all risks" terms, but did not contain a *Sue and Labour Clause*, consequently the Underwriters were reluctant to make any payment in respect of the costs. The question, therefore, was whether expenses incurred to safeguard the goods were only recoverable under a *Sue and Labour Clause*, or whether they were simply recoverable as expenses necessarily incurred in consequence of, and to avert, a peril insured against. The Australian Marine Insurance Act included the same provision as S.78(4) of the English Act, and Mr. Justice Manning could see no reason why the duty to take reasonable measures to minimise a loss should be carried out by the assured at his own expense. The case seemed to support the view that particular charges could be recovered under the policy quite apart from the *Sue and Labour Clause*, provided the total claim did not exceed the policy limit.

However, some doubt was cast on this view in the later case of *Integrated Container Service Inc. v. British Traders Insurance Co. Ltd.* (1981) when Mr. Justice Neill expressed great diffidence in being unable to follow the decision of Mr. Justice Manning, as he would have been reluctant to imply a term not shown in the policy, unless it could be demonstrated to be one that the parties intended to form part of the contract. However, he was saved from this difficulty, as the policy he was considering did, in fact contain a *Sue and Labour Clause*, and he decided that the charges in dispute were recoverable under that clause.

When the market came to revise the standard clauses, it was perhaps quite natural that Underwriters would take the opportunity to modernise the provisions of the *Sue and Labour Clause*, and to spell out the duties of the assured more immediately, so as to emphasise that the onus is upon them to act as if uninsured. The spirit of the clause, together with the provisions of the Marine Insurance Act, and the attendant *Waiver Clause*, are now incorporated under the sub-section headed *Minimising Losses*, viz:

MINIMISING LOSSES

16   It is the duty of the Assured and their servants and agents in respect of loss recoverable hereunder

16.1   to take such measures as may be reasonable for the purpose of averting or minimising such loss, and

16.2   to ensure that all rights against carriers, bailees or other third parties are properly preserved and exercised and the Underwriters will, in addition to any loss recoverable hereunder, reimburse the Assured for any charges properly and reasonably incurred in pursuance of these duties.

17   Measures taken by the Assured or the Underwriters with the object of saving, protecting or recovering the subject-matter insured shall not be considered as a waiver or acceptance of abandonment or otherwise prejudice the rights of either party.

It can be seen at once that there is no longer any mention of suing and labouring as such, and that Clause 16 can be taken as it is, without any reference to S.78 of the Marine Insurance Act, which was specifically related to the *Sue and Labour Clause* in the S.G. Form. However, insofar as the Underwriters agree to pay, in addition to any loss, the reasonable costs of measures taken for the purpose of averting or minimising a loss recoverable under the policy, the supplementary nature of the *Sue and Labour Clause* has been preserved. Consequently, charges coming within the scope of the clause will continue to be paid whether the measures are successful or not, and in addition to a total loss. The value agreed in the policy is, of course, (according to S.27(3) of the Marine Insurance Act), conclusive as between the insurer and assured in the absence of fraud, consequently it is not possible to apply under-insurance to such charges without a special provision in the terms of the contract. While the essential features of the old clause have not been disturbed, nevertheless a welcome clarification has taken place in regard to the costs which an assured can incur in preserving Underwriters' rights of subrogation, or in endeavouring to obtain a recovery from negligent carriers, or bailees, on their behalf. In the past these have often been a source of contention, a situation which Underwriters have now seen fit to remedy.

Underwriters have always maintained that they are only liable for charges which are reasonable, and obtained a judicial pronouncement to this effect in *Lee v. Southern Insurance Company* [1870]. This was in connection with an insurance on freight, where the ship having stranded, the shipowner decided to discharge the goods and forward them by rail. There was, however, every expectation of refloating the vessel, so that the goods could be reloaded and forwarded to destination in the original manner. Subsequent to the actual refloating and repair of the vessel, the Court ruled that the insurers should only bear the expenditure which would have been incurred had the cargo been re-shipped, this being the more economical method.

The question of whether reasonable measures have been taken by the assured to avert or minimise a loss came under close scrutiny in the previously mentioned case of *Integrated Container Service Inc. v. British Traders Insurance Co. Ltd.*. The facts of the matter were that the plaintiffs leased container and trailer equipment to a Japanese firm, who moved cargo to and from Japan, Taiwan and the Phillipines where they had depots, and were required, as bailees, to maintain insurance on the property. In 1975, when they had more than a thousand containers on hire, the firm was found to be insolvent and ceased trading, consequently the policy they were required to provide lapsed through non-payment of premium. In a subsequent rescue operation the plaintiffs managed to trace and recover all but two of the containers, which had been scattered over the Far East, their costs amounting to approximately $134,000 in respect of customs and storage charges, removal to their own depots, travelling expenses of those engaged in the rescue work, and legal fees for advice obtained from Japanese lawyers to secure the release of the property.

The plaintiffs had taken out a contingency policy to indemnify them in the event of their being unable to recover from the lessees for loss or damage to the containers, this being against "all risks" as per the Institute Container Clauses, the S.G. policy form to which they were attached containing the usual *Sue and Labour Clause*. In addition, Clause 9 of the Container Clauses stated that it was "the duty of the Assured and their Agents in all cases, to take such measures as may be reasonable for the purpose of averting or minimising a loss and to ensure that all rights against carriers, bailees or other third parties are properly preserved and exercised"—a provision which is very similar to that in the present standard cargo conditions.

The Underwriters were prepared to pay for the lost containers, and for the repair costs to damaged units, but denied liability with regard to the recovery costs as, in their view, there was no question of any insured peril operating to cause the loss, these being incurred solely on a commercial undertaking to retrieve containers from a bankrupt hirer.

As already intimated, Mr. Justice Neill ruled, in the Commercial Court, that such costs were recoverable under the suing and labouring clause, this judgment being based on his finding that the insurance cover effected was an insurance on goods, and not merely a policy offsetting the liability of the lessees. After the case had been referred to the Official Referee to decide what sue and labour costs were recoverable, however, the Underwriters appealed and raised other points in their defence, their main contention being that there was no evidence to show that a loss would "very probably" have occurred within the currency of the policy, in the absence of the measures taken. As can be seen from the previous article the Underwriters were attempting to rely on the words used by Lord Justice Brett in *Lohre v. Aitchison.*

The Court of Appeal was not impressed with this argument. While none of the containers was in immediate danger of being disposed of or physically damaged, it would inevitably follow that, if the assured had not exerted themselves, they would not have recovered the containers. Either the containers would be sold towards satisfaction of unpaid charges by port authorities or warehousemen, or they would eventually be annexed by third parties as articles apparently abandoned by the true owners. The embracing picture which covered all the containers was that they had been effectively abandoned by their custodians, and, until they were recovered they were lost, and at the mercy of whatever should befall them. They were thus exposed to the risk of loss or damage from some cause or other, and since the Court was concerned with a policy which covered "all risks", the insurers were liable to indemnify the assured for moneys laid out to avert a claim which might result from the existence of a threat of loss or damage, no matter if that threat resulted from the insolvency of the lessees.

In any case the Court observed that there was nothing in the clauses or in the Marine Insurance Act which required the assured to show that a loss would "very probably" have occurred. In the view of the Lord Justice Eveleigh it would place an assured in a dilemma to demand such a high degree of proof, as he would have to make up his mind whether he could satisfy that burden or do nothing and take the risk that insurers would be able to show that he should have acted in defence of the goods. "As the right to recover expenses is a corollary of the duty to act, in my opinion the assured should be entitled to recover all extraordinary expenses reasonably incurred by him where he can demonstrate that a prudent assured person, mindful of an obligation to prevent a loss, would incur expense of an unusual kind ... Someone has to be trusted to be reasonable in this situation and insurers have imposed that responsibility on the assured. It seems to me that it would be wholly unreasonable to penalize an assured on the basis that, while he has shown that a reasonable man would have done as he did, yet in the light of all that has transpired the loss would not, as we now know, have been probable. In the vast majority of cases at least the assured will not incur extraordinary expenditure unless he feels it incumbent upon him to do so." He did not think it was open to insurers by searching enquiries and detailed analysis to assert that as a matter of ultimate truth they would never have been liable.

It is interesting to note that while Underwriters, under the new clauses, undertake to reimburse the assured for any charges properly and reasonably incurred in pursuance of their duties, in addition to any recoverable loss, unlike the standard hull clauses there is no upper limit stated. This appears to leave it open to argue that when expenditure is incurred at the outset with a reasonable hope of a successful outcome, but the optimism is eventually found to be misplaced, Underwriters are liable for the amount involved even if this turns out to be more than the value of the goods insured. However, it can equally be argued that any attempt to avert or minimise a loss for which Underwriters would be liable can only be effective up to 100% of the insured value, consequently a situation might arise where it would be better to obtain the agreement of the Underwriters to continue with the operation.

In a potential total loss situation the *Waiver Clause* serves to protect the position of both parties, its intention being to make it clear that neither the assured nor the Underwriters are to be prejudiced by action taken to safeguard the property. In these days of rapid communication, however, probably its main function in modern practice is to allow the cargo insurers to step in and take charge of the operations without giving the impression that they have acquiesced to an abandonment of the goods by the assured.

Where, as the result of an insured marine peril, the goods are left stranded at an intermediate port, special provision is made for the forwarding charges to destination under Clause 12. This clause recognises that the subject-matter of cargo insurance is not merely the cargo itself, but also the adventure contemplated, and if that adventure is frustrated there is a total loss under the policy. If, in the circumstances, the reasonable course is to forward the goods to destination, obviously a constructive total loss will be avoided.*

---

* See also Clause 13, the *Constructive Total Loss Clause*.

Chapter 8

PRESERVING CONSISTENCY OF INTERPRETATION

The exalted idea that the use of standard English conditions in a contract would automatically ensure the application of English law and jurisdiction has been under attack in recent years. Here it is explained why marine Underwriters have taken steps to protect their position.

Tucked in neatly at the end of the standard cargo clauses is a new provision stipulating that the insurance is subject to English law and practice (Clause 19). Since the terms and conditions have for so many years been devoid of any reference to the applicable law and practice, one may wonder why it is now deemed advisable to include such a provision.

At the turn of the century it was probably true to say that if a standard English form was used in a contract, the Courts would assume that the parties intended English law to apply. Thus, in the case of *Greer v. Poole* [1880] Mr. Justice Lush observed: "It is no doubt competent to an Underwriter on an English policy to stipulate if he thinks fit that such policy shall be construed and applied in whole or in part, according to the law of any foreign, state; and the policy does so stipulate as regards general average. But except when it is so stipulated the policy must be construed according to our law ..." In 1894, in the case of the *Industrie*, to which the Courts have made frequent reference, the Court of Appeal was prepared to pay particular regard to the fact that the parties had used an English printed form of charter-party, so as to. give rise to an inference that the proper law of the contract was English law.

It must be stressed, however, that these rulings occurred at a time when British merchant shipping dominated the oceans to such an extent that London was the natural centre to resolve many maritime disputes. This exalted position was further enhanced by the fact that judgments could only be made in sterling — a stable currency which was considered to have no equal. Even in 1961 Lord Denning was prepared to describe sterling as a currency "of whose true-fixed and resting quality there is no fellow in the firmament."

As the case in question, that of *In re United Railways of Havana and Regla Warehouses*, is relevant to the pattern of events which followed, it is pertinent to mention that the Courts were concerned with a money debt in US Dollars, due under a contract the proper law of which was held to be the law of Pennsylvania, the debtor (the United Havana Railways Co.) being English, while the creditor was American. The House of Lords decided that the provable sum in US Dollars had to be converted into sterling at the rates of exchange prevailing when the relevant sums fell due and were not paid (the breach-date rule). While the case did nothing to upset established precedent, at least it did lend authority to the principle that in determining the proper law of a contract containing no express choice of law, the task of the Court is to ascertain the intention of the parties from the terms and nature of the contract and the general circumstances of the case and, if no intention can be inferred, to identify the system of the law with which the transaction has its closest and most real connection.

But now the winds of change were blowing, and in the 1970's the English Courts began to develop different attitudes. Britain's entry into the Common Market, for instance, meant that we were subject to the terms of the Treaty of Rome, and other European Courts could allow a plaintiff to claim payment of a sum of money in a foreign currency and obtain judgment in that currency. Coupled with the fact that sterling was no longer a stable currency, and its value could vary greatly between the time of the breach date and the date of judgment or payment, Lord Denning in the Court of Appeal in *Schorsch GmbH v Hennin* felt compelled to think again in 1975, and gave judgment for a German company in its national currency of Deutschmarks, thereby overturning the decision of the House of Lords fourteen years earlier. As he later confessed in his book *The Discipline of Law*: "The Court of Appeal ought to have followed the *Havana* case and refused the German company's appeal. But I am afraid we did what a great sailor once did. We turned a blind eye to the *Havana* case. We were guilty of what Lord Wilberforce afterwards described as 'some distortion of the judicial process'." Nevertheless, he felt that, eventually, a good end was attained, albeit by a bad means, for the dramatic effect of the judgment was to cause the House of Lords to depart from its own decision in the *Havana* case, when the time came to deliver judgment in *Miliangos v. George Frank (Textiles) Ltd.* [1976]. This the Lords were able to do under their own 1966 Declaration, which recognises that too rigid an adherence to precedent can lead to injustice in a particular case and unduly restrict the proper development of the law. Not surprisingly they later decided to extend judgments in foreign currencies to cases of tort and breach of contract (the *Despina R* and the *Folias* [1979]).

Returning now to the question of deciding the proper law of a contract, this point was deliberated upon at some length in *Compagnie Tunisienne de Navigation S.A. v. Compagnie d'Armement Maritime S.A.,* which, after a series of adventures, reached the House of Lords in 1970. This case concerned a contract between a Tunisian company and French shipowners for the transport of specified quantities of crude oil from one Tunisian port to another. It was made on a standard English form in the English language with typed clauses added, and contained a London arbitration clause. Disputes having arisen, arbitrators found on a preliminary point that the proper law of the contract was French law, but in the Court of Appeal it was held that English law applied because of the inclusion of the London arbitration clause. In the House of Lords, however, it was decided that the proper law was French law.

The precise route by which each of their Lordships reached that conclusion differed, but it was generally agreed that some importance should be attached to an arbitration clause providing for arbitration in a particular country when considering what was the proper law of a contract. Nevertheless, they held that this did not have the overriding effect which previous Courts had attributed to such a clause, and the words of Lord Morris of Borth-y-Gest probably sum up their opinion most conveniently. "The circumstances that parties agree that any differences are to be settled by arbitration in a certain country may and very likely will lead to an inference that they intend the law of that country to apply. But it is not a necessary inference or an inevitable one though it will often be the reasonable and sensible one. Before drawing it all the relevant circumstances are to be considered." In this case they relied on their finding that French law had the closest and most real connection with the transaction.

While the Commercial Court has been ready to provide a service for foreign litigants who wish to take advantage of the skill and experience of the first class lawyers and judges available in this country, it has at the same time been somewhat reluctant to allow foreign Courts to adjudicate in cases where English law is applicable. This reluctance was expressed very strongly by Mr. Justice Kerr in the case of *B.P. Exploration Co. (Libya) Ltd. v. Hunt* [1976] when he said: "Having arrived at the conclusion that the proper law to be applied in the present case is English law, I consider this to be the predominating factor to be borne in mind. Unless there be other considerations of overwhelming weight which militate against the English Courts, which in my view do not exist in the case, I think that the appropriate forum for deciding the rights of the parties under English law are the Courts of this country."

However, there was a growing awareness of the development of rival jurisdictions, and a natural unwillingness to challenge their competence, which gradually brought about a change of attitude, so much so that, in the Court of Appeal in the *Elli 2* [1985], Lord Justice May felt constrained to say: "... each of these cases involves a question of balancing competing considerations. For myself I would respectfully not go quite so far as Mr. Justice Kerr, and hold that the fact that the proper law to be applied is English law is a 'predominating factor' in these cases."

In the absence of any agreement between the parties it is now the practice of the Courts to pay close consideration to the Rules of the Supreme Court to first establish whether the contract is by its terms, or by implication, governed by English law—the "jurisdiction point". If the Court is satisfied on that score, then it can exercise its discretion to assume jurisdiction provided it can be sufficiently demonstrated that the case is a "proper one" for service of the writ in another country. This is appropriately referred to as the "discretion point" and leads to much discourse on the subject of *forum conveniens*.

So far as marine policies are concerned, it is recognised that the S.G. Form and the standard English clauses, produced and developed in the London insurance market, have achieved a world-wide currency. This is partly due to the long history, the great experience, the professional expertise, and the high standing of that market, combined with the traditional dominance of London as a commercial centre. It has also been helped by the process of imperial development which has led to the adoption of the Marine Insurance Act, 1906, in far corners of the globe. The result has been that in Western Europe, Australia and New Zealand, South Africa, Singapore, North Yemen, Israel, various parts of Africa, Indonesia, China and elsewhere, the standard form of English marine policy has been in regular use. Similar use has been made in the Gulf and the Middle East. Sometimes there would be an express choice of jurisdiction, but frequently there was no such choice, and the policy wording would remain as in the schedule to the Act, often with the Institute Clauses added, but sometimes translated into the appropriate language. Did this mean that, with the absence of express law or jurisdiction, the parties were subject to English law with its potential consequences under our law on jurisdiction? Or, to put it another way, did the use of the English standard conditions indicate that the parties to the insurance intended to subject the contract to English law or to establish a close and real connection with England? These questions were debated at length in the case of the *Amin Rasheed Shipping Corporation v. Kuwait Insurance Co.* which reached the House of Lords in 1983.

The plaintiffs were the owners of a small cargo vessel of landing craft type, named *Al Wahib*, which, in February 1980, entered a minor port in Saudi Arabia just south of Kuwait. Apparently the master was thought to be using the vessel to try and smuggle diesel oil from Saudi Arabia to the United Arab Emirates, consequently the master and crew were seized by the Saudi Arabian Authorities and imprisoned. Although they were later released, the vessel remained where it was, apparently confiscated.

As the owners were insured with the defendant insurance company on the terms of Institute War and Strikes Clauses (Hulls) they claimed for the loss of their vessel, but this was declined by the insurers under the exclusion in the clauses relieving them for "loss, damage or expense arising from ... arrest, restraint, or detainment ... by reason of infringement of any customs regulations". The accusation of smuggling was strongly denied by the owners, who sought redress through the English Courts, contending that there was an intention to incorporate English law into the contract, particularly as one of the exclusions referred to "... any claim for expenses arising from delay except such expenses as would be recoverable in principle in English law and practice under the York-Antwerp Rules 1950", this being a reference to general average. To this end they obtained an order made *ex parte*, granting leave to serve proceedings upon the insurance company in Kuwait. The Kuwait Insurance Company then sought to set aside these proceedings on the grounds that the Court had no jurisdiction to give leave for such service; alternatively they argued that the Court should exercise its discretion against permitting such service on the ground that Kuwait and not England was the appropriate forum for trial of the action.

In the Commercial Court Mr. Justice Bingham ascertained that the text of the policy form very closely followed the language of the statutory form of English marine policy, although this had not been adopted in its entirety. Even so, he thought that the standard form had become part of the *lingua franca* of international marine insurance, and the more international and generally used the form and its attached clauses became, so they tended to be less specifically English. While the contract was arranged by brokers in London, the policy was made and issued in Kuwait, and provided for claims to be payable there. He could see no reason why the Kuwaiti Courts would encounter difficulty in giving the policy its correct commercial interpretation, as a Kuwaiti judge, like any other, faced with a question of construction on which domestic authority was lacking, would seek assistance from any jurisdiction in which there was helpful authority, and would be able to inform himself of the interpretation with which some phrases in the policy had become encrusted. Accordingly he concluded that the proper law of the contract was Kuwaiti, and therefore the Court had no jurisdiction to order service of suit on the insurers in Kuwait. Strictly speaking this left him without any need to consider the discretion point, but, mindful that his decision on the proper law of the contract might be held to be wrong, he expressed the opinion that the factual question of whether the vessel was involved in smuggling activities, which was the main difficulty, could be determined as well in Kuwait as in England, possibly better. On this basis, he would have exercised his discretion against upholding service, and the result would have been the same.

In the Court of Appeal there was a diversity of opinion. Sir John Donaldson, M.R., held in favour of the assured on both the jurisdiction and the discretion points. Lord Justice May found in favour of the assured on the jurisdiction point, but against them on the discretion point. Lord Justice Goff found against the assured on the jurisdiction point, and therefore refrained from expressing any opinion on the discretion point, despite the fact that his two brethren were divided on it. The result was that the appeal failed but created a wide variety of judicial reasoning.

When the case proceeded to the House of Lords, however, their Lordships were unanimous in finding that not only was English law the proper law of the contract, but also that Kuwait was the best forum for trying the case.

In the leading judgment Lord Diplock said that the obsolete language of the Lloyd's S.G. policy as scheduled to the Marine Insurance Act, 1906, made it impossible to discover what were the legal incidents of the mutual rights and obligations accepted by the insurers and the assured as having been brought into existence by the contract, unless recourse was had not only to the rules for construction of the policy contained in the first schedule, but also to many of the substantive provisions of the Act. In the absence of an indigenous law of Marine Insurance in Kuwait, English law was the only system of private law by reference to which it was possible for a Kuwaiti Court to give a sensible and precise meaning to the language that the parties had chosen to use in the policy. In holding that a Kuwaiti Court was nevertheless a *forum conveniens* for the dispute he ruled: "My Lords, the jurisdiction exercised by an English Court over a foreign corporation which has no place of business in this country, as a result of granting leave ... for service out of the jurisdiction of a writ on that corporation is an exhorbitant jurisdiction, i.e. it is one which under general English conflict rules, an English Court would not recognize as possessed by any foreign Court in the absence of some treaty providing for such recognition. Comity thus dictates that the judicial discretion to grant leave ... should be exercised with circumspection in cases where there exists an alternative forum, viz. the Courts of the foreign country where the defendant does carry on business, and whose jurisdiction would be recognized under English conflict rules."

He then went on to say that the onus of persuading the Court to exercise its discretion was upon the would-be plaintiff, as the exhorbitance of the jurisdiction sought to be invoked was an important factor to be placed in the balance against granting leave. "It is a factor that is capable of being outweighed if the would-be plaintiff can satisfy the English Court that justice either could not be obtained by him in the alternative forum; or could only be obtained at excessive cost, delay or inconvenience. In the instant case, the assured failed to satisfy Mr. Justice Bingham that any of these factors in favour of granting leave to compel the insurers to submit to the exhorbitant jurisdiction of the English Court were of sufficient moment to satisfy the onus."

While there was substantial agreement by the other Law Lords, Lord Wilberforce felt that, in considering the discretion point, the Court should take into account the nature of the dispute, the legal and practical issues involved, such questions as local knowledge, availability of witnesses and their evidence and expense.

In subsequent cases the Courts have had occasion to wonder whether the tests laid down by Lord Diplock on the discretion point were intended to be restrictive or exhaustive, but have concluded, by taking them in conjunction with the views of Lord Wilberforce, that all the relevant facts and circumstances must be taken into account in the interests of justice, e.g. the *Spiliada* [1985].

By making the new cargo clauses subject to English law and practice, Underwriters have taken a useful step towards avoiding disputes on this aspect of the contract, and to ensure that existing case law and the Marine Insurance Act, 1906, will be fully applied, even if some other jurisdiction is involved.

Of course, the Rules of the Supreme Court would still impose upon a plaintiff the burden of showing good reasons why service of a writ, calling for appearance before an English Court, should, in the circumstances, be permitted on a foreign defendant. Indeed, the E.E.C. Convention on Judgments in Civil and Commercial Matters enables defendants domiciled in E.E.C. countries to have the trial in their own Courts, and it is clearly desirable for the parties to the insurance contract to stipulate which jurisdiction should apply.

The London market has not overlooked this fact, and reference to the marine policy form will reveal the words "This insurance is subject to English jurisdiction". Thus, so far as their own policies are concerned, they have closed the door on "forum shopping", and special agreement will be necessary if any other law or foreign jurisdiction is required.

Chapter 9

INCREASED VALUE POLICIES

The introduction of the Increased Value Clause into the standard cargo clauses gives the author the opportunity to discuss P.P.I. Policies — and their disadvantages.

As may be recalled, the formation of the South Sea Company in 1711 was destined to lead to a period of wild speculation and corruption. In conjunction with the Anglo-Spanish Treaty of 1713, a plan was produced for redistributing the National Debt and offering better terms to the national Exchequer, in return for which a monopoly of trade with South America and the Pacific Islands would be secured. When this got under way in 1719, there followed an extraordinary hysteria for investment, the constant flow of funds justifying new issues of stock to such an extent that the naive public was encouraged to participate in more and more implausible projects, and even the Government became involved with its schemes. When the mania reached its peak in 1720, and the "bubble" finally burst, it was left to Sir Robert Walpole, Britain's first prime minister, to extricate the nation out of its difficulties.

Unfortunately greed and fraudulence continued to characterise the years which followed, and in marine insurance wagering and gaming contracts were prevalent. Such contracts, being purely speculative, could be accompanied by the natural temptation to enter into conspiracies to bring about the required ends. To repress this tendency, the Marine Insurance Act ("Gambling Act") of 1745 was passed, having as its objective the prohibition of policies taken out by persons with no direct interest in a loss. It particularly related to policies on British ships and their cargoes which were taken out by way of gaming or wagering, or which were written "interest or no interest", or "without further proof of interest than the policy", or "without benefit of salvage to the insurer". Such policies, of course, were known as "P.P.I. Policies" i.e. "Policy Proof of Interest".

Despite the prohibition, and the fact that such insurances would be "null and void to all intents and purposes", they continued to be used, and the Courts would, in some cases, be prepared to resolve disputes under them. Thus, in *Buchanan v. Faber* [1899], where a genuine insurable interest existed, the Court consented with the agreement of the parties, to try the case as if the policy did not contain a *P.P.I. Clause*. On the other hand, in the case of *Gedge v. Royal Exchange Assurance Corporation* [1900], the Court took the view that they could not ignore the presence of the clause because there was, in fact, no insurable interest, the insurance being a purely speculative one under which a total loss was payable in the event of the vessel failing to arrive by a certain date. The Underwriters disputed the subsequent claim on the grounds of the concealment of the lack of insurable interest, and the Court held that no action was maintainable by the assured on a contract rendered illegal by the 1745 Act.

In practice, of course, P.P.I. policies serve a very real need and are commonly effected on such interests as increased value, disbursements, anticipated profits and the like, where the nature of the interest may be difficult to define with accuracy and the *quantum* may be hard to fix. Their advantage is that in the event of loss by an insured peril, the production of the policy is deemed to be sufficient proof of interest entitling the assured to recover from Underwriters.

Possibly the Legislature had this in mind when the 1745 Act (19 Geo.2.c.37) was repealed under the second schedule to the Marine Insurance Act, 1906, and replaced by the provisions of S.4 of that Act reading:

(1) Every contract of marine insurance by way of gaming or wagering is void.

(2) A contract of marine insurance is deemed to be a gaming or wagering contract-

    (a) Where the assured has not an insurable interest as defined by the Act, and the contract is entered into with no expectation of acquiring such interest; or

    (b) Where the policy is made "interest or no interest," or "without further proof of interest than the policy itself," or "without benefit of salvage to the insurer," or subject to any like term:

61

> Provided that, where there is no possibility of salvage, a policy may be effected without benefit of salvage to the insurer.

While the Act served to bring all marine insurances within its ambit, not merely those on British vessels or their cargoes, it no longer prohibited P.P.I. policies, it merely made them "void". The Marine Insurance (Gambling Policies) Act, 1909, went a step further, however, and made it a criminal offence for any person to procure a contract of marine insurance without having a *bona fide* interest (or the expectation of acquiring such an interest), and for employees of a shipowner, not being part owners, to effect P.P.I. policies. Thus, there remained no objection to policies falling within S.4(2)(b) of the Marine Insurance Act, 1906, provided there existed a *bona fide* interest, or the expectation of acquiring such interest; they simply remained, at law, unenforceable, although perfectly legal.

As a result of this disability it became the practice to pin the *P.P.I. Clause* to such policies to facilitate removal in case the parties wished to resort to the Courts. This procedure was sanctioned by the Underwriters in the Clause itself:

> This slip is no part of the policy, and is not to be attached thereto, but is to be considered as binding in honour on the Underwriters; the assured however having permission to remove it from this policy should they so desire.
>
> Full interest admitted; the policy being deemed sufficient proof of interest. This insurance is without benefit of salvage.

Although Underwriters are morally bound to observe the clause most scrupulously, and policies with the clause pinned or stapled on are referred to as "honour" policies, nevertheless, at times there can be differences of opinion. In *Cheshire and Co. v. Thompson* [1918], for instance, there was a dispute with Underwriters over the question of non-disclosure of a material fact by the brokers. The assured therefore availed themselves of the liberty to remove the clause and took proceedings against the Underwriters. The Court, being unaware that the contract came within S.4(2)(b) of the Marine Insurance Act, held in favour of the Underwriters who had adhered to their implied agreement not to plead or disclose the fact that the policy was written P.P.I.. It was only when the assured was subsequently obliged to take action against the brokers for negligence that the nature of the policy came to light.

Unfortunately, in the only three cases recorded in the text books on the subject of P.P.I. policies since the passing of the Marine Insurance Act, the Courts have been consistent in their view that such policies remain void whether the clause is detached or not. In *Cheshire and Co. v. Vaughan Bros. and Co.* [1919], which concerned the claim against the brokers just mentioned, it was held that no action for damages could be maintained over a policy which was itself void. The suggestion that S.4(2)(b) of the Marine Insurance Act should, by implication, not apply if insurable interest could be shown to exist was rejected by McCardie, J. on the grounds that the intent of the Section was "to provide a statutory condemnation both of contracts in which there is no insurable interest and of contracts which use words which might well suggest that no insurable interest existed."

Again, in *re London County Commercial Re-Insurance Office* [1922] Lawrence, J. held that the removal of the slip could not render the policies valid if they were null and void when issued. In that case, however, claimants were under difficulty because their claims had to be presented to the liquidator of the company concerned, who felt unable to honour the agreement. They were able to claim for the returns of premium, however, the policies not being illegal, merely void, the consideration for which the premiums had been paid having wholly failed (vide S.84(1) of the M.I.A.).

The third case, that of *Edwards and Co. Ltd. v. Motor Union Insurance Co.* [1922] was concerned with Underwriters' subrogation rights under a freight policy. This again came before McCardie, J. who refused to recognise such rights on a P.P.I. policy, which he described as a document "stricken with sterility by Act of Parliament."

Despite the obvious disadvantages of insuring on P.P.I. terms, however, "honour" policies have continued to survive on cargo shipments, particularly on commodities which increase in value during the voyage, and which may change hands several times whilst *en route*. If the buyer has insufficient details of the primary insurance, policies for the "increased value" will be arranged with a different set of Underwriters, simply worded "To pay as cargo" to indicate that any loss covered by the primary cargo policy will be met proportionately by the increased value Underwriters.

It must be emphasised, nevertheless, that there is no privity of contract between the Underwriters on the two policies. The primary policy agrees that the goods are of a certain value, this being binding on the parties to the contract in the absence of fraud, including those to whom the assured has assigned his rights. Thus, the primary Underwriters, besides providing an indemnity for any loss or damage to the goods based on the value shown in their policies, will also have to bear the survey fees entirely, and all the sue and labour or other special charges incurred in quantifying the claim.

On the other hand, the primary Underwriters are able to maintain subrogation rights up to the full value of their policies, so as to preclude the increased value Underwriters from participating in recoveries normally obtained from third parties. This was made abundantly clear in the case of *Boag v. Standard Marine Insurance Co. Ltd.* [1936] which concerned a cargo of wheat originally insured for a value of £685. While the ship was on her voyage the price of wheat rose considerably, and the owners took out an increased value policy with different Underwriters for £215. In the course of the voyage, the vessel grounded and the cargo was jettisoned, consequently both sets of Underwriters paid the amount of their policies in full. Based on an estimated sound arrived value of £900, the Underwriters became entitled to a recovery of approximately £532 when the general average adjustment was made, and the increased value Underwriters claimed a proportion of this allowance. The Court held that the subrogation rights vested in primary insurers could not be prejudiced by the policy subsequently taken out with the increased value Underwriters, and the primary insurers were entitled to receive the whole of the salvage. Not surprisingly, therefore, there has been a tendency to place increased value policies "without benefit of salvage".

The position is far from satisfactory, and Underwriters took steps to ease the situation by introducing an "Increased Value Clause" in certain of the Trade Clauses to bring about co-insurance between the primary and increased value insurers. This concept has now been extended throughout the market by the introduction of a similar clause in the standard conditions.

The first part of the clause relates to the primary insurance and reads:

> 14.1 If any Increased Value insurance is effected by the Assured on the cargo insured herein the agreed value of the cargo shall be deemed to be increased to the total amount insured under this insurance and all Increased Value insurances covering the loss, and liability under this insurance shall

be in such proportion as the sum insured herein bears to such total amount insured. In the event of claim the Assured shall provide the Underwriters with evidence of the amounts insured under all other insurances.

Under this wording it can be seen that the primary Underwriters limit their liability to the proportion that the sum insured by their policies bears to the total sum insured by all the policies in existence. While the agreed value of the cargo is deemed to be increased to the aggregate sum thus reached, there would not be complete privity of contract between all the parties without a similar agreement in the increased value policies. The second part of the clause is therefore specifically for use with increased value policies:

14.2 Where this insurance is on Increased Value the following clause shall apply:

The agreed value of the cargo shall be deemed to be equal to the total amount insured under the primary insurance and all Increased Value insurances covering the loss and effected on the cargo by the Assured, and liability under this insurance shall be in such proportion as the sum insured herein bears to such total amount insured.

In the event of claim the Assured shall provide the Underwriters with evidence of the amounts insured under all other insurances.

Following the introduction of these clauses, enabling the individual policies to rank equally with each other in respect of claims and recoveries, London Underwriters have recommended that increased value insurances should no longer be accepted on a P.P.I. basis, or written "without benefit of salvage". They have also sought the co-operation of other markets to try and achieve uniformity of practice.

The United Nations Conference on Trade and Development (UNCTAD) have been extremely critical of the statutory rule making English marine policies void when written on a P.P.I. basis, even if insurable interest exists, and have suggested that a more enlightened approach should be adopted. Under French law, for instance, if the insurer wishes to contest the existence of a valid insurable interest after issuing a P.P.I. policy, the burden of proof is on him to show that no such interest exists; In America P.P.I. policies are enforceable to the extent that the assured can prove insurable interest.

Even more remarkable is the fact that in the non-marine market in the U.K. such policies do not seem to suffer from the same defect as their counter-parts in the marine market. In non-marine insurance the position would appear to be controlled by the Gaming Acts of 1845 and 1892, under which it is submitted by *Arnould* that non-marine policies expressly admitting interest are not void, if the insured has, or expects to acquire, an interest showing that he did not intend to make a wager. In this respect *Wilson v. Jones* [1867] is cited, Willes, J. stating that the Act of 1845 "has no application to a contract upon a matter in which the parties have an interest."

Why there should remain this discrimination against P.P.I. policies effected on marine risks in this country is not at all apparent. Speaking at a seminar held in London in 1979, Mr. Donald O'May, who acted as legal adviser to the Technical and Clauses Committee during the revision of the clauses, expressed the hope that Underwriters would use their influence to promote a reform in the law. This, he suggested, could be achieved by a short and simple statutory provision, possibly by an amending section in the next Finance Act.

At the present time, however, while "honour" policies will, no doubt, continue to provide a convenient means of insuring some types of cargo risks, their lack of recognition by the Courts has obvious drawbacks. Plainly it should not be necessary for the parties to the contract to be tempted to remove the *P.P.I. Clause* is an endeavour to deceive the Court into delivering judgment on a point at issue. It is always possible that, if he is astute enough, the judge will hold the policy up to the light and discover some suspicious staple or pinholes — as is alleged to have happened on a previous occasion. Is that not a gamble?

Chapter 10

DISTRESSED CARGO

With the proliferation of cases where vessels fail to deliver their cargoes at destination for reasons unconnected with the normal perils of the sea, Underwriters have taken steps to restrict their liability. Kenneth Goodacre looks at the opposing views over the new clause centred on the insolvency or financial default of the sea carriers.

Public awareness of the famine in Africa caused the press to report recently that an EEC-funded Oxfam shipment of wheat destined for the Sudan had been held up at Piraeus because of a contractual dispute caused by the liquidation of the vessel's charterers.

The shipment was part of the cargo on the *Pasni Bay* which had been loaded at Hamburg early in July, 1985, but later in the same month, after the charterers had gone out of business, the shipowners were obliged to seek the assistance of the International Maritime Bureau to try and resolve the situation. Apparently the shipowners had only received a small proportion of the charter hire and it was necessary for the cargo interests to provide further funds if they wished the voyage to continue, otherwise the most likely outcome would be the forced sale of the vessel.

This is but one of the many examples from the last decade, where cargo owners have found themselves with the problem of completing the adventure, simply because the carriers have become insolvent, or somebody has defaulted in the payment of the freight. The usual result is for the vessel to put into the nearest port and abandon the voyage, or for the shipowner to leave the cargo at an intermediate port if the cargo owners fail to provide the outstanding freight. At the end of the day, however, whatever sort of rescue operation becomes necessary, the cargo assured will want to know whether he can recover the additional expenditure from his insurers if he holds a policy covering "All Risks".

In the past this has been rather debatable. In an early case, that of *London and Provincial Leather Processes, Ltd. v. Hudson* [1939] it was held that the term "All Risks" was sufficient to cover the wrongful conversion of a consignment of skins sent to a dressing firm in Germany, who sub-contracted part of the work. The sub-contractors subsequently exercised a lien on the skins for money due to them and the dressing firm went bankrupt. As a result of this the German administrator in bankruptcy seized other skins belonging to the plaintiff and illegally retained them. "I am unable to see why," said Lord Justice Goddard, "if goods which are insured against all risks are converted so that the true owner, the assured, is deprived of possession of his goods, he is less entitled to recover under the policy then he would be if the goods were stolen."

Mention can also be made of the more recent case of *Integrated Container Service Inc. v. British Traders Insurance Co. Ltd.* [1981], which concerned a claim under the Institute Container Clauses — Time (All Risks). This case was fully described in an earlier article in this series on the subject of minimising losses, but it can be recalled that many containers were left scattered over the Far East, having been abandoned by the lessees in consequence of their insolvency. As a result the owners of the containers were put to considerable expense to trace and recover their property. These disbursements were held to be recoverable under "all risks" conditions as sue and labour charges, having been incurred to avert a claim which might have resulted from the existence of a threat of loss or damage, no matter if that threat had originated from the insolvency of the lessees.

Under the old standard cargo conditions much the same situation applied, for it must be remembered that "... the primary subject of the insurance is the goods as physical things, but there is superimposed an interest in the safe arrival of goods. This is very old law ..." (per Lord Wright in *Rickards v. Forestal Land, Timber and Railways Company*, 1941). It has long been recognised that the adventure may be lost even though the goods are neither damaged nor lost, nor taken from the assured's possession or control. Thus, if goods are left short of destination by reason of an insured peril there is the possibility of a constructive total loss, and if expenditure is reasonably incurred to avert or minimise such a loss, the assured has every expectation of being reimbursed by the Underwriters who have benefited by the action taken. The question, however, has always been whether the insolvency of a carrier can be regarded as the operation of a risk covered by the insurance, and lawyers have found it difficult to regard a situation where cargo is left in an unexpectedly distressed position as anything but a fortuity.

However, one can see straight away that cargo Underwriters would become less and less willing to act as financial guarantors against bad debts and broken contracts as the number of claims gradually increased.

Concern on this subject was expressed by Mr. Gordon Edwards at a seminar organised by Lloyd's of London Press in London in 1978, when, as head of Lloyd's Underwriters' Cargo Claims Department, he gave the example of a vessel on a passage from Italy to New York which was found to have water leaking from the boiler. The vessel hove to while the boiler tubes were plugged and then proceeded, but, as the starboard boiler was still leaking, she returned to port. The next day the vessel failed again, and within 24 hours suffered a small fire followed a little later by a complete breakdown of the electrical power. After putting into Gibraltar for further repairs, the engine again broke down and she was towed to Lisbon. Here she spent 14 weeks on a variety of repairs, but, after sailing, quickly ran into further trouble, with the catalogue of misery continuing until the owners announced they had no money and, in any case, the vessel was now a constructive total loss. As it was a one ship company, there was no redress for cargo, there being no value in the vessel; also she was heavily mortgaged and there were various priority creditors.

Generally speaking, he felt that the assured had considerable ability to control the manner in which his cargo was carried. "If he puts his property to a freight forwarder, he can, and should, as a prudent uninsured owner enquire as to what is the nature of carriers to be used; whether the contract with the shipowner is with himself, the freight forwarder or charterer; whether the vessel belongs to a reputable owner, with respectable vessels in which there is some value, and which can be attached by legal process if the owner should for one reason or another become short of funds."

Following on this he made the point that if an assured puts his goods into cheap packing which does not withstand the hazards of a normal voyage, in law this is considered to be an inherent vice of goods, and, therefore, an excepted peril. Should it not be regarded as an inherent defect of the voyage, then, if the assured puts his goods into the hands of a carrier who does not have the capacity to fund the contractual obligation? It seemed to him that the choice of parties with whom to do business was one which was at the very heart of business acumen, and often the factor determining success or failure. It was something over which the assured cargo owner had control, and if he did not exercise that control with such acumen or sound judgment, it could be said the lack of endeavour could be a negligence which was contributory to the loss. This was most material to Underwriters and would affect their judgment in accepting or rating a risk. It could also be argued that, to the extent that the circumstances affected the liklihood of loss arising from insolvency, the cause of loss flowed from events present before shipment and therefore before Underwriters were at risk.

Whatever the merits of the opposing views, Underwriters decided during the revision of the standard clauses that it would be best to encourage the assured to use only credit-worthy and reputable sea carriers. Accordingly, a new and controversial exclusion was introduced into the new clauses, so that in no case would the insurance cover:

> 4.6. loss damage or expense arising from insolvency or financial default of the owners managers charterers or operators of the vessel.

While the clause will undoubtedly help to avoid the use of poor quality tonnage, and make an assured wary of contracting for transportation of his cargo at a cheap rate — especially when this is below the cost of bunkers and port expenses — it has invoked criticism on the grounds that it can serve to penalise innocent shippers or consignees because of the indiscretions of the relatively few. Lloyd's Underwriter, Mr. Alan Jackson, who was Chairman of the Technical and Clauses Committee at the time of the revisions, attempted to allay these fears at the conference held by the International Union of Marine Insurance in September 1982. Recognising concern over the new exclusion he stressed that it was aimed only at those shippers who were interested solely in obtaining the cheapest freights and using what he called "fly-by-night" carriers. He said the clause ought not to be applied where the person insured had taken reasonable steps to ascertain that the carriers had the necessary resources.

Foreign insurers, however, who habitually use the English clauses in order to facilitate the placement of reinsurance in the London market, have pointed out that the shipping industry itself is not able to provide an adequate first class service to all destinations of the world. In developing countries, where the availability of vessels may be limited to comparatively older ships, mostly tramps, or the consignment is less than a container load, it seems evident that the shipper often has little or no control in the selection of the vessel. In these circumstances, such insurers are reluctant to abandon the innocent victims.

Another source of criticism has been in regard to the association of loss, damage or expense with the use of the words *arising from* insolvency or financial default. The words "arising from" are wider than "proximately caused by" in the sense in which that expression is used in S.55(1) of the Marine Insurance Act, 1906, and there is an implication that Underwriters are not only concerned with the avoidance of direct losses emanating from the failure of the carriers, but also with any other claim which can be considered to be a link in the chain of events consequent on such failure. Thus, if the goods are left unprotected at an intermediate port and rainwater damage or theft ensues, Underwriters could well argue that the insolvency or financial default of the carriers was a contributory cause of the loss, and therefore the claim was caught by the exclusion.

Suffice to say there was a strong current of feeling against the clause, and it is significant that when the revised trade clauses began to emerge another version appeared in the Institute Commodity Trades Clauses, which stipulated that in no case would the insurance cover:

> 4.6　loss damage or expense caused by insolvency or financial default of the owners managers charterers or operators of the vessel where, at the time of loading of the subject-matter insured on board the vessel, the Assured are aware, or in the ordinary course of business should be aware, that such insolvency or financial default could prevent the normal prosecution of the voyage.
>
> This exclusion shall not apply where this insurance has been assigned to the party claiming hereunder who has bought or agreed to buy the subject-matter insured in good faith under a binding contract.

It can readily be seen that this version of the clause is far more amenable to an assured who, although making reasonable enquiries, remains unaware *at the time of loading* that the carriers may not be able to complete the voyage. An even wider concession is granted to the assignees of the policy, who have no role in arranging the transport and no means of knowing the state of mind of the actual shipper. It is to be noted, nevertheless, that this concession is tied to the basic principle of good faith, and should the assignees have notice of possible insolvency or financial default on the part of the carriers, it is unlikely the provision will afford them any defence. Like any exclusion clause, however, the burden of proof is on the insurers to show that its terms are applicable.

The substitution of the words "caused by" in place of "arising from" suggests that Underwriters have conceded a drafting error in the original text. All the same it is difficult to envisage circumstances in which the exclusion clause can apply to the B and C clauses, which cover only certain specified perils. It is, of course, always possible that, in the intriguing situations which continually occur in marine insurance, the operation of an insured peril in the wake of the failure of the carrier would be held to be so foreseeable or inevitable as to make the insolvency or financial default the dominant and effective cause of the subsequent loss, damage, or expense. Such a contingency would appear to be extremely remote, but much will depend on the facts of the matter.

Although there is now an alternative wording in use Underwriters have indicated they have no immediate plans to amend the basic clauses to incorporate the revised exclusion. Evidently they feel that they should be able to exercise their discretion in this respect, and any amended terms will be a matter of negotiation.

Where, *as a result of the operation of a risk covered by the policy*, the insured transit is terminated at a port or place other than that to which the goods are covered, Underwriters undertake, by Clause 12 of the standard conditions, to reimburse the assured for the reasonable extra charges incurred in unloading, storing, and forwarding the goods to the insured destination, but such charges are specifically denied if they arise from the insolvency or financial default of the owners, managers, charterers, or operators of the vessel.

It is therefore incumbent on the assured to refer to the provisions of the *Termination of Contract of Carriage Clause* (Clause 9) in which it is stipulated that where, owing to circumstances beyond his control, either the contract of carriage is terminated at a port or place other than the destination named in the policy, or the transit is otherwise terminated before the normal expiry of the insurance at destination, then the policy will also terminate. In that case the cover will cease unless prompt notice is given to the Underwriters and continuation of the risk is requested, subject to any additional premium they may require.

If that is done the goods will be insured until they are sold or delivered at the port or place of termination, or, unless otherwise specially agreed, until the expiry of 60 days after arrival there, whichever first occurs.

Alternatively, if the goods are forwarded to the original destination, or to some other destination, within that period of 60 days (or any agreed extension) cover will continue until ceasing in the usual way under the provisions of the *Transit Clause*.

It will be absorbing to follow any developments in the wording of this particular exclusion clause. The assured will naturally be looking for some amelioration of its terms, yet, on the other hand, since it is apparent that operators of land conveyances are also prone to failure might we not see the day when more stringent conditions will be imposed?

Chapter 11

SEAWORTHINESS ADMITTED (1)

Here the author studies the extent to which Underwriters sought, under the old cargo clauses, to protect the assured from adverse conditions of carriage, defects in the vessel, and misconduct on the part of the carriers. In a subsequent article the present attitude of Underwriters will be examined.

When the first Institute Cargo Clauses were issued in 1912, they contained a *Bill of Lading Clause* reading as follows:

> Including all liberties as per contract of affreightment. The Assured are not to be prejudiced by the presence of the negligence clause and/or latent defect clause in the Bills of Lading and/or Charter Party. The seaworthiness of the vessel as between the Assured and the Assurers is hereby admitted.

The first part of this wording has since found its way into the *Transit Clause*, where under section 8.3 of the current clauses it can be seen that Underwriters agree that the insurance shall remain in force during any variation of the adventure arising from the exercise of a liberty granted to shipowners or charterers under the contract of affreightment, thus protecting the Assured in this respect.

The second part of the wording owed its presence to the fact that in earlier years it was quite uncommon for the contract of affreightment to contain exceptions relieving the carriers from liability for any claim arising from their negligence, or from a latent defect in the vessel. In those days an Underwriter who had settled a claim on cargo by reason of sea perils could rely on having a substantial prospect of obtaining a recovery from the carriers if the loss or damage could be shown to have been induced by such negligence or latent defect. It was therefore a question of how material it was for the Underwriter to know whether the contract of affreightment contained the exceptions. As they became more widespread, however,

Underwriters introduced the concession to remove any doubt on the point, and today it is not even considered necessary.

A similar situation could be found in the *Craft, &/c., Clause*, which in 1912 read:

> Including risk of craft, raft, and/or lighter to and from the vessel. Each craft, raft, and/or lighter to be deemed a separate insurance. The Assured are not to be prejudiced by any agreement exempting lightermen from liability.

Here again the last part of the clause emphasised the importance of the custom upon which the parties to the insurance were able to contract. It owed its origins to the case of *Tate v. Hyslop* [1885] up to which time it was largely the practice for lightermen to remain common carriers i.e. liable for everything except Act of God, justifiable jettison, and King's Enemies, consequently the premium was higher if arrangements existed by which the lightermen protected themselves against additional risks. In the case in question it was found that the lighterage contract had been granted at a reduced rate on the understanding that there would be no recourse against the lightermen for loss or damage to the goods, consequently Underwriters had no rights of recovery. It was held that there had been a concealment of a material fact which enabled the insurers to avoid liability, hence the clause was introduced.

Strangely enough, although it has been the practice of lightermen to carry goods with almost complete immunity over a considerable period, the clause survived until the revisions in 1982, the only difference being the use of the words "Including *transit by* craft ..." instead of "Including *risk of* craft ...", the substitution having taken place in 1920. With the abandonment of the S.G. Form and the Memorandum franchise, also the wide acceptance of the very limited recovery prospects against lightermen, the *Craft Clause* has been considered to be outmoded, and this, too, has disappeared.

Having disposed of the reasons why most of these early provisions have been discarded, attention can now be directed at the purpose of Underwriters in admitting seaworthiness of the vessel as between themselves and the Assured, this being the third part of the *Bill of Lading Clause* shown above.

Since most cargo insurances are placed on a voyage basis, the relevant sections of the Marine Insurance Act, 1906, applicable to voyage policies, will apply, and it must first of all be emphasised that such cargo policies are subject to an implied warranty of seaworthiness of the ship, not only at sailing but also, if the voyage is by stages, at each stage:

39.   (1)   In a voyage policy there is an implied warranty that at the commencement of the voyage the ship shall be seaworthy for the purpose of the particular adventure insured.

      (2)   Where the policy attaches while the ship is in port, there is also an implied warranty that she shall, at the commencement of the risk, be reasonably fit to encounter the ordinary perils of the port.

      (3)   Where the policy relates to a voyage which is performed in different stages, during which the ship requires different kinds of or further preparation or equipment, there is an implied warranty that at the commencement of each stage the ship is seaworthy in respect of such preparation or equipment for the purposes of that stage.

Failure on the part of the Assured to comply with the exact conditions of a warranty discharges the insurer from liability for all losses as from the date of the breach, and it is no defence to show that the breach was remedied, and the warranty complied with before a loss occurred, unless there is some express provision in the policy to the contrary (see Sections 33 and 34 of the M.I.A.).

Underwriters were mindful of the fact that a strict interpretation of the law could place the innocent cargo owner in an invidious position, as his only recourse for loss or damage to the goods would be against the carrier, even if such loss or damage was not connected with the unseaworthiness or unfitness of the vessel, but would have formed a legitimate claim on the policy except for the breach of warranty. The original intention of the clause admitting the seaworthiness of the vessel, therefore, was probably to do away with the otherwise implied warranty of seaworthiness, leaving the Assured free to show that an insured peril had operated so as to substantiate a claim against Underwriters. However, the presence of such a clause has been construed by the Courts as making insurers liable for losses, due to the sinking of the vessel, as a "peril of the sea" although the sinking was the direct result of unseaworthiness.

In this respect the very old case of *Parfitt v. Thompson* [1844] serves to show that the clause had ancient origins. In the case in question the Underwriters under a voyage policy on ship admitted the vessel was seaworthy, but, at the trial held at the Bristol Assizes before Mr. Justice Patteson and a special jury, the Underwriters attempted to show that the vessel was lost in consequence of her unseaworthy state, contending that their admission of her seaworthiness merely precluded them from contesting the fact in case the loss had happened by the perils of the sea. The judge, however, was of the opinion that the defendant's admission of seaworthiness was an admission for all purposes, and made it immaterial to consider whether the vessel was in a decayed or seaworthy condition during the voyage.

In later proceedings Chief Baron Pollock said: "I cannot think the parties intended that if the unseaworthiness alone were the cause of her loss, the plaintiff should have no right to recover on the policy. But it seems to me that if the vessel had foundered in a calm sea, from a leak occasioned by rottenness, on the day after the making of the policy, the Underwriters would have been liable."

Much reliance was placed on that case in *Cantiere Meccanico Brindiso v. Janson* [1912]. Here a floating dock was insured for a voyage from Bristol to Brindisi under a policy which contained the words "seaworthiness admitted", the Assured honestly believing it was fit for the journey contemplated. This belief was misplaced for, on reaching the Bay of Biscay, the wall and pontoons parted amidships in a fresh breeze so that the dock sank in two pieces. In the first Court Mr. Justice Scrutton held that a proposal to an Underwriter on the basis of an insurance "seaworthiness admitted", while not doing away with the necessity for the disclosure of all material facts, should put the Underwriter on inquiry if he wants to investigate the particular details of a risk. The Court of Appeal upheld his decision in favour of the Assured, maintaining that the words could be taken to mean that either the warranty of seaworthiness was to be taken as fulfilled, or that the risk of unseaworthiness was one which the Underwriter accepted, the result being that if the vessel was lost by unseaworthiness the Underwriter was liable, and it was no defence to say that it was not fit to contend against the ordinary perils of the sea.

Cargo Underwriters were evidently content to bear any extra burden imposed on them by the clause in the event of the carrying vessel sinking because of unseaworthiness, for later on they were prepared to extend the clause to cover the situation where the vessel was scuttled. This arose from the famous case of *Samuel and Co. v. Dumas* [1924], which became known as "the case of the innocent mortgagee". Here the vessel was scuttled by the master with the connivance of the shipowner, and the question was whether the mortgagee, who had taken out an insurance for his own benefit could recover as a principal, being in no way connected with the fraud. It was held by the House of Lords that there was no loss by a peril of the sea, but rather, as Viscount Finlay put it: "... a peril of the wickedness of man ..." Since there was no operation of an insured peril, it was established that the innocent mortgagee, and, by parity of reasoning, the innocent cargo-owner, could not recover as for a loss by perils of the sea when the ship was deliberately cast away with the privity of her owners.

Shortly after this decision the London Market took steps to mitigate the position of the innocent parties, and in cargo policies added extra provisions to the *Bill of Lading Clause*, which for a great number of years read as follows:

> The Assured are not to be prejudiced by the presence of the negligence clause and/or latent defect clause in the Bills of Lading and/or Charter Party. The seaworthiness of the vessel as between the Assured and the Underwriters is hereby admitted and the wrongful act or misconduct of the shipowner or his servants causing a loss is not to defeat the recovery by an innocent Assured if the loss in the absence of such wrongful act or misconduct would have been a loss recoverable on the Policy. With leave to sail with or without pilots, and to tow and assist vessels or craft in all situations, and to be towed.

In 1963, however, when the cargo clauses underwent a general revision, the Clause was considerably reduced, being then described as the *Seaworthiness Admitted Clause*. Consequently, it was in the fashion shown below, that the meaning and intent of the Clause came under the close consideration of the Courts in the case of the *Salem*, which was finally concluded in the House of Lords in 1983:

> The seaworthiness of the vessel as between the Assured and Underwriters is hereby admitted. In the event of loss the Assured's right of recovery hereunder shall not be prejudiced by the fact that the loss may have been attributable to the

wrongful act or misconduct of the shipowners of their servants, committed without the privity of the Assured.

The *Salem* was, of course, a super-tanker used for a gigantic fraud. It was in December, 1979, that she loaded 195,000 tons of crude oil in the Arabian Gulf for carriage from Kuwait to Italy, and then, whilst sailing down the east coast of Africa changed her name to *Lema* by painting out the first two letters and adding one at the end. Instead of going straight down to the Cape she turned off at Durban where she made fast to a single buoy mooring 1½ half miles offshore. There she pumped 180,000 tons of the oil through hoses into the tank farms ashore, leaving only 15,000 tons in the ship. *Salem* then took in seawater to take the place of the oil, and set off again on her voyage round the Cape – looking to all the world as if she still had a full cargo of oil. In a calm sea off Dakar and Senegal there was a series of explosions and she began to sink. As a British tanker, the *British Trident*, was not far away, she put out her lifeboats and picked up the crew before the *Salem* went to the bottom. The Captain of the *British Trident* took a film of the sinking, which came in useful afterwards to find out why she sank. It was soon established that she had been scuttled. The Shell International Petroleum Co., who had quite innocently bought the oil on c.i.f. terms soon after the vessel left Kuwait, found themselves a great deal out of pocket and therefore claimed on the insurers. But this was on the standard S. G. Form of Lloyd's Policy with the Institute Cargo Clauses (F.P.A.) attached.

As to the wrongful misappropriation of the cargo by the shipowner, it was decided that this was not covered by the standard form, nor was there any provision in the F.P.A. Clauses. This left the question of whether the loss of the 15,000 tons in the actual sinking could be "deemed" to have been by a peril of the sea by reason of the second sentence of the *Seaworthiness Admitted Clause*.

It was common ground that this sentence, although not in the original form issued on the London Market in 1925, was designed for the benefit of innocent cargo-owners to surmount the House of Lords decision in *Samuel and Co. v. Dumas* [1924]. While the Court thought that the wording of the sentence incorporated in the F.P.A. Clauses in the case of the *Salem* was not the most apt to express that intention, nevertheless Underwriters were prepared to concede that the clause should entitle Shell to have a loss caused by the scuttling of the ship treated as a loss proximately caused by a peril of the sea.

The difficulty was, bearing in mind that the cargo had already been misappropriated, could it be said that this part of the cargo was proximately lost by a peril of the sea?

The final word on this point was left to Lord Roskill, who, in delivering judgment on behalf of all the Law Lords said: "No doubt the balance of the cargo would not have been lost but for the fraud or fraudulent conspiracy. But that alone does not make either of those causes the proximate cause of the loss any more than the fact that the seizure of the ship in *Cory v. Burr* [1883] would not have happened without the prior barratrous acts of smuggling by those on board the ship made the ship a loss by barratry and not by seizure."* He found it difficult to accept the concept of fraud or fraudulent conspiracy, as distinct from overt acts done in furtherance of that fraud or fraudulent conspiracy, as the proximate cause of a loss, neither was he satisfied that when the *Salem* sailed from Kuwait the fraud of fraudulent conspiracy was bound to succeed — or to put it another way, the cargo was "doomed". Having regard to the concession made on behalf of Underwriters by the clause, therefore, the final loss was by perils of the seas.

Perhaps Shell International were able to count themselves lucky to a certain extent, as part of the cargo only remained on board due to problems experienced by the vessel with her pumps during discharge ...

Not so lucky were the shipowners in another case, who by inadvertence, had their insurance drawn up on a cargo policy to which were attached the Institute Cargo Clauses incorporating the clause admitting seaworthiness. They were unaware at the time of taking out the policy that their vessel had stranded and was unseaworthy, and sought to take advantage of the clause. It was held by the Irish Court of Appeal, confirming the decision in the King's Bench Division, that the Institute Cargo Clauses were solely referable to cargo and were therefore inapplicable in the circumstances (*McDermott v. National Benefit Life Assurance Co.,* 1921).

* This case is reported on pages 179/180.

Chapter 12

SEAWORTHINESS ADMITTED (2)

Concluding his remarks on this subject, the author points out that the standard cargo clauses no longer admit the seaworthiness of the vessel, and do not specifically protect the assured against the wrongful acts of the shipowners.

It is a remarkable fact that until 1982 there was no specific reference in the cargo clauses to the seaworthiness or fitness of craft used in the conveyance of the goods, the *Seaworthiness Admitted Clause* and its predecessors merely confining themselves to the admission of seaworthiness of the *vessel*. It was probably intended that the clause should be construed to apply to any craft employed in the transport, bearing in mind the case of *Lane v. Nixon* [1866], in which it was decided that, where a claim arose upon goods landed at destination, there was no implied warranty of seaworthiness as to the craft. In that case Mr. Justice Byles said: "... where the insurance is upon cargo, the owner has his remedy against the shipowner, or he may refuse to put his goods on board, if the vessel be not seaworthy, but how different is the case of lighters or means of disembarkation at the other end of the voyage."

Unfortunately there was no codification of this decision in the Marine Insurance Act, which remains strangely silent on the subject of craft risk, although it does acknowledge that when goods are insured until "safely landed" they must be landed in the customary manner at the port of discharge, and within a reasonable time after arrival (Rule for Construction No. 5). Nowadays, of course, the clauses provide for the insurance to continue "during the ordinary course of transit" until termination of the risk, as defined.

While Section 39 of the Marine Insurance Act makes it clear that the implied warranty of the seaworthiness of the *ship* applies to each stage of the voyage, there does not appear to have been any intention to override the decision in *Lane v. Nixon*, and, in modern practice, it is generally accepted that there is no implied warranty of seaworthiness of craft at destination. For the same reason it is also believed that there is no warranty of seaworthiness or fitness of the craft at shipment, or during transhipment, but unless it can be said that the point is governed by *Lane v. Nixon*, which does not appear to be the case, there is no decision to the effect.

On the other hand, although the Act refers only to seaworthiness of the *ship*, it has been held that the implied warranty applied to a voyage insurance on two dumb Danube barges, which were lost during a towage across the Black Sea. The owners of the barges contended that the loss was due to bad weather, but it was held by Roche, J. that the weather was not exceptional, and that the barges were unseaworthy at the commencement of the voyage by reason of their steering badly, having too little freeboard, and insufficient bulkheads. The owners were not entitled to recover. (*Harocopus v. Mountain*, 1934).

Although the wording of the Marine Insurance Act may not be sufficiently clear on all the aspects of unseaworthiness in relation to cargo policies, therefore, it is submitted that the present intentions of Underwriters can readily be deduced from the *Unseaworthiness and Unfitness Exclusion Clause* reading as follows:

5   5.1   In no case shall this insurance cover loss damage or expense arising from
   unseaworthiness of vessel or craft,
   unfitness of vessel craft conveyance container or liftvan for the safe carriage of the subject-matter insured,
where the Assured or their servants are privy to such unseaworthiness or unfitness, at the time the subject-matter insured is loaded therein.

5.2   The Underwriters waive any breach of the implied warranties of seaworthiness of the ship and fitness of the ship to carry the subject-matter insured to destination, unless the Assured or their servants are privy to such unseaworthiness or unfitness.

Attention may first of all be drawn to the second part of the clause, which is now more closely related to the Marine Insurance Act. It has already been demonstrated in the previous article that Sections 39(1)(2) and (3) of the Marine Insurance Act make provision for the seaworthiness of the ship, and for its fitness to encounter the ordinary perils of a port, but it is here pertinent to quote further Sections. Section 39(4) explains what is meant by "seaworthy" thus:

> A ship is deemed to be seaworthy when she is reasonably fit in all respects to encounter the ordinary perils of the seas of the adventure insured.

However, from the cargo owner's point of view, the qualification contained in Section 40(2) is also of considerable importance:

> In a voyage policy on goods or other moveables there is an implied warranty that at the commencement of the voyage the ship is not only seaworthy as a ship, but also that she is reasonably fit to carry the goods or other moveables to the destination contemplated by the policy.

The immediate effect of Clause 5.2 is, therefore, to nullify the sections of the Act relating to the implied warranties of seaworthiness of the ship, and its fitness to carry the cargo to its intended destination, always supposing that the Assured and their servants are ignorant of any such defect. If, however, with their knowledge and consent, the goods are carried in an unseaworthy ship, or one that is unsuitable for its transport, then the warranties will apply, and the Underwriters can take advantage of the fact to avoid any claims arising, even when such claims are caused by insured perils.

It is noticeable that this provision is somewhat different from the old *Seaworthiness Admitted Clause* insofar as the present clause does not purport to treat the vessel as seaworthy, but only relaxes the strict obligation on the part of the Assured to ship the goods in one which is both seaworthy and fit for the purpose. In the absence of a clause admitting seaworthiness it would, under the old clauses, have been difficult on occasions to substantiate a claim for a "peril of the sea", as illustrated by the case of *Sassoon and Co. v. Western Assurance* [1912]. In this case the plaintiffs were the owners of a wooden hulk, which was moored in a tidal river and used by them as a store for some opium. Due to its decayed state, the hulk sprang a leak and the opium was damaged by water percolating through. The weak place was covered by copper sheathing, so the plaintiffs were not aware of its condition. Although the policy covered "perils of the sea", it evidently did not contain the clause as to seaworthiness being admitted, and the Judicial Committee of the Privy Council did not allow the claim. Lord Murray, in delivering their judgment, said: "There was no weather, nor any other fortuitous circumstances, contributing to the incursion of the water; the water merely gravitated by its own weight through the opening in the decayed wood, and so damaged the opium. It would be an abuse of language to describe this as a loss by perils of the sea. Although sea water damaged the goods no peril of the sea contributed either proximately or remotely to the loss."

With a fresh approach to the insured perils in the new clauses, there is no longer any problem in determining whether a peril of the sea has operated, for the words are now defunct. Instead, under the Institute Cargo Clauses (C) we have cover for any claim *reasonably attributable* to the "vessel or craft being stranded grounded *sunk* or capsized", while the Institute Cargo Clauses (B) not only cover those perils, but also pay for claims caused by the "entry of sea lake or river water into vessel craft hold conveyance container liftvan or place of storage." Accordingly, without any special exclusion enabling Underwriters to decline claims arising from unseaworthiness or unfitness of the vessel or craft, they will remain liable for the named perils consequent on the defective condition. This is made evident by Clause 5.1, where the Underwriters make it clear that they only seek to avoid liability in the event that the Assured or their servants are privy to the unseaworthiness or unfitness at the time the goods are loaded. In a situation similar to that in the case of *Sasoon and Co. v. Western Assurance*, therefore, Underwriters should respond, under the "B" Clauses, for damage caused by the entry of water, but not under the "C" Clauses unless the damage could be said to be reasonably attributable to the vessel or craft being sunk. Of course, under the "A" Clauses the entry of water would, undoubtedly, be regarded as the exceptional circumstance which the Courts seek to find in applying the meaning of "All Risks".

Since the new clause places much emphasis on the need for the Assured or their servants not to be privy to any unseaworthiness or unfitness of the means of transport, possibly it will be useful to comment on the terms used.

Whether a vessel can be adjudged to be seaworthy must depend on the facts in relation to a given insured venture. It is not just a question of whether she is "tight, staunch and strong", but whether she is properly manned and provisioned, has her equipment (such as wireless, lights, anchors etc.) in good order, and her machinery in good repair. She needs to have proper navigational instruments and correct charts; to be loaded "within her marks" and for the cargo to be properly stowed; also she should be adequately bunkered. It is also fairly obvious that although a vessel may be perfectly seaworthy for trading in the Mediterranean, she could be hopelessly unsuited to face the rigours of the North Atlantic in the winter. On top of her ability to cope with the ordinary perils of the seas is the requirement that she is in every way equipped to carry the particular cargo. In the case of coal or scrap metal probably little preparation would be required, but in a special trade, such as the carriage of chilled or frozen meat, clearly the refrigerators and refrigerating machinery would assume importance.

The meaning of the word "privity" was discussed in great detail in the *Eurysthenes* [1976], when the Court of Appeal decided that, although the expression meant with "knowledge and consent", this was not necessarily the same as "wilful misconduct". It was indicated by their Lordships that "knowledge" did not only mean positive knowledge but also the sort of knowledge expressed in the phrase "turning a blind eye". Accordingly, if a man, suspicious of the truth, turns a blind eye to it, and refrains from enquiry, so that he should not know it for certain, then he is to be regarded as knowing the truth. Alternatively, negligence in not knowing the truth is not equivalent to knowledge of it. Applying these dicta to the clause under review it is reasonable to assume that if the Assured and their servants are not aware of the facts, or do not realise that they render the means of transport unseaworthy or unfit for the safe carriage of the goods, then they ought not to be held privy to it, even though they were negligent in not knowing.

In the past it has been difficult to draw a line between acts of privity committed by the Assured *personally*, and those of his servants. It has been held on many occasions that in construing the meaning of "Assured", or the "owners" of the property, one has to decide who may be considered the *alter ego* of the company. Lord Denning in the case of *Bolton Co. Ltd. v. Graham and Sons, Ltd.* [1957] likened a company to a human body, which has a brain and nerve centre controlling what it does, but also has hands to hold the tools and act in accordance with directions from the centre. Those people in a company who are nothing more than hands to do the work are merely servants who cannot be said to represent the mind or will of the company.

Unfortunately, it can be difficult to discover who represents the mind and will in some circumstances, and it becomes necessary to study the functions of the directors and managers. In more recent cases, such as the *Marion* [1982], the Courts have stressed the need for adequate staff supervision by the directors of a company over their instructions to their subordinate managerial staff, and delegation of duties must be carried out in an effective manner.

In the standard cargo clauses, however, Underwriters have avoided this nice point by adopting a stricter attitude and relating the act of privity to both the Assured and their servants. Originally it was proposed to include their agents as well, but this proposal was dropped after representations were made by other sections of the market, thus it can be assumed the exclusion does not apply to freight forwarders, container operators and the like, whose services are engaged by the Assured, but not controlled by them.

As the position stands under the new basic clauses, therefore, in the event of a claim arising from an insured peril, the burden of proof will be on the insurers to show that (i) the vessel, craft, conveyance, container, or liftvan, was unsuitable for its purpose, (ii) the Assured or their servants were aware of its condition when the goods were loaded therein, and (iii) there was some causal connection between the defective condition and the operation of the insured peril. Since a consignee might collect the goods on arrival at destination, attention must also be drawn to the fact that the exclusion could bite if his own vehicle is not up to standard.

As with the exclusion for insolvency or financial default of the carriers, so the Federation of Commodity Associations managed to negotiate more acceptable terms for tne *Unseaworthiness and Unfitness Exclusion Clause.* Under the Institute Commodity Trades Clauses this reads:

5   5.1   In no case shall this insurance cover loss damage or expense arising from

      5.1.1   unseaworthiness of vessel or craft or unfitness of vessel or craft for the safe carriage of the subject-matter insured, where the Assured are privy to such unseaworthiness or unfitness, at the time the subject-matter insured is loaded therein

      5.1.2   unfitness of container liftvan or land conveyance for the safe carriage of the subject-matter insured, where loading therein is carried out prior to attachment of this insurance or by the Assured or their servants.

5.2   Where this insurance has been assigned to the party claiming hereunder who has bought or agreed to buy the subject-matter insured in good faith under a binding contract, exclusion 5.1.1. above shall not apply.

5.3   The Underwriters waive any breach of the implied warranties of seaworthiness of the ship and fitness of the ship to carry the subject-matter insured to destination.

A careful comparison will show that certain steps have been taken to protect the innocent consignee, to whom the policy has been assigned. Thus, by section 5.2. the assignee will not be responsible if the Assured (but not their servants or agents) fail to load the cargo in a seaworthy or fit vessel or craft, even if this is with the latter's knowledge and concurrence. It is noticeable that this concession is not granted in the case of defective containers, liftvans, or land conveyances, where the loading is controlled by either the Assured or their servants, and in any event Underwriters are not prepared to accept liability when claims arise from goods being loaded in unsuitable means of carriage prior to the attachment of the insurance. In this respect the provision equates very much with the exclusion of bad stowage in containers or liftvans in Clause 4.3 of the standard clauses.

Although there is no mention, in Clause 5.3, of the waiver of the implied warranties being nullified by the privity of the Assured or their servants to any unseaworthiness or unfitness of the ship, it must be remembered that Underwriters might still have a defence against non-disclosure of a material fact, or even by reason of wilful misconduct of the Assured, if the circumstances justify such a course.

A notable omission from the new clause as compared with the old *Seaworthiness Admitted Clause* is the provision protecting an innocent Assured from the wrongful acts or misconduct of the shipowners or tneir servants. At first glance this would appear to be a withdrawal of a valuable concession, and the situation merits closer consideration.

In the *Salem* case, the provision was useful in helping the Court to arrive at the conclusion that the 15,000 tons of oil, remaining on board when the vessel was scuttled, could be deemed to be lost by a peril of the sea, but, since the present clauses do not contain the term, this difficulty no longer arises. Thus, we have a similar position as with losses arising from unseaworthiness or unfitness of the means of transport i.e. the policy will provide cover against the insured perils, unless there is any special exclusion.

Under the "A" Clauses, therefore, the scuttling of the vessel, and its subsequent disappearance below the waves, would be treated as one of the perils undertaken by Underwriters granting "All Risks" terms. In the case of the "B" and "C" Clauses, however, although they initially offer cover for claims attributable to the vessel being "sunk", they have taken the precaution of inserting a special clause (4.7) which excludes:

> deliberate damage to or deliberate destruction of the subject-matter insured or any part thereof by the wrongful act of any person or persons.

This clause is particularly aimed at removing liability for arson, scuttling, sabotage, or any form of malicious act involving the goods. Nevertheless, the Assured is given the option of deleting the clause by payment of an additional premium so as to incorporate a *Malicious Damage Clause*, which reads:

> In consideration of an additional premium, it is hereby agreed that the exclusion "deliberate damage to or deliberate destruction of the subject-matter insured or any part thereof by the wrongful act of any person or persons" is deemed to be deleted and further that this insurance covers loss of or damage to the subject-matter insured caused by malicious acts vandalism or sabotage, subject always to the other exclusions contained in this insurance.

This clause, it will be noted, not only deletes the exclusion of deliberate damage or destruction, but also adds positive cover for loss or damage caused by malicious acts, vandalism, or sabotage.* Scuttling of the vessel for personal gain would not appear to fall into any of these new risks, and, that being the case, resort will have to be made to the original peril of the vessel being sunk, albeit by the wrongful act of the master or crew.

Cargo Underwriters are naturally anxious to protect their rights of recovery against carriers, and it is perhaps opportune to mention that a *Not to Inure Clause* continues to remain in the cargo clauses

* as to the operation of the "other exclusions" see page 208

because some carriers are able to insert a condition in their contracts of carriage, under which they insist on having the benefit of any insurance on the property, thereby divesting themselves of any financial responsibility for damage to the goods from an insured peril. Such a condition, where the contract of carriage is subject to the Hague Rules, is null and void, but in other cases, notably when the goods are being carried to and from the sea-going vessel, it is possible for a "benefit of insurance" clause to appear. Underwriters therefore seek to render the clause ineffective by inserting the following provision in the standard clauses:

15. This insurance shall not inure to the benefit of the carrier or other bailee.

In this way Underwriters aim to preserve their rights of subrogation.

Chapter 13

GENERAL EXCEPTIONS IN THE CARGO POLICY.

Now Kenneth Goodacre takes a closer look at some of the exclusions in the cargo clauses, and shows how they compare with the provisions of the Marine Insurance Act.

In the old cargo clauses emphasis was placed on the fact that Underwriters were not prepared to admit claims for loss, damage, or expense proximately caused by delay, or inherent vice or nature of the subject matter insured, even under "All Risks" conditions. These exclusions served to echo the provisions of the Marine Insurance Act, and merely brought them to the attention of the Assured, so that they would be fully aware of the situation.

In the new clauses this idea has been extended to other provisions of Section 55 of the Act so as to clarify the statutory position relating to wilful misconduct of the Assured, and such inevitable losses as ordinary leakage, loss in weight or volume, or ordinary wear and tear. At the same time the opportunity was taken to incorporate new exclusions relating to the insolvency or financial default of the carriers, the use of nuclear weapons and the like, and also to state Underwriters' attitude towards bad packing, as well as bad stowage in containers or liftvans. The *General Exclusions Clause* appears in the Institute Cargo Clauses (A) as follows:

EXCLUSIONS
4   In no case shall this insurance cover
    4.1   loss damage or expense attributable to wilful misconduct of the Assured
    4.2   ordinary leakage, ordinary loss in weight or volume, or ordinary wear and tear of the subject-matter insured
    4.3   loss damage or expense caused by insufficiency or unsuitability of packing or preparation of the subject-matter insured (for the purpose of this Clause 4.3 "packing" shall be deemed to include stowage in a

container or liftvan but only when such stowage is
carried out prior to attachment of this insurance or by
the Assured or their servants)

4.4 loss damage or expense caused by inherent vice or
nature of the subject-matter insured

4.5 loss damage or expense proximately caused by delay,
even though the delay be caused by a risk insured
against (except expenses payable under Clause 2 above)

4.6 loss damage or expense arising from insolvency or
financial default of the owners managers charterers or
operators of the vessel

4.7 loss damage or expense arising from the use of any
weapon of war employing atomic or nuclear fission
and/or fusion or other like reaction or radioactive force
or matter.

These exclusions are also common to the "B" and "C" Clauses,
but it will be recalled from the previous article that these two sets
contain an additional exclusion for deliberate damage or deliberate
destruction of the subject-matter insured, which was discussed at that
time. Also previously reviewed in these pages was the exclusion relating
to the insolvency or financial default of the sea carrier, and no further
comment is necessary.

The new provision in connection with the use of any atomic or
nuclear weapon, maintains uniformity with the standard hull clauses
in which the exclusion has appeared for some time, being currently
designated the *Nuclear Exclusion Clause*. In fact, the War Clauses
for hull, freight and cargo interests have excluded claims arising from
the *hostile* use of such weapons for a number of years, because
Underwriters felt that the cumulative destruction which could be
caused from this source might well prove disastrous, even beyond their
ability to pay. Evidently they thought that they might find themselves
faced with obligations arising from the detonation of such weapons
where no hostility is intended, and have taken steps to close a possible
loop-hole in the cover afforded. Consequently, neither the marine
nor the war clauses presently in operation protect the Assured from
losses emanating from the use of these weapons, whatever the reason.*

As mentioned earlier, the exclusion regarding delay was present
in the old clauses, but in its form then it did not quite complement

* But see commentary on War Clauses at page 201

Section 55(b) of the Marine Insurance Act because, although it was stated that the insurance did not extend to cover loss, damage, or expense proximately caused by delay, the words in the Act "although the delay be caused by a peril insured against" were missing. Reference to the present clause will show that this omission has been rectified by the addition of similar words; accordingly it is made abundantly clear that Underwriters have resisted attempts to make delay a legitimate concern of the marine insurance policy, preferring to avoid claims for loss of market or those caused by inherent vice, when there is no physical damage to the goods as a direct result of an insured peril. In this respect they maintain the position obtained in two old cases.

In *Taylor v. Dunbar* [1869], due to delay caused on the voyage by a tempest, a cargo of meat became putrid and was jettisoned. It was held that the loss was proximately caused by neither a peril of the sea nor jettison, but entirely by the delay. In *Pink v. Fleming* [1890], a collision with another vessel necessitated the discharge of a cargo of oranges and lemons, so that repairs to the carrying vessel could be carried out. Some of the fruit was badly damaged by natural decay arising from the delay in the voyage, and some from the extra handling involved, but as Bowen, L.J. said: "The proximate cause of the loss was not the collision, or any peril of the sea, but the perishable character of the cargo combined with the handling and delay."

In the French market it appears possible to obtain cover for losses arising from similar circumstances to those appertaining in *Pink v. Fleming*, based on the premise that, since the insurer is aware of the perishable nature of the cargo he is insuring, he should not be permitted to use the exclusion of inherent vice when an insured peril occurs which permits those characteristics to operate, even if such characteristics only manifest themselves as a result of a delay caused by the insured peril. The Norwegian Plan also contains a clause expressly covering physical loss of or damage to goods caused by delay. These factors have led to UNCTAD considering a draft provision for their proposed international wording which includes coverage for physical loss or damage to the goods when delay is caused by an accident to the means of transport, or by the destruction of ports, airports, roads or railway lines.

Under the Institute Clauses, however, the only concession is in respect of expenses falling due under the *General Average Clause* (Clause 2). This acknowledges the fact that, under the York-Antwerp

Rules (which generally govern a general average act), expenses are allowed by reason of the prolongation of the voyage when a carrying vessel has to resort to a port of refuge in time of peril, and the cargo can be called upon to pay an appropriate contribution.

As regards the exclusion for loss, damage or expense attributable to the wilful misconduct of the Assured, the most obvious example of the operation of this clause would be where a conspiracy is entered into with the master to defraud the cargo Underwriters of the value of goods alleged to have been lost with a vessel deliberately cast away. It is readily apparent that such an attempt would invalidate the insurance by reason of a breach of good faith, but in other situations the issue may not be so clear-cut.

In the case of *Papadimitriou v. Henderson* [1939], for instance, the War Risks Underwriters on ship and freight attempted to show that there was wilful misconduct on the part of the owners in allowing the vessel to proceed from Odessa to Marseilles with a cargo of lorries and spare parts consigned to agents of the Spanish Republican Government. It was said that there were warnings of possible interference by insurgent warships off Cape Bon, and that the vessel was insufficiently documented to prove her neutrality. Although there seems to have been an intention to return to Piraeus the vessel was in fact captured 160 miles east of Malta and taken to Majorca, where the cargo was classed as contraband, and the vessel condemned as prize. In the action to recover under the policies Lord Justice Goddard held that there was no wilful misconduct on the part of the owners, and the vessel was properly documented. In any case, there was no more reason to suppose that the vessel was condemned for carrying irregular papers than that she was condemned for carrying contraband. Underwriters were held liable for the insured value of the vessel, also the indemnity fixed by the policy for the anticipated freight.

In a later case, an aircraft was on a flight from London to Lagos via Bordeaux but, owing to low cloud, the pilot was unable to land at Bordeaux and the route book did not contain sufficient information about the alternative airfields of Toulouse or Marignane. As he had enough fuel, the pilot decided to return to England, but later changed his mind and diverted to Le Bourget, Paris. Here the weather was unsuitable and he was directed by Le Bourget airport to land at Comeilles, Paris. However, due to the difficulty in contacting that airport by wireless, he made his way back to England across the Channel, only to run out of fuel and crash in Kent.

In the subsequent claim lodged by a passenger for injury sustained, the airline sought to limit liability under the Carriage by Air Act, 1932, but the plaintiff alleged that the accident was due to the wilful misconduct of the defendants or their servants or agents, and under Article 25 they were not entitled to avail themselves of the limitation provisions. Mr. Justice Barry, in his directions to the Jury, said that wilful misconduct was misconduct to which the will was a party, and was something wholly different in kind from mere negligence or carelessness, however gross that negligence or carelessness might be. In order to establish wilful misconduct the plaintiff had to satisfy the Jury, not beyond reasonable doubt, but satisfy them that the person who did the act knew that he was doing something wrong, and knew it at the time, and yet did it just the same, or alternatively that the person who did the act did it quite recklessly not caring whether he was doing the right thing or the wrong thing, quite regardless of the effect of what he was doing upon the safety of the aircraft and the passengers. In the event, because of the series of mishaps which contributed to the crash, the Jury were unable to agree and were discharged. Later it was stated that a settlement had been reached out of Court. (*Horobin v. British Overseas Airways Corporation, 1952*).

It is, perhaps, significant that UNCTAD have not used the term "wilful misconduct" in compiling their own international clauses, and the proposed exclusion reads:

> Loss, damage, liability, or expense resulting from the personal act or omission of the Assured done with the intent to cause such loss, damage, liability or expense, or recklessly and with knowledge that such loss, damage, liability or expense would probably result.

As already indicated, the *General Exclusions Clause* was partly framed to make it clear to the Assured that insurers wish to maintain the defences provided by the Marine Insurance Act in respect of losses of an expected nature. Actually, the exclusions in the clause are somewhat different from the provisions of Section 55(2)(c) of the Act reading:

> Unless the policy otherwise provides, the insurer is not liable for ordinary wear and tear, ordinary leakage and breakage, inherent vice or nature of the subject matter insured, or for any loss proximately caused by rats or vermin ...

The absence of any reference in the exclusion clause to losses proximately caused by rats or vermin is indicative of a different attitude towards today's trading conditions compared with those in operation at the time the Act was drawn up. With modern methods of dealing with pests it can no longer be said that rats or vermin are regular passengers on a ship, and direct damage to cargo by pests from without is now considered by most Underwriters to be a risk of an accidental or fortuitous nature, rather than being in the class of expected damage. This consideration should be taken into account when dealing with claims under "All Risks" terms. Of course, if the vermin are present in the cargo when the risk commences, and simply manage to thrive in suitable conditions on the voyage, then the Underwriters are able to plead the defence of inherent vice.

Mention should perhaps be made at this point of the famous case of *Hamilton, Fraser and Co. v. Pandorf and Co.* [1887]. Here rats gnawed through a lead pipe (serving as a discharge from a bathroom in the vessel) in order to gain access to a cargo of rice. In the subsequent rolling of the vessel on the voyage seawater entered through the hole causing damage to the rice, making it necessary to ascertain whether, at law, such damage was occasioned by a peril of the sea. Although the case was brought to determine whether the shipowners were liable to the cargo-owners under the terms of the Bill of Lading, it was recognised that the same principles would have applied under a policy of insurance, and the activities of the rats were treated as a remote cause. Lord Watson, in the House of Lords, made the following observation: "If the respondents were preferring a claim under a contract of marine insurance, expressed in ordinary terms, I should be clearly of the opinion that they were entitled to recover, on the ground that their loss was occasioned by a peril of the sea within the meaning of the contract."

In similar circumstances under the present clauses, therefore, there would be a claim under the "B" Clauses for damage caused by the entry of seawater into the vessel, and also under the "A" Clauses, as the accidental incursion would provide the exceptional circumstance required by "All Risks" conditions.

Another omission from the *General Exclusions Clause,* as compared with the Marine Insurance Act, is that of "ordinary breakage". Although it might be expected that shipments of fragile items, such as glass, would arrive with some measure of breakage it has not been customary in the past to make any fixed deduction in respect of this, and if the policy covered breakage, or all risks of loss or damage, Underwriters would pay the breakage claim in full. The reasoning behind this lay in the fact that, if the goods were properly packed, the breakage would usually be caused by careless handling in the course of transit; one could therefore reasonably argue that such breakage must necessarily be fortuitous, and recoverable as an insured peril.

On the other hand, it is well known that certain commodities will be expected to suffer loss in weight in course of transit due to natural causes, such as sifting, seepage, or the drying out of the moisture content, and this fact needs to be taken into account when assessing shortages. In other cases, losses also arise through evaporation or by absorption of liquid cargoes into the casks in which they are shipped, such losses being dependent upon climatic conditions and the nature of stowage during transit. Leakage can arise where barrels or casks suffer from shrinkage of timbers. Such "ordinary" losses can usually be eliminated from claims calculations by weighing a representative number of sound packages on delivery, or by comparing the details of bulk cargoes with those of previous shipments, so as to arrive at the normal percentage of loss. Since consignees of goods do not always appreciate that the question of ordinary loss has an important bearing on their claim, the clarification of Underwriters' rights should prove helpful.

Naturally the matter of the suitability or sufficiency of the packing itself is an important consideration, and, resulting from two cases heard in 1955, it is well recognised that bad packing is in the nature of inherent vice. In *Berk v. Style*, the plaintiffs sought to recover the expenses of re-bagging a large number of bags of kieselguhr (infusorial earth), found to be torn or broken on discharge at a Thames wharf, on the grounds that the expenditure was incurred in avoiding a claim under the policies. The kieselguhr was packed in paper bags each containing 56 lbs. and it was contended by the insurers that the seams opened because of lack of adhesive to keep them firmly closed during ordinary handling. Mr. Justice Sellers agreed that the bags were defective on shipment and inadequate to endure the normal wear and tear of handling and carriage. The special expenditure incurred was due to the inherent vice of the bags, and, as such was not recoverable under "all risks" conditions which did not extend to cover a certainty. As it was certain that the bags in the condition in which they were shipped could not safely have held their contents in the course of necessary handling and transport, the claim was dismissed.

The other case, that of *Gee and Garnham Ltd. v. Whitall*, concerned several shipments of thin aluminium kettles from Hamburg to the U.K. On arrival many kettles were found to be dented, but this damage was ascribed to the way the kettles were packed, so that the handle of one kettle pressed into the side of another. In addition stains were found to be present on the aluminium, which were found to be caused by the moisture in the wood wool used in the packing. This was less seasoned than usual because of a shortage at the time. Mr. Justice Sellers also presided in this case, and held that the damage must have occurred either before transit started or owing to inadequate packing. Accordingly the loss came within the exception of "inherent vice" and was not recoverable.

Concern about the standard of packing is now expressed by Underwriters by the inclusion of a new provision in the clauses, which also reflects the hazards of modern methods of transport. Not only have they impressed on the Assured that the goods should be suitably packed and prepared for the contemplated journey, but also that stowage in containers and liftvans should be properly carried out before the commencement of the insurance, or when undertaken by the Assured or their servants. Naturally, if a container or liftvan is improperly stowed, so that shifting can take place, the goods can repeatedly rack the sides and doors, eventually rendering themselves valueless. In heavy seas, with a ship rolling 25 to 30 degrees, a container can swing through an arc of about 50 feet, to and fro for hours on end. Nevertheless, when goods, properly packed and prepared, have commenced transit, and are subsequently stowed in a container or liftvan by parties other than the Assured or their servants, Underwriters have taken into account that such stowage is as much a risk to the Assured as bad stowage in a vessel's holds, and special dispensation is given in those circumstances. If a container or liftvan is in such a state that it is unfit to carry the goods safely, protection is afforded to the insurers by Clause 5.1, if they can show that the Assured or their servants were privy to the unfitness at the time the goods were loaded therein.

In the next article the author will
describe the difficulties which can
be experienced in overriding some
of the exclusions.

Chapter 14

INSURANCE AGAINST INHERENT VICE.

To what extent do cargo insurers cover losses by heat, sweat, mould, mildew and spontaneous combustion? The author investigates.

It is often said that for every insurable risk there is always an Underwriter willing to write it for an appropriate premium. Nevertheless, there is also an element of caution, and careful attention is paid to exclusion clauses.

In marine insurance the Act of 1906 permits insurers to underwrite losses on any legal adventure, except those attributable to the wilful misconduct of the assured. Thus, if the policy so provides, liability on cargo policies can be undertaken for any loss proximately caused by delay, or for ordinary leakage and breakage, inherent vice or nature of the subject matter insured; otherwise such losses are expressly excluded by Sections 55 (2)(b) and (c) of the Act.

The problem of over-riding these exclusions centres around the choice of the appropriate words. In the case of *Sassoon and Co. v. Yorkshire Insurance Co.* [1923] for instance, a consignment of tin-lined cases of cigarettes, shipped from Glasgow to Baghdad, was insured against the ordinary marine risks but including damage by freshwater mould or mildew. On arrival at destination all the cigarettes were found to be mildewed, with the tin linings of the cases rusty both on the inside and on the outside. There was no indication of any outside violence or damage to the cases. The Underwriters resisted the claim on the grounds that the mildew was the result of an inherent vice in the goods, and suggested that it was caused by too high a moisture content in the cigarettes when they were packed, rather than from any external cause.

Doubts were expressed both in the High Court and the Court of Appeal as to whether the specific inclusion of mould or mildew was sufficient to extend the policy to cover inherent vice, but the question

99

remained unanswered because the assured was able to provide sufficient evidence about previous shipments to persuade the Court that the rusting had commenced externally, allowing water to gain access to the contents. Lord Justice Atkin said, however: "It seems to me conceivable, if apt words are used, that an assured might cover a loss occasioned by mould which he does not know enough about to know whether it will or will not happen during the voyage, and which in fact may happen during the voyage but which may not happen during the voyage".

Of course, there is something to be said for the view that the intention of the parties is to obtain cover for the stipulated kinds of damages whatever the cause. If one takes spontaneous combustion as an example, it must always be due to the inherent nature of the goods, and to that extent the policy must cover inherent vice, or the insurance against spontaneous combustion would be meaningless. Such protection has for many years been available under the standard conditions for shipments of coal.

On the other hand, one can understand an Underwriter being wary of undertaking questionable losses without proper safeguards, and in cases where cover is afforded for leakage or shortage, either an appropriate premium must be charged to take care of the normal loss for the voyage contemplated, or a suitable excess must be applied. But in most cases it would seem reasonable to suppose that the object of the special terms is to provide cover against particular vices which do not always occur, thus providing the element of risk which Underwriters prefer.

Quite clearly, however, the relationship between inherent vice and inevitability of damage, as defences to a claim under the Marine Insurance Act, can be elusive. Reference to 'Arnould' will show that the editors attempted to define the situation as follows:

"... the defence of inherent vice can only be excluded by express words or by necessary inference, i.e. by covering a peril which would only be caused by inherent vice. For example, where tinned goods are insured against 'blowing of tins', it is submitted that the defence of inherent vice is thereby excluded. But if the peril is one which (like mould and mildew) can be caused by some external agency, even though more commonly caused by inherent vice, the better view is that only damage from an external cause is covered."

Some of the difficulties in ascertaining whether goods have suffered from inherent vice during transit were touched upon by Mr. Gordon Edwards, head of the Cargo Department, Lloyd's Underwriters' Claims Office, at a seminar held in London in 1976. In one particular case a shipment of walnuts had been insured, *inter alia*, against inherent vice, and at destination the public health authorities refused to allow them to be imported owing to the presence of mould. This mould was not visible to the naked eye and was only detected when the nuts were subject to examination under a microscope. Nuts purchased in highly reputable stores at the same time revealed a similar or higher degree of mould, and given the fact that there was no legislation covering tolerable levels of mould growth in walnuts, the question was therefore at what point could it be said that there was damage caused by inherent vice. The effective cause of the loss was the executive act of the health authorities which would produce a claim under the War Clauses as a "restraint of princes" except for the fact that no cover is provided for land based goods according to the Waterborne Agreement in the clauses.

He went on to suggest that brokers should clearly state what they mean when presenting a risk and Underwriters should insist that they do. "If 'inherent vice' is required to be insured against — use the term. If you want to insure against heat from inherent defect, say so. Phraseology such as '... including heat, sweat and spontaneous combustion ...' is descriptive of damage which can be caused both extrinsically and inherently."

Possibly at that time he was already involved with some claims on cargoes of soya beans shipped to Antwerp in the summer of 1973, these being insured specifically against the risk of heat, sweat and spontaneous combustion only — referred to more briefly as HSSC policies. The beans arrived in a damaged state, leading in 1979 to the case of *Soya G.m.b.h. v. White* to determine whether Underwriters were liable.

These shipments had their origins in the fact that in 1973, serious flooding took place in the Mississipi basin, which greatly disrupted the production and supply of several commodities, and resulted in the United States government imposing an embargo on the export of soya beans. This led to a great shortage of soya beans for the European market, consequently importers sought alternative sources, one of which was Indonesia. Although the Indonesians had always grown soya beans, these had only been exported to Europe in insignificant quantities some years previously. One Dutch firm, which traded extensively with Indonesia, included soya beans under its open cargo cover for the first time, and insured a shipment on W.A. terms only. When the vessel arrived in Antwerp the cargo was found to be damaged on the surface but not significantly; nevertheless the importers felt it would be prudent to procure insurance against HSCC risks on two other shipments in course of preparation. This was an option allowed under the open cover at a special additional rate, and the brokers duly carried out their instructions, at the same time advising the Underwriters of the negligible damage to the initial shipment. This information was later accepted by the Court as a correct description of the condition of the cargo.

When the next two shipments arrived, however, the soya beans were in a heated and deteriorated condition, the depreciation varying between 12½ per cent. and 45 per cent., resulting in a loss of over $700,000. The Underwriters denied liability on the grounds of inherent vice, asserting that the goods were shipped with an excessive moisture content of over 14 per cent. from a hot and humid climate, and the condition when shipped was such as to make heating and resulting damage inevitable during the voyage.

It was common ground between the experts that if soya beans are shipped with a moisture content below 12 per cent. microbiological activity cannot occur, and there is no risk of heating from that source. On the other hand, if the moisture content is above 14 per cent., microbiological activity is bound to occur. Between these two percentages there is a "grey area" where heating may or may not occur, depending on factors during the voyage.

Mr. Justice Lloyd, in the Commercial Court, decided on the best evidence available that the moisture content was well under 13 per cent. when shipped, and, as it was possible for such cargoes not to suffer any damage on a voyage of 45 days, the damage was not inevitable, therefore the proof of the occurence (heating) was sufficient proof of a casualty. In delivering judgment in favour of the plaintiffs he said: "Where there is an insurance against risks of heating and heating occurs because of the conditions under which the soya beans were carried on the particular voyage, I am entitled to hold that the cause of the damage was the conditions under which the soya beans were carried, even though the conditions were normal, and even though nothing untoward occurred. I would only be obliged to find that inherent vice was the proximate cause if the soya beans were such that they could not withstand any normal voyage of that duration."

However, in the Court of Appeal a less strict rule was adopted. Lord Justice Donaldson thought that the test of inherent vice in a policy of insurance should be similar to that under a contract of affreightment, and stated that in his judgment: "... a loss is proximately caused by inherent vice if the natural behaviour of the goods is such that they suffer a loss in the circumstances in which they are expected to be carried ..."

On this basis he was able to accept Mr. Justice Lloyd's finding that the cause of the loss was the condition under which the beans were carried, but disagreed with his conclusion that this did not constitute a loss proximately caused by inherent vice. Their Lordships were unanimous in holding that the policy did not cover inevitable loss or damage by heat, but it was an insurance which clearly covered inherent vice provided always that the heat and sweat were risks and not known certainties. Therefore the appeal failed.

The case proceeded to the House of Lords, where Lord Diplock delivered judgment on behalf of their Lordships. He held that the standard HSSC policy did "otherwise provide" so as to displace the *prima facie* rule of construction laid down by S.55 (2)(c) of the Marine Insurance Act relieving insurers from liability for inherent vice, to the extent that such inherent vice consisted of a tendency for the goods to become hot and sweat, and the risk would not have to be triggered off by an external cause. He was unable to agree with the proposition contained in "Arnould" (already quoted) which he thought was misleading. It was simply a question of construction of the policy concerned whether particular kinds of inherent vice were covered.

Did this mean then that their Lordships' decision was to the effect that inherent vice of these particular kinds would be recoverable even if they were inevitable, although unknown to the assured? This question was left open when Lord Diplock said: "I should make it clear that since in your Lordships' House the concurrent findings of fact that the moisture content of the soya beans fell within the grey area was accepted so that deterioration from heat and sweat in the course of the voyage was *not* inevitable, it has not been necessary for your Lordships to consider whether the insurers would have been liable under HSSC policy if, unknown to the assured the moisture content of the beans on shipment had been so high as to make such deterioration inevitable. On that question, on which we have heard no argument, I express no opinion."

It seems somewhat remarkable that, some 80 years after the passing of the Marine Insurance Act, it is still debatable what Underwriters intend to cover when writing these special perils. In these circumstances perhaps it is appropriate to revert to some of the remarks made in the Court of Appeal.

Lord Justice Waller summed up his feelings by saying: "In my opinion this clause is designed to cover this form of damage to cargoes. It is an insurance against these particular forms of inherent vice and may well also cover heat or sweat damage from extraneous causes. The next question that arises is whether there was a risk or whether in fact there was a certainty. This was a policy covering a risk and it would not therefore cover a certainty."

Lord Justice Donaldson expressed the view that there was no reason why known certain losses could not be the subject matter of a contract of indemnity; merely that very clear words would be required, since it was a highly improbable contract for someone to make in the course of his business as an insurance Underwriter. But he perceived the following difference between words describing the cause of loss and those describing the loss itself: " 'Heat' of course describes a cause of loss and not the loss itself. If the Underwriter chooses to define the risk by reference to the loss itself, e.g. 'leakage' or 'leakage from any cause whatsoever' or 'loss of volume', it is even more likely that the true construction of the contract is that the risk of the defined type of loss is insured regardless of how it is caused, and, in particular, of whether or not it is caused by the inherent vice or nature of the subject matter insured."

It seems apparent, with the divergence of opinion amongst even the most eminent men in the profession, that to secure any guarantee of cover against inherent vice, express words need to be used, assuming, of course, that the extent of the peril is known to both the assured and Underwriter. If the certainty of a loss is known to the assured and not to the Underwriter, other defences will be open, e.g. fraud, non-disclosure or, possibly, loss by the act of the assured in knowingly exposing the subject matter to certain loss. Obviously there is no substitute for a proper understanding of the intentions and requirements of the parties to the contract at the crucial time of negotiation.

Chapter 15

GENERAL AVERAGE (1)

Continuing his series on the standard cargo clauses the author looks at the subject of general average. In the first of two articles he concentrates on the oldest form of sacrifice, that of jettison.

In discussing the essential features of general average, it is first of all desirable to know what the subject is about. Most claims under cargo policies are the direct result of the operation of an insured peril, and consequently fall into the category of losses of a fortuitous nature. General average is distinguishable by the fact that, in time of common peril, some extraordinary sacrifice or expenditure is deliberately incurred for the safety of the adventure as a whole.

An early reference to such a sacrifice is to be found in the Bible, where, in the Acts of the Apostles (Chapter 27), there is recorded the voyage of Paul, who, in A.D. 61, was being taken from Caesaria, in Samaria, to Rome, in order that he could make an appeal to the Emperor Nero. Accompanied by a Roman centurion and certain other prisoners, he boarded a ship which first hugged the coast as far as Sidon, but then sailed towards Cyprus as the winds were not favourable. Eventually they reached the Turkish city of Myra, where the centurion found a ship from Alexandria, which was bound for Italy, and put them on board. This vessel carried a cargo of wheat and was large enough to take 276 persons — "two hundred threescore and sixteen souls".

Slow progress was made for some time and with winter coming on it was decided to sail to a haven in Crete which would provide shelter for the season. Unfortunately they were caught in a tempestuous wind, and being unable to bear into it were forced to let the vessel drive. The next day they threw out some of the cargo, and on the third day cast out the ship's tackling with their own hands. They sighted neither the sun nor the stars for many days, and began to give up hope.

On the fourteenth night, having been driven off the island of Malta, they took soundings which made them fear they would be forced upon the rocks; accordingly they threw four anchors out of the stern. This allowed them to have their first good meal since the trouble started, and then, in better spirits, to jettison the cargo of wheat. When daylight came they discovered a creek with a shore where it was possible to ground the ship, and so they took up the anchors, freed the rudder bands, hoisted the mainsail, and were able to run the ship aground so that the forepart stuck fast. However, the hinder part was broken by the violence of the waves, so some swam ashore while the rest used boards or pieces of the ship. Thus, they all escaped safely to land.

Jettison is, of course, one of the most well-known acts of general average, and is recognised as such by the early laws of the sea. Often quoted is the ancient Rhodian law which states: "Where jettison of goods takes place for the purpose of lightening a ship, let that which has been jettisoned on behalf of all be restored by the contribution of all." This gives some clue that general average is based on equity. Those who have been unfortunate enough to have their goods thrown overboard, are entitled to a contribution from those who have been able to benefit from the sacrifice. It follows, therefore, that no contribution will be forthcoming unless something is saved, and in the case of Paul the Apostle, where both ship and cargo were lost, the general average contribution was not collectable. It would also be unfair if the owner of the goods sacrificed were to be fully recompensed, as he would then be better off than those who had been obliged to contribute towards his loss. To overcome this anomaly, he is expected to put in his share of the kitty.

This old rule was adopted by the Romans in the Digest of Justinian which dates from about 530 A.D., this code having been rediscovered at Amalfi, a small town in Italy, on its conquest by the Pisans in 1135. In the celebrated sea code known as the Rolls of Oleron, this ancient custom is once more stated, and it is worthy of mention that this code, which was held in great importance and authority for centuries, was copied into the Black Book of the English Admiralty, and confirmed by an Act of Parliament in 1402.

How this came about is of some interest. Queen Eleanor (Duchess of Aquitane) was divorced by Louis VII of France, and then married Henry II of England. Henry already had an extensive empire, which, in addition to England, included Normandy, Anjou, Maine and

Terraine in France. By his marriage to Eleanor he also acquired Poitou, Guienne, and Gascony, so that he held most of the British Isles and about one-half of France. It was on this occasion that the Island of Oleron, situated in the Bay of Biscay, passed into possession of the English Crown, and it is said that their son, Richard I, gave his sanction to the code when returning from the Crusade. These Rules are preserved among the records of the High Court of Admiralty in the Public Record Office, London.

In earlier days merchants were apt to travel with their goods. They could bargain with the ship's master over the carriage and freight, and would sell or exchange their wares at foreign ports on a very personal basis. Consequently it was well within the bounds of possibility for the master to settle questions of general average before the interests parted company. Article 8 of the Rolls of Oleron sanctioned his actions in the matter of jettison by giving the example of a ship leaving Bordeaux, and having been caught in a storm, is unable to escape without throwing out goods from the hold. The master was bound to advise the merchants that it was necessary to throw out the wines and other goods for the common safety, whereupon the merchants had to consider the reasons and give their consent. However, if there was any disagreement, the master had authority to jettison whatever seemed to him to be reasonable, but, on coming ashore safely, would have to swear himself and a third of his crew on the Holy Gospels that the jettison was not carried out in malice, but for the sake of the ship, the goods, the wines, and those on board.

The Rule further provided that the cargo sacrificed should be valued in the same fashion as that saved, and the loss should be divided among the merchants, the ship and the freight. In respect of the freight, however, it was recognised that, sometimes, part of this formed the mariners' wages, and in that case one tonne for each man was freed from contribution. But if any mariner failed to defend himself on the sea like a man during the voyage this concession was withdrawn. In Article 32 it was also ordained that if there were at least two cups of silver in the ship they ought to contribute towards jettisoned property, but if there was only one cup it should not be brought into the contribution if it was used at the table for the service of the mariners. Robes and linen which had not been worn or cut for clothing were expected to contribute towards a jettison.

No doubt the mariners were quite keen on carrying shipments of wine, as it was a custom of the sea for the merchants to give them at each port of call, or on each day of a double feast, a pot of wine — or even two or three pots. Although the mariners had no legal right to demand such a favour, Article 29 set out to support the custom by stressing that the merchant could indulge in this courtesy according to his pleasure.

As can be surmised, general average was in existence long before marine insurance became established. It is not known for certain when this branch of insurance was introduced to this country, but it is generally agreed that in the Middle Ages there were two great bands of traders. One set of merchants — the Hanseatic League — traded from the Baltic towards the south, while the other — the Lombards — operated from the Mediterranean northwards. The principal centre for these traders was Bruges in Belgium, where in 1310 a Chamber of Insurance was formed for the purpose of providing the merchants with security against the risk of loss arising from sea perils, this being instrumental in allowing trade to flourish. It is believed that this system could have been copied by English merchants.

Obviously marine insurance was well established in this country by the Elizabethan era, for it was in 1601 that the first Act relating to marine insurance became law. Here can be found the classic definition of the purpose of this type of insurance, for in the Preamble it is stated:

> "And whereas it hath been time out of mind an usage amongst merchants, both of this realm and of foreign nations, when they make any great adventure (especially into remote parts) to give some consideration of money to other persons (which commonly are in no small number) to have from them assurance made of their goods, merchandises, ships and things adventured, or some part thereof, at such rates and in such sort as the parties assurers, and the parties assured can agree, which course of dealing is commonly termed a policy of assurance ... it cometh to pass upon the loss or perishing of any ship, there followeth not the undoing of any man, but the loss lighteth rather easily upon many than heavily upon few, and rather upon them that adventure not than those that do adventure, whereby all merchants, especially of the younger sort, are allured to venture more willingly and more freely."

As a contribution to general average was a liability attaching to a merchant's goods, this risk was naturally included in the marine insurance policy, and so it came about that for some centuries general average contributions have been paid by Underwriters following an adjustment showing the position of the interested parties.

Strangely enough there was no proper definition of general average in the English Courts until 1801, when Mr. Justice Lawrence used the following words in *Birkley v. Presgrave*:

"All loss which arises in consequence of extraordinary sacrifices made, or expenses incurred, for the preservation of the ship and cargo comes within general average, and must be born proportionately by all who are interested."

This case concerned the vessel *Argo* which was caught by a violent squall when entering her port of discharge, making it necessary to let go the anchor. For further security she was fastened to the south pier by a warp, but this parted. Extra cable was paid out to allow the vessel to drift alongside the north pier where she was fastened with hawsers and tow-lines normally used for mooring purposes. The master also cut the cable, as he feared the *Argo* would be fallen on by another vessel drifting down on her, and used this to provide extra mooring to the pier; during this operation the other moorings parted.

The shipowner claimed as general average not only the value of the cable cut, but also the value of the hawsers and tow-lines. It was agreed the value of the cable could be allowed, this having been appropriated to a different use from that originally intended, so as to contribute towards the preservation of the ship and cargo; but so far as the hawsers and towing lines were concerned it was found they had merely been used for the purpose for which they had been provided, and did not fall within general average.

This case appears to have laid the foundations of general average in English law, being used as a test to see if the following conditions were satisfied:

(1) The act had to be voluntary.
(2) The sacrifice or expenditure had to be extraordinary.
(3) The act had to be intended for the common safety of ship and cargo.
(4) The measures taken had to be incurred in an emergency.

A further test was also applied—whether the sacrifice or expenditure was reasonable.

It was generally thought, before 1868, that Underwriters' liability towards general average would be restricted to the eventual contribution established by the adjustment, even when the merchant's own goods were jettisoned. In other words, the merchant was expected to recover the contributions from his co-adventurers in respect of goods sacrificed before applying to his Underwriters for his own proportion of the loss. But, in that year, in the case of *Dickenson v. Jardine,* a decision was given which completely disturbed the existing arrangements, and succeeded in causing much confusion. The vessel *Canute*, while on a voyage from Foochow to London with a cargo of 641 packages of tea, struck on a reef, and in the time-honoured fashion 607 packages were jettisoned in order to refloat her. The policy, in the usual form, specifically covered the risk of jettison, and the merchant claimed the insured value of the packages sacrificed from his Underwriters directly. They were quite indignant, maintaining that their only liability was for general average contribution. The Court held, however, that the owner of the goods, having expressly insured them against jettison had two remedies; one for the whole value of the goods against the Underwriters, the other for a contribution in case the vessel arrived safely in port. "And he may avail himself of which he pleases, though he cannot retain the proceeds of both so as to be repaid the whole of his loss twice over." In the event of a direct claim on the policy, therefore, Underwriters are entitled to take over the rights of the Assured, and make their own claim in general average by way of recoupment.

With the advent of steamships, there was obviously room for the growth of different kinds of sacrifice, the most prominent being damage done to machinery in forcing the vessel off the ground, provided she was in danger of running serious risk if she remained there.

Unfortunately, the allowances which could be made in general average varied considerably according to the laws of different nations, but in a series of cases heard in this country during the 19th century it was clearly established that the Adjustment should be made according to the law and practice of the place where the adventure ended.

British Underwriters, of course, wished to apply British law to policies issued by themselves, consequently there was much conflict about the extraordinary allowances which were sometimes made in foreign statements. With the enormous diversity of the law and practice in the various countries it become apparent from the inconveniences which were found to arise that it was desirable to bring about a measure of international uniformity on the subject, and with this object in mind an Association was formed under the title "The Association for the Reform and Codification of the Laws of Nations." This Association held a meeting at York in 1864, and another at Antwerp in 1877, when a code of Rules was agreed for stating general average, being known as the York-Antwerp Rules. Later on, in 1890, when the Association again met at Liverpool, the code was revised, and the Rules, known as the York-Antwerp Rules 1890, were adopted. The adjustment of general average as between the shipowner and the owner of the cargo thus became dependent upon a clause in the contract of affreightment dealing with the matter, but it will usually be found at the present time that provision has been made to deal with general average on the basis of the York-Antwerp Rules.

Although they did not form a complete code, and some points were still left to be treated in accordance with the law of destination, at least they serve to ease the situation, and for many years Underwriters were willing to include the following provision in their cargo clauses:

> "General Average and Salvage Charges payable according to Foreign Statement or per York-Antwerp Rules if in accordance with the contract of affreightment."

Rather curiously, the Rules, as eventually adopted, contained a stipulation that no jettison of deck cargo was to be made good as general average. This was something of a departure from the previous practice under which timber cargo, carried on deck in accordance with the custom of the trade, and jettisoned for the common safety at a time of peril, was allowed in general average as if such cargo had been jettisoned from below deck. The new provision meant that, as no contribution was due from the other interests, the Underwriter of the deck cargo, having provided insurance for the entire loss, was put at a disadvantage compared with the old system.

The injustice imposed by the Rule, however, soon raised protests, and, since 1924, the jettison of any cargo carried in accordance with the recognised custom of the trade has been allowed in general average when sacrificed for the common good. In the container age, where purpose built vessels might not be employed, it can still be necessary for a shipowner to prove that his practice of stowing containers on deck amounts to such a custom.

Chapter 16

GENERAL AVERAGE (2)

Concluding his comments on general average the author now studies the relationship between the York/Antwerp Rules and the liability of cargo Underwriters under the terms of their policies.

The liability of Underwriters towards a general average loss was conveniently summarised by the Marine Insurance Act, when the pre-existing case history was codified in 1906. Section 66(1) indicates that such a loss is one caused by or directly consequential on a general average act, and includes a general average expenditure as well as a general average sacrifice.

It is in S.66(2) that the first statutory definition of a general average act is to be found, this reading as follows:

"There is a general average act when any extraordinary sacrifice or expenditure is voluntarily and reasonably made or incurred in time of peril for the purpose of preserving the property imperilled in the common adventure."

Here we have all the ingredients which distinguish general average from other partial losses, the former embracing losses or expenses incurred by the deliberate act of man in an emergency, for the common benefit, while the latter are usually concerned with the operation of the elements, or other transport risks, causing loss or damage to the subject-matter itself. Generally speaking, therefore, general average arises at a time when it becomes essential that some action should be taken beyond the ordinary duty of the master to the shipper, in the interests of the safety of the whole adventure.

An ingenious example of a general average act is given in *Emerigon*, being concerned with a French vessel which had been pursued all day by an enemy ship and was in danger of being captured. When darkness fell the Master set his long boat adrift with a lighted lantern fixed to a rapidly fitted mast and sail. The lights of the ship were then extinguished and the course altered. Borne away by the wind the longboat drifted off, followed by the enemy, allowing the ship to escape. The sacrifice of the longboat was held to be a general average loss.

The definition in the Marine Insurance Act was closely adhered to by that first introduced into the York-Antwerp Rules as Rule "A" in 1924, and which has remained unchanged up to the present time. Although the Rule refers to any extraordinary sacrifice or expenditure which is "intentionally and reasonably made or incurred for the common safety for the purpose of preserving from peril the property involved in a common maritime adventure", there is no practical difference in the two definitions, the word "intentionally" being preferred to "voluntary" as being more decisive.

The current York-Antwerp Rules, adopted in 1974, give specific examples of cargo sacrifices. Thus, apart from the jettison of goods carried in accordance with the recognised custom of the trade (Rule I), damage done by water which goes down an opening made for the purpose of carrying out a jettison for the common safety, will be made good as general average. In fact, an allowance will be made in general average for damage done to either ship or cargo in consequence of any sacrifice made for the common safety (Rule II).

Measures taken for the purpose of extinguishing a fire on board the ship are the subject of Rule III. Under this Rule damage to the ship or cargo, by water or other means used in the extinguishing operations, including damage by beaching or scuttling a burning ship, will also be made good as general average. However, no compensation can be claimed in general average for any damage caused by smoke or heat, such damage being treated, for practical purposes, as part of the fire.

In a case where a ship is intentionally run on shore for the common safety, whether or not she might have been driven on shore, Rule V provides that the consequent loss or damage shall be allowed in general average. Where a voluntary stranding necessarily results in damage to the cargo, there seems to be no reason why such damage should not be made good in general average, as it would in any event fall to be considered under Rule "A".

Loss or damage sustained by cargo during the course of discharge or reshipment, when use is made of barges to lighten a vessel which has gone ashore, is specifically admitted as general average under Rule VIII.

Closely allied to this Rule is Rule XII, which states that damage to or loss of cargo caused in the act of handling, discharging, storing, reloading and stowing shall be made good as general average, when the cost of such measures is admitted in general average.

The most common use of this Rule arises when the vessel has to put into a port of refuge as a result of some extraordinary circumstance which renders that necessary for the common safety. If the handling or discharge of cargo is also necessary for the common safety, or to enable repairs to the ship to be carried out for the safe prosecution of the voyage, such charges are admitted as general average under Rule X, likewise the costs of storage, insurance if reasonably incurred, and the reloading and stowage of the cargo.

Rule XII can, however, give rise to some difficulty as the damage or loss sustained by the cargo is only related to the *act* of handling, discharging etc. and thus is restricted to misfortunes occurring during the actual process of moving the goods. Although Rule "C" would serve to allow, in general average, losses, damages or expenses which are directly consequential on a general average act, it has to be borne in mind that such consequences are not infinite, but are dependent on an assessment of what can be regarded as the natural and reasonable result of the act, i.e. those consequences which flow in an unbroken chain from the act. In particular, the Rule excludes entirely any loss or damage sustained by the cargo through delay, and any indirect loss whatsoever, such a loss of market. Thus, if the storage facilities are adequate, adjusters are not likely to admit as general average losses occurring in storage when unexpectedly caused by fire, theft, storm, flood, or even by negligence on the part of someone leaving open the doors or windows of a warehouse and so permitting rain to enter. On the other hand, if it is known that the facilities for storage are inadequate, and the possibility of certain kinds of risks are foreseeable, e.g. rain through a leaking roof, the subsequent loss or damage may well qualify for an allowance in general average.

In view of the fact that loss or damage cannot always be allowed as general average following the discharge of the goods at a port of distress, average adjusters will often take the precaution of insuring them whilst in store, in which case the premium can be included in the general average disbursements.

It is here pertinent to remark that the standard cargo clauses have traditionally covered loss or damage to the cargo reasonably attributable to discharge at a port of distress, and this protection has been maintained in the present (B) and (C) clauses under Clause 1.1.5, subject, of course, to the exclusions which are detailed subsequently.

Since, in the majority of cases, such loss or damage would be recoverable as general average, the clause will serve to benefit the assured mainly in circumstances where the original vessel is condemned short of destination and the voyage ended. The shipowner will simply notify the cargo interests that they must or can remove their property, and the subsequent discharge will not qualify as general average. The purpose of including the clause would, therefore, appear to be to admit cases of loss or damage which cannot be recovered either as general average, or under one of the other perils insured against. In any event it stresses that Underwriters are directly liable for claims emanating from discharge at a port of distress, whether recoverable in general average or not.

The extent to which loss or damage can be *reasonably attributed* to discharge at a port of distress will naturally turn on a question of the facts. In studying this clause UNCTAD have pointed out that it could give rise to difficulties of interpretation, particularly in relation to loss during storage, or due to theft or rain damage. "The difficulty is one of causation, in that it is not clear whether the assured has to show merely that the loss or damage occured at the port of distress, or that loss or damage was the result of an increased risk because of particular hazards at the port of distress, or that the loss was reasonably attributable to the act of discharging at a port of distress, i.e. excluding subsequent storage and reloading." It is suggested that it might be better to specify more precisely what perils are covered at the port of distress.

It can be anticipated that in some general average situations it will be necessary to store the cargo ashore for a considerable period while repairs to the vessel are carried out, during which time the storage costs can rapidly escalate. Since all the parties to the adventure will be obliged to contribute towards such costs, it may prove advantageous to forward cargo to destination by alternative means, and so save money. This form of economy, known as a "substituted expense", is well recognised in practice, and is covered by Rule "F" of the York-Antwerp Rules, which reads:

116

"Any extra expense incurred in place of another expense which would have been allowable as general average shall be deemed to be general average and so allowed without regard to the saving, if any, to other interests, but only up to the amount of the general average expense avoided."

Of course, it can be argued that the separation of the cargo from the vessel puts an end to the common adventure, and therefore cargo can escape contribution to the subsequent expenses of a general average nature incurred by the shipowner to enable the vessel to continue her voyage. To overcome this legal nicety, it is the custom of average adjusters to obtain the approval of the parties to place themselves as nearly as possible in the same position as if the cargo had been forwarded in the original vessel. Such approval is embodied in a "Non-Separation Agreement", and ensures that the shipowner can include in the adjustment all the port of refuge expenses, the wages and maintenance of the master, officers and crew, also the fuel and stores consumed during the prolongation of the voyage, as allowed under Rules X and XI of the York-Antwerp Rules; to which the cargo will make a rateable contribution.

For many years Underwriters followed the principle that they were not liable for a general average loss or contribution where the measures taken were not incurred for the purpose of avoiding, or in connection with the avoidance of, a peril insured against, this principle being embodied in S.66(6) of the Marine Insurance Act. In many cases, such as when a fire breaks out on board, the peril to the cargo is immediately apparent, but circumstances often arise in which the vessel is not actually in the grip of a disaster, but, say, merely disabled by an engine breakdown, or fast aground in calm water. It is obvious, however, that if nothing is done, there will remain the potential danger of loss from the weather turning hostile, and the benefit of tug assistance or salvage services becomes readily apparent as a means of avoiding such a peril. The contribution towards such measures, when put into operation for the common safety would therefore become recoverable as general average under the cargo policy as an expense incurred in avoiding a peril of the sea.

With the disappearance of the term "perils of the sea" with the S.G. Form of Policy, and the emergence of specific perils under the new (B) and (C) clauses, Underwriters have considered it worthwhile to reword the *General Average Clause* (Clause 2) which now reads:

> "This insurance covers general average and salvage charges, adjusted or determined according to the contract of affreightment and/or the governing law and practice, incurred to avoid or in connection with the avoidance of loss from any cause except those excluded in Clauses 4, 5, 6, and 7 or elsewhere in this insurance."

The essential difference is that Underwriters undertake to respond to a claim for general average contribution, except when arising from the causes specifically excluded. Underwriters have pointed out that the coverage will not differ materially from that previously afforded, but the indemnity is now stated in broader terms aligned to modern practice.

The war and strikes exclusions are balanced up by the coverage given by the War and Strikes Clauses which are normally attached to cargo policies, but, as already mentioned, loss or damage sustained by the cargo through delay, also loss of market, are in any event excluded from general average under the terms of the York-Antwerp Rules (Rule "C").

Although salvage charges are defined in S.65(2) of the Marine Insurance Act as "charges recoverable under maritime law by a salvor independently of contract", the practice is to treat all salvage services, undertaken for the common benefit, as general average. Rule VI of the York-Antwerp Rules, 1974, states as follows:

> "Expenditure incurred by the parties to the adventure on account of salvage, whether under contract or otherwise, shall be allowed in general average to the extent that the salvage operations were undertaken for the purpose of preserving from peril the property involved in the common maritime adventure."

This Rule was first introduced in 1974 in order to maintain international uniformity on the subject, as it could be argued in some countries that each interest was liable to contribute to salvage charges independently of the other, and strictly speaking there was no element of general average. The new Rule ensures that all salvage services, whether of an entirely voluntary nature, a contractual hire basis, or on Lloyd's Form of Salvage Agreement, are treated as general average, subject to the proviso that the expenditure was incurred for the common benefit. Therefore, although salvage awards are often based on salved values at the place where the services end, the final contributions will be calculated by the average adjuster on the "actual net values of the property at the termination of the adventure", in accordance with Rule XVII of the York-Antwerp Rules.

So far as cargo is concerned, the Rule stipulates that its value will basically be that at the time of discharge by reference to the commercial invoice rendered to the receiver, but if there is no such invoice the shipped value will be utilised. The cost of insurance and freight must be included, unless the freight is still at risk. Naturally, any loss or damage suffered by the cargo prior to or at the time of discharge will be deducted, and in the special case of goods being sold short of destination, they shall contribute upon the net proceeds of sale. Any made good must, of course, be added, and this will be computed in a similar way, as provided in Rule XVI. Before the Rules were revised in 1974, average adjusters were often obliged to adopt the expediency of taking the invoice value plus a reasonable percentage of profit because of difficulties in ascertaining market values. The present basis, although somewhat arbitrary, does at least result in the simplification of procedures.

Another advantage is that the contributory value of the cargo will not, in the ordinary way, exceed its insured value, since a sudden rise in market value will no longer be an influencing factor. S.73(1) of the Marine Insurance Act specifies that, subject to any express provision in the policy, the measure of indemnity for any general average contribution is the full amount of such contribution if the cargo is insured for its full contributory value, otherwise the indemnity payable by the insurer must be reduced in proportion to the under insurance. Under the present system of calculating the contributory value such cases will be comparatively rare.

Some Underwriters feel that when the new clauses were being drafted up, the subject of general average could have been studied with a view to eliminating the concept altogether, allowing losses and expenses to fall on those interests which are actually affected, so as not to involve the entire marine adventure. This is a theme which surfaces from time to time, by reason of the fact that adjustments of general average can be seen to remain complex, time-consuming and expensive. Furthermore, there is a growing tendency for cargo interests to challenge liability for contribution on the grounds that the general average arose from unseaworthiness of the vessel, and that the shipowners failed to exercise due diligence before and at the beginning of the voyage to remedy the defect. This can lead to litigation, and, as the Hague Rules throw the burden of proof on the carrier to show that due diligence was, in fact, exercised, can be extremely onerous when the adjustment is not completed until some years after the event. To some extent, therefore, it might be said that general average partly owes its survival to the willingness of the P. and I. Clubs to shoulder the costs of any dispute, and to pay the contribution themselves if necessary.

However, general average is unlikely to disappear unless there is international agreement to abolish it throughout the maritime community. Evidently the detailed and protracted consultation required to achieve this aim has already proved too formidable a deterrent.

Chapter 17

THE MERRY-GO-ROUND OF COLLISION LIABILITY.

When vessels negligently collide, and involve cargo owners in damage to their goods, who eventually pays? Here the difference between American and English law, which resulted in a special clause being inserted in cargo policies, is explained.

The *"Both to Blame Collision" Clause*, the third of the standard cargo clauses, owes its presence to an astonishing difference between English and American law with respect to the rights of innocent cargo owners when two vessels are in collision — all the more remarkable as the position has developed from the same sources of law of the two countries. The clause itself reads:

> This insurance is extended to indemnify the Assured against such proportion of liability under the contract of affreightment "Both to Blame Collision" Clause as is in respect of a loss recoverable hereunder. In the event of any claim by shipowners under the said Clause the Assured agree to notify the Underwriters who shall have the right, at their own cost and expense, to defend the Assured against such claim.

To explain the purpose of the clause it is perhaps best to go back to the common law relating to the joint and several liability of joint tortfeasors. In more understandable language it means that when an innocent party suffers injury by the contributing negligence of two or more persons, he may recover his damages in full from any one of them, or from them all jointly. If he sues only one person, and proves negligence, he can recover the whole extent of his damages from that one, who then has no right of recovery from the other parties, as there is no contribution between joint tortfeasors.

The early Admiralty Courts modified the harshness of this rule for the benefit of ship operators by allowing a right of contribution between joint tortfeasors to the extent that where two or more parties were negligent, the total damages caused by their combined negligence should be divided equally between them. Thus, in a collision situation where both vessels were at fault, an innocent party who had suffered injury or damage to his property could claim recompense in full from either vessel, and the vessel which had been required to make the payment could then recoup one-half of the sum paid from the other vessel. This development is said to have its origins in the Rolls of Oleron in which Article 15 of the text copied into the Black Book of the Admiralty provided that if a ship was lying anchored in a roadstead and was struck by another vessel under way, the damages would be divided equally between the owners of the two vessels, assuming that the captain and the merchants on the ship under way could swear on oath that the collision was accidental. The reason given for this quaint judgment was that if the master of an old ship knew that he could recover full damages, he might be tempted to place his vessel in the way of a better ship, but would be dissuaded by knowing that the damages would be shared between the two vessels.

When the early settlers landed in America they naturally adopted the prevailing law of their mother country, and so for many years the law of both countries developed in harmony. The divided damages rule in cases of mutual fault was firmly established in England in the *Woodrop-Sims* in 1815, and confirmed nine years later by the House of Lords in *Hay v. LeNeve*. In America the rule was approved by the Supreme Court in the case of the schooner *"Catherine" v. Dickinson* in 1854, when, rather influenced by the decisions in the English Courts, it was decided it would "induce care and vigilance on both sides, in the navigation." Subsequently, in the case of the *Atlas* (93 U.S. 302), the Supreme Court upheld the principle that an innocent owner of a cargo was not bound to pursue both colliding vessels, though both might be at fault, but was entitled to a decree against one alone for the entire amount of his damages.

It was around this time that the law regarding the rights of cargo owners began to drift apart in the two countries. In 1861, in the case of the *Milan*, heard in England, where contractual exemptions from liability for negligence were beginning to be permitted to the carrier, Dr. Lushington allowed the innocent cargo owner only one half of his damages against the colliding vessel, when the carrying vessel was partly to blame. This decision was thought by some authorities to be illogical and unsound, as it prevented the innocent owner of cargo on board either ship from recovering from the wrong-doing owner of either ship more than a part of his loss. Nevertheless the ruling continued to find favour with the Admiralty Courts and became part of our statue law under subsection (9) of section twenty-five of the Supreme Court of Judicature Act, 1873 (36 and 37 Vict.,c.66), being confirmed and applied in the case of the *Drumlanrig* [1910].

In the United States, however, adherence to the old system continued. Until 1893 it was considered to be against public policy for common carriers of goods by water to be allowed to insert any stipulation in the contract of carriage exempting themselves from liability for damage to the goods occurring from their own negligence. Consequently the cargo owner could recover his damages in full from either of the colliding vessels, subject to the right of contribution between tortfeasors as laid down in the Admiralty Courts. Thus, each vessel would pay half the damages in the final analysis, unless one vessel was able to limit liability, in which case the balance became recoverable from the other.

Due to the proliferation of bills of lading issued by foreign shipowners containing exemptions from liability for negligence, Congress was prompted in 1893 to enact the Harter Act in order to alleviate the position for shipowners transporting goods to or from ports in the United States. Provided the shipowner had exercised due diligence to make the vessel seaworthy, neither the vessel, her owner, or her charterers would be held responsible for damage or loss resulting from faults or errors in navigation or in the management of the vessel.

The immediate result was that a cargo owner could no longer automatically recover his damages from the carrying vessel consequent on a negligent collision, but it was soon established, in the case of the *Chattahoochee* (173 U.S. 540), that he would still have a right to claim 100 per cent. from the other negligent vessel. Furthermore the non-carrying vessel would, by the divided damages rule, be able to include one-half of such damages in the set off between the two vessels, so that, indirectly, the carrying vessel would still contribute 50 per cent towards the cargo claim. The Supreme Court concluded that "the relations of the two colliding vessels to each other remain unaffected by this Act, notwithstanding one or both of such vessels be laden with a cargo."

This, of course, gave rise to the strange situation that, if the carrying vessel was entirely to blame for the collision it could escape liability towards the cargo altogether, whereas, if it were only partly to blame it would eventually be called upon to pay 50 per cent of such liability.

The next step towards divergence between the two systems occurred in 1911 when the Maritime Conventions Act was passed in this country to give effect to the Brussels Convention of 1910. At that time a new attitude was adopted when both vessels were to blame for a collision; instead of both vessels being deemed equally to blame, apportionment of damages was to be governed by the degree in which each vessel was in fault, and in cases where it was not possible to establish different degrees of fault the liability would be divided equally. It was also confirmed that only in cases of loss of life or personal injury would the liability of the owners of the vessels be joint and several. Since the contract of carriage would invariably exempt the carrying vessel from liability to its own cargo consequent on negligent navigation, the only recourse was for the innocent cargo owner to claim against the non-carrying vessel according to its degree of fault. There the matter would end.

The United States, however, were opposed to any proposal to alter the basic principle under which the cargo owner could claim 100 per cent from the colliding vessel, neither were they prepared to depart from the divided damages rule, consequently the Brussels Convention was never adopted in America, and the position remained that in the set off between the two vessels, the carrying vessel could ultimately be called on to contribute 50 per cent towards the damage to her own cargo notwithstanding the exemption otherwise afforded by the Harter Act. This sum was recoverable from the vessel's P. & I. Club.

The principles laid down in the *Chattahoochee* were thus quietly followed in America for about forty years until the case of the *Toluma* in 1935 (A.M.C. 412), when a dispute arose as to whether general average expenditure, which had been incurred to avert or minimise the peril arising from a collision, was to be treated in the same way as other collision damages. The Supreme Court held that they were, and so, by following the existing procedures, the carrying vessel became liable for 50 per cent of the general average contribution due from its own cargo.

At this stage shipowners and their P. & I. Underwriters evidently thought that cargo owners were enjoying too much of a privileged position, and drew up a clause for insertion in Bills of Lading under which the cargo owners were required to indemnify the carriers for

124

liability in respect of their goods as a result of a collision. This clause, by reason of its origins, was first referred to as the *Toluma* Clause, but soon became known as the "Both-to-Blame Collision" Clause:

> If the ship comes into collision with another ship as a result of the negligence of the other ship and any act, neglect or default of the master, mariner, pilot or the servants of the carrier in the navigation or in the management of the ship, the owners of the goods carried hereunder will indemnify the carrier against all loss or liability to the other or non-carrying ship or her owners insofar as such loss or liability represents loss of, or damage to, or any claim whatsoever of the owners of said goods, paid or payable by the other or non-carrying ship or her owners to the owners of said goods and set-off, recouped or recovered by the other non-carrying ship or her owners as part of their claim against the carrying ship or carrier.

The clause was apparently adopted by carriers following the North Atlantic Freight Conference of 1937, by which time both England and America had confirmed certain statutory exemptions from liability towards the cargo on board, by means of their respective Carriage of Goods by Sea Acts. To some extent, therefore, it could be said that the clause accomplished in the United States a similar distribution of cargo loss to that achieved by the Brussels Convention of 1910 in practically every other maritime country in the world, except that, by the divided damages rule, the cargo owner's indemnity would always be 50 per cent. of his recovered claim from the non-carrying vessel. At any rate, it was only natural that Underwriters would assume liability, by the insertion of a special clause in their policies, for the amount which cargo owners had managed to recover from the non-carrying vessel, but were then obliged to hand over to their own carrier. This achieved the same position as if only 50 per cent. had been recovered from the non-carrying vessel in the first place.

While it might be thought that, by inserting the clause in their Bills of Lading, shipowners had corrected an unfortunate situation peculiar to the United States, in fact there was much opposition to the change. Obviously the individual shipper had no opportunity to repudiate the document agreed upon by the trade, even though he had actually examined it, and there was resentment about the lack of equality of bargaining power which had long been recognised in American law. It was felt that so definite a relinquishment of what the law gave the cargo could hardly be found reasonable without direct authorisation of the law.

Nevertheless the validity of the clause was not challenged until several years later, following a collision which occurred in New York harbour in November, 1942, between the *Nathaniel Bacon* (owned by the United States) and the Belgian motor vessel *Esso Belgium*. As a result of the collision both vessels and the cargo on board the *Nathaniel Bacon* sustained damage. It was agreed both vessels were at fault. In the merry-go-round which followed, an action was brought by the United States, as owners of the *Nathaniel Bacon* and as bailees of her cargo, against the *Esso Belgium*, seeking to recover for the damage done to the *Nathaniel Bacon* and her cargo. There was also a cross-action filed by the owners of the *Esso Belgium*, seeking to recover from the United States for the damage sustained by the *Esso Belgium*, including the amount they might be held liable to pay for damage to the cargo on board the *Nathaniel Bacon*. The United States then impleaded the owners of the cargo on board the *Nathaniel Bacon*, seeking indemnity from them pursuant to the provision of the "Both-to-Blame" Clause in the Bills of Lading.

The District Court held that the owners of the cargo on board the *Nathaniel Bacon* were liable to indemnify the United States, as carriers, under the "Both-to-Blame" Clause, but on appeal by the cargo owners, the Court of Appeal held that such a clause in a Bill of Lading violated both the historical and the legislative background of the protection afforded by Acts of Congress, and was contrary to the public policy of the United States. It allowed carriers to be legislators beyond justification. In 1952, the Supreme Court upheld that decision, maintaining there was no indication that either the Harter Act or the Carriage of Goods by Sea Act was designed to alter the long established rule that the full burden of the losses sustained by both ships in a both-to-blame collision was to be shared equally. If that rule was to be changed, Congress, not the shipowners, should change it. The clause was declared invalid (*United States of America v. Atlantic Mutual Insurance Co.,* A.M.C. 659).

While this case settled the law so far as Bills of Lading were concerned, it was not felt that the position under charter parties was affected, since cargo owners were free to negotiate the terms of the charter with shipowners. The use of the "Both-to-Blame" Clause in charter parties was, however, tested in 1976 in the case of *American Union Transport Inc. v. United States of America* (A.M.C. 1480), when its validity was confirmed. Consequently there remains a need for cargo owners to be indemnified by their Underwriters in those instances where the *"Both-to-Blame Collision" Clause* still applies.

But that is not the end of the story. The U.S. Courts had begun to have doubts about their divided damages rule, which seemed to them to provide a means of avoiding having to make a division of damages on the merits of the case, and, on some occasions did not serve to achieve even rough justice. In 1975, therefore, the Supreme Court, in the *Mary A. Whalen*, finally came round to adopting the system of proportional fault. As Mr. Justice Stewart said: "An equal division of damages is a reasonably satisfactory result only where each vessel's fault is approximately equal and each vessel thus assumes a share of the collision damages in proportion to its share of the blame, or where proportionate degrees of fault cannot be measured and determined on a rational basis. The rule produces palpably unfair results in every other case." (*United States v. Reliable Transfer Co. Inc.,* A.M.C. 541).

This change of heart, it must be emphasised, did nothing to alter the ability of innocent cargo owners to claim 100 per cent of their damages from the colliding vessel (see e.g. the *Anco Princess* [1978] 1 Lloyd's Rep. 293). The position is that now, in the set off between the two vessels involved, the carrying vessel will pay for the damages to its own cargo according to its degree of blame, and, if the "Both-to-Blame" Clause is in the charter party, indemnity can be sought from the cargo owners for the proportion so paid.

Cargo owners, no doubt, find this all very irksome, but if they are insured they have a simple remedy. Better to claim against the Underwriters in the first place, and let them deal with the problems afterwards ...

Chapter 18

DURATION OF THE RISK (1)

This is the first of three articles dealing with the period of cargo Underwriters' liability. In this part Kenneth Goodacre discusses the commencement of the risk, and the "ordinary course of transit".

It has previously been recorded that, under the *Insurable Interest Clause* (Clause 11) in the standard cargo clauses, the assured must have an insurable interest in the subject-matter at the time of loss in order to recover under the insurance. The Clause also stresses that Underwriters are only liable for insured losses occurring during the period specified by the insurance, accordingly the stipulations relating to the duration of the risk are of paramount importance.

In bygone days cargo Underwriters were only prepared to insure the goods during the ocean voyage. The standard S.G. policy form — so recently discarded — covered the goods from the time when they were actually on board the ship until they were discharged and safely landed. Rule for Construction No. 4 of the Marine Insurance Act indicates there was no liability for the goods while in transit from the shore to the ship, consequently there was no protection for the assured for any period the cargo was in lighters for transport to the ship prior to loading. On the other hand Rule for Construction No. 5 provided for the use of lighters at destination by stipulating that the goods should be landed in the customary manner and within a reasonable time after arrival at the port of discharge, otherwise the risk ceased. If, therefore, the merchant despatched his own lighters to a point further than usual in order to obtain possession of his goods earlier, that would be a divergence from the customary lighterage necessary for discharge, and would terminate the insurance.

Transhipment was also frowned upon by insurers, who would frequently have little idea of the state of the on-carrying vessel, and special provision would be necessary. An exception was granted in the case, where by the operation of an insured peril, the voyage was interrupted at an intermediate port or place under circumstances which would justify the master in transhipping the goods and sending them on to their destination, or simply landing and reloading them (see Section 59 of the Act).

While such restrictions may have been admirably suited to earlier times, the reasonable demands of business required that Underwriters should provide more realistic cover, undertaking the inland risks as well, consequently they became willing to include all transport risks under what used to be known as the *Warehouse to Warehouse Clause.*

In the first Institute Clauses (W.A. and F.P.A.), published in 1912, the period of cover was described as follows:

> ... from shippers' or manufacturers' warehouse until on board the vessel, during transhipment if any, and from the vessel whilst on quays wharves or in sheds during the ordinary course of transit until safely deposited in consignees' or other warehouse at destination named in policy.

It was also made clear by a separate *Craft Clause* that the cover included the risk of craft, raft or lighter both at the port of loading and discharge, thus the period of transit was to be continuous between the termini stated in the policy, whether the carriage of the goods was by means of road, railway, canal, lake, river or sea. The criterion was that they would be subject to the "ordinary course of transit", i.e. carried in the customary manner, by the usual route, and with reasonable despatch, to the destination. Any unreasonable delay or any deviation from the normal route would give the Underwriters the opportunity to terminate the insurance.

In this regard the Underwriters were protected by the Marine Insurance Act in a number of ways. Section 48, for instance, provides for the adventure to be prosecuted with reasonable despatch, and if no lawful excuse can be raised, the insurers are discharged from liability as from the time any delay becomes unreasonable.

Section 46 also stipulates that where a ship, without lawful excuse, deviates from the voyage contemplated by the policy, the insurer is discharged from liability as from the time of the deviation, and it is immaterial that the ship may have regained her route before any loss occurs. Although the S.G. Form itself was worded to allow the vessel to "touch and stay at any ports or places whatsoever", Rule for Construction No. 6 indicates that the words did not authorise the ship to depart from the course of her voyage between the ports of departure and destination. Section 47 of the Marine Insurance Act also says that where several ports of discharge are specified in the policy, the ship must proceed to them in the order designated by the policy, but where the policy simply states to "ports of discharge" within a given area, she must proceed to them in their geographical order.

Clearly these early provisions were designed to ensure that the risk undertaken by the insurer would be one within his contemplation, based upon the supposition that everything which was usual and necessary would be done. Nevertheless, there was recognition that certain unexpected events could arise which ought not to prejudice the insurance, these being set out in Section 49 of the Act. Thus deviation or delay was excused when caused by circumstances beyond the control of the master or employer, an obvious example being stress of weather or some other insured peril. Another excuse would be when it was reasonably necessary to comply with an express or implied warranty — particularly relevant if seaworthiness was involved. Regard for the safety of the ship (which might have to resort to a port of refuge), the saving of human life, and the need to obtain medical or surgical aid for anyone on board the ship, were all sufficient excuses for the vessel to deviate or incur delay, but no dispensation was allowed if the purpose was merely to save other property. If barratry was one of the perils insured against, the policy would remain in force if any deviation or delay was caused by the barratrous conduct of the master and crew.

Naturally it was possible to import special terms into the policy, by arrangement with Underwriters, so as to maintain the insurance in force during any deviation or delay, and, in the earliest clauses, provision was specifically made for the assured to be held covered, at a premium to be arranged, in case of deviation, protection also being given in the event of any variation of the adventure arising from any liberty granted to the carriers by the contract of affreightment. But, whatever excuse was authorised, the Act made it a condition that when the cause had ceased to operate, the ship should resume her course, and prosecute her voyage, with reasonable despatch.

In the present standard conditions the duration of cover is expressed in the *Transit Clause*, under which clause 8.1. maintains the position which has been in operation since before the last war i.e. that *the insurance attaches from the time the goods leave the warehouse or*

place of storage at the place named for the commencement of the
transit, and continues during the ordinary course of transit ...

On the face of it the words seem clear enough. By relating the commencement of the transit to the time when the goods leave the
designated warehouse or place of storage, Underwriters have ensured
that they are not responsible for any loss or damage during the period
the goods are merely being transferred from the manufacturers'
premises to a packers' warehouse prior to export, neither will they
incur any liability while the goods are in store awaiting the
commencement of the transit. Such risks would have to be specifically
covered. Nevertheless there are occasions when doubts can arise as
to whether the goods can be said to have "left" the warehouse or place
of storage for the commencement of the transit.

While this particular point does not appear to have required the
attention of an English Court, several cases have been contested in
America.

In *Plata American Trading Inc. v. K.L. Lancashire* [1957], for
instance, a consignment of 501 tons of tallow was insured from
Houston to Hamburg, being in the storage tanks of the Marco
Chemical Company before commencing transit. The bill of lading
was made out for the full quantity, having been certified by an
experienced cargo inspector and surveyor named Martin. In fact only
375 tons were delivered at destination, and, on investigation, it was
proved that this was all that had been received on board. It transpired
that the chemical company had three storage tanks which were inter-
connected so that the tallow could run from one tank to another.
All these tanks were connected with a gauge pump through which
the tallow had to flow before it would reach the final hose from which
it would be deposited into the ship's tanks. In the ensuing action by
the buyers against the representative Lloyd's Underwriters, the
steamship line, and the surveyor, the New York Supreme Court was
satisfied that the missing tallow did not pass beyond the gauge pump,
and concluded that the remainder had been diverted by the chemical
company by transferring it from one tank to another by means of
the inter-connecting pipes.

Dealing with the claim against the Underwriters Mr. Justice
Coleman stated: "We need not go so far as to say that the tallow
should actually have passed into the ship's tank before the risk
attached; that would make the 'Warehouse to Warehouse' clause
meaningless. But certainly until tallow passed through the gauge

pump it was still in Marco's plant. It was only after it had passed through the pump for the final passage into the vessel that it was in transit — only then had it reached the point of no return — and only 375 tons left Marco's custody and possession. It is fiction to talk of 501 tons or of any quantity beyond 375 tons or of any balance. There was no balance. If the tallow had been loaded on trucks from the tanks to be deposited on the pier, it would not be in transit while the trucks were still within Marco's establishment. Similarly it was not in transit here and the risk had not attached."

In the event judgment was given against Martin for the amount which the buyers had overpaid by reason of his negligence.

Another case worthy of mention is that of *Kessler Export Corporation v. Reliance Insurance Company of Philadelphia* [1963]. Here goods had been loaded through the back of a vehicle which was partly inside a warehouse, the front part remaining outside across the pavement, so that some of the goods, at least, had passed over the warehouse boundary. Because it was too late to depart, the vehicle was backed into the warehouse, only to be stolen during the weekend. It was decided that the goods had not left the warehouse for the commencement of the transit.

The meaning of the word "transit" has, however, been the subject of some deliberation in the English Courts in disputes arising on "Goods-in-Transit" policies. As these are more concerned with the liability of road carriers the period of transit, is, of course, dependent on the particular terminology employed, but they do provide some interesting observations on the part of the learned judges concerned.

In *Sadler Brothers Company v. Meredith* [1963] the Court had to consider Underwriters' liability under a policy covering loss of "goods and/or merchandise of all kinds including machinery in transit by commercial vehicles operated by the insured." The vehicle was loaded with cleaning materials with the intention of taking them to the docks as soon as the remaining matters had been completed, but, on police instructions, it was moved round the corner and parked about 70 yards from the insured's premises, whence it was subsequently stolen. On the question of whether it could be said the goods were in transit Mr. Justice Roskill said: "I think here 'transit' means the passage or carriage of goods from one place to another and I think the goods were still being carried and, therefore, were still in transit from the one place to the other even though the lorry in which they were being carried was temporarily parked."

In another case, that of *Crow's Transport Ltd. v. Phoenix Assurance Co. Ltd.* [1965], the manufacturers of a consignment of gramophone records, Decca, had sent the goods in their own lorries to a road hauliers' premises in Holloway, London, for delivery in Gateshead. The London manager took the cartons down some steps to a place which he believed to be safe, and left them there to be loaded on the next lorry for Gateshead. During the 20 minutes he was away for lunch several of the cartons were stolen.

On this occasion the hauliers had a goods in transit policy which provided cover for "the subject matter insured belonging to or in the custody or control of the Insured whilst being loaded upon carried by or unloaded from the Vehicles described herein ... and whilst temporarily housed during the course of transit whether on or off the Vehicles ..." The insurers denied that, at the time of the loss, the goods were in the course of transit.

The County Court judge held that the goods were not in the course of transit because, in his opinion, the course of transit did not begin until some step had been taken by the hauliers towards loading the goods on to a vehicle. In the Court of Appeal, however, Lord Denning was much in favour of the instances put forward during the argument. When one takes a parcel to the Post Office or a railway station, hands it over and obtains a receipt, the goods are in transit from the moment when the Post Office or railway take them. They are in transit by the Post Office or the railway's vehicles, as the case may be, because from that moment onwards everything that is done is incidental to that transit. It seemed to him, in the present case, that from the moment the carriers accepted the goods and took them down the steps, they were temporarily housed awaiting loading on to their vehicles. It was an incident of transit by those vehicles, and therefore the goods were in transit by the insured's vehicles.

Lord Justice Danckwerts, in agreeing with Lord Denning, made the point that, when Decca sent the goods in their own lorries to the hauliers' premises, they had already started on their journey to Gateshead, and remained in transit until they reached their destination. While that part of the journey to the hauliers' premises was not covered by the policy, when the goods arrived there they had to be unloaded and, as a practical matter, it was obvious that they might occasionally be carried from one vehicle to another, but, much more probably, be put down temporarily on the ground or some place where it would be convenient. They might be kept there for a few minutes, or it might be for hours, or it might be for a day, but it was part of the transit and plainly covered by the words "temporarily housed during the course of transit whether on or off the Vehicles."

A somewhat similar problem arose in *A. Tomlinson (Hauliers) Ltd. v. Hepburn* [1964]. The plaintiffs had been engaged to carry a consignment of cigarettes from the manufacturers' premises in Nottingham to premises in City Road, London. The lorries arrived after working hours and were taken into the depot but not unloaded. They remained in the depot under the protection of a night-watchman, and would have been unloaded the next morning by employers of the depot, assisted by the carriers' driver and his mate. At some time in the evening the lorries and cigarettes were stolen, without any negligence on the part of the carriers, the lorries being found abandoned and empty a day or so later. On this occasion the goods were insured "whilst being carried and/or in transit anywhere in the United Kingdom including loading and unloading. Including risk during halts and/or whilst garaged and/or elsewhere overnight." The insurers contended that the goods were off risk at the time of the loss.

In the Commercial Court it was submitted that, having reached their City Road destination, the lorries and the goods had completed their transit, but that the policy would be re-attached for a short period the following morning while the goods were being unloaded. It was argued that once inside the depot, and the drivers had left their cabs, the security staff became responsible for the goods.

Mr. Justice Roskill, who was again involved, was not impressed. "In my judgment, the cover afforded by this particular policy continues right down to the point of time at which unloading from the lorry is completed. Any other view seems to produce great practical difficulties. The Court should be slow to construe a policy as covering risks in what one might call fits and starts."

The Court of Appeal upheld his decision that the goods were covered at the time of the loss, saying that in any ordinary case the goods would remain on risk until completion of the unloading, and that, in any event, the loaded lorries were, within the meaning of the policy, garaged overnight at the City Road premises.

Taking an overall view of the decisions it would seem reasonable to suggest that cover under the standard cargo clauses commences once the goods are removed from the warehouse or place of storage for the furtherence of their carriage to destination. The risk will, accordingly, continue while the goods are being loaded on to a lorry, railway wagon, or other conveyance, and whilst thereon before moving off, if it is the intention to proceed on the journey without undue delay, or if the custody and control of the goods has passed to independent carriers. Once the journey has commenced the "ordinary course of transit" will include temporary parking, temporary housing, unloading at the place of destination, and until delivery is effected at the final warehouse or place of storage.

In some circumstances where it is difficult to determine the confines of a "place of storage" e.g. a private railway siding, an open site, a silo, or a land tank, it may be necessary to refer to the custom of the manufacturers or the merchant, but in such cases it is obviously desirable to clarify the intentions of the parties to the contract of insurance by express provision.

Understanding that the assured have little means of regulating the movement of their goods once they have left their custody. Underwriters have provided considerable dispensation in respect of matters outside their control by stipulating in Clause 8.3 that, subject to the provisions elsewhere regarding the termination or continuance of the risk, *the insurance shall remain in force during delay beyond the control of the assured, any deviation, forced discharge, reshipment or transhipment and during any variation of the adventure arising from the exercise of a liberty granted to shipowners or charterers under the contract of affreightment.* It is here to be noted that this protection is automatically provided, without requiring the assured to give notice to the Underwriters or to pay an additional premium. Nevertheless, attention is drawn to the necessity to avoid delay wherever possible by Clause 18, which states:

It is a condition of this insurance that the Assured shall act with reasonable despatch in all circumstances within their control.

This clause serves to reiterate Section 48 of the Act on the subject of unreasonable delay. There is no provision for the assured to be held covered in the event that the goods are delayed for their own convenience, consequently early notice should be given to Underwriters, and their consent obtained to extend any such periods in storage, customs and the like, if the continuation of cover is not to be prejudiced.

Chapter 19

DURATION OF THE RISK (2)

In the second of this three part series the author explores the circumstances which terminate the risk under the standard cargo clauses.

In the previous article it was shown that the original *Warehouse to Warehouse Clause* contained no time limits, the only restriction being that the goods should be in the ordinary course of transit. Underwriters began to find, however, that they had been on risk for extensive periods after discharge, particularly when carriage to the interior happened to be by limited means. For some years prior to the last war, therefore, they deemed it necessary to confine the period of transit, after discharge from the overseas vessel, to 15 days if the destination was within the port area, and 30 days if it were outside. Any prior delivery naturally terminated the insurance in the usual way. Delay in excess of the time limits, arising from circumstances beyond the control of the assured, and any unusual transhipment, could be covered at a premium to be arranged.

Due to the increased marine risks arising out of wartime conditions, various surcharges to basic cargo rates were introduced in January 1940, and, in May, 1942, a new clause, the *Unlimited Transhipment Clause* — later to become the *Wartime Extension Clause* — was issued. This gave assureds (subject to the payment of a surcharge) the option of cover against unlimited transhipment and unlimited delay in situations which could not be controlled by them. Nevertheless it was found in practice that many assureds did not take up this offer and additional premiums were seldom paid under ordinary circumstances except where claims brought to light some delay or extra transhipment. In 1943, therefore, it was decided to make the surcharges for extended cover compulsory, and they had to be added to all basic marine rates without option to the shippers, in addition to the other marine surcharges arising out of wartime conditions.

These "Combined Marine Surcharges", as they were called, remained in effect until July, 1949, when the return to more normal conditions made their use appear to be superfluous, and the then current "C.M.S." rates were merged with the basic rates. In due course, owing to competition and other factors, these combined rates gradually became reduced in many cases to the level of the original basic rates, or even lower, so that there was; in fact, no longer any additional premium being paid for the additional cover. However, the clauses continued to remain in use as it was not considered that brokers or their clients would tolerate a return to the more restricted *Warehouse to Warehouse Clause*.

The *Wartime Extension Clause* was superseded by the *Extended Cover Clause* in 1952, but was followed by a period of increasing agitation in Underwriting circles for some restriction of the very wide extension of cover granted. This matter was brought to a head by very long delays — sometimes up to six months — which were occurring in 1955 on the west coast of South America due to currency restrictions and delays in customs. As a result new *Extended Cover Clauses* were issued in 1956, under which the period of cover after discharge was limited to 60 days, this being felt to be an acceptable compromise. However, there was no "held covered" provision, because, in the light of the difficulty already experienced in obtaining the appropriate additional premium in all applicable cases, Underwriters were not prepared to make an automatic extension available. Instead, it was left to the shipper to approach the Underwriters for a grant of some reasonable extension of the 60 days limit at the time of the inception of the risk, so that a suitable additional premium could be paid beforehand — and that is the position still appertaining today.

The next major change came in 1963, when Underwriters undertook to clarify the meaning of "final warehouse". Problems could arise at destination in a variety of ways because of differing conditions at ports of discharge, among which was the practice of the port authorities to put the goods in a transit shed at the ship's berth and allow the importers a certain number of days of grace before charging storage. If the consignees were not able to take delivery due to lack of space in their own premises, they might well use the storage facilities at the port to advantage thus preventing the normal flow of transit to the intended destination. On other occasions they would be inclined to use the wharf shed as a means of allocation and distribution to several customers, making it difficult to decide which was the final warehouse.

The latter point was considered by Mr. Justice McNair, in the case of *Overseas Commodities v. Style* [1958], which concerned the import of two consignments of canned pork butts from France "to final warehouse at any port or ports, place or places in the United Kingdom via London." The conditions included blowing of tins, also inherent vice and hidden defect, but condemnation by the authorities was restricted to three months from the date of arrival in final warehouse, making it important to identify where the transit had terminated. In his judgment, on the facts of the case, "the final warehouse contemplated by this clause is the final warehouse in this country at which the goods arrived and were made available to the plaintiffs for distribution as part of their stock as importers." Accordingly he ruled that on one shipment the final warehouse was at the wharf where the goods were discharged, while on the other it was at a goods station in London.

The question of whether a transit shed should be considered as a final warehouse came up many years ago in *Westminster Fire Office v. Reliance Marine Insurance Company* [1903] when a shipment of jute arrived at Dundee from Calcutta, and was insured "including all risk of craft to wharf or export vessel at port of discharge, and, in the event of the goods being temporarily placed upon the quay, it is agreed to hold the same covered whilst there and until delivered to the export vessel or at any wharf or warehouse within the limits of the port." In accordance with the practice of the port some parcels of the jute were landed and placed in "transit sheds" on the quay in order that they might be sorted and weighed, the consignee not having made up his mind at that time as to the ultimate destination of the jute, which he was endeavouring to sell. According to the by-laws of the port, the goods could not remain in the sheds for more than 48 hours, but this rule was not strictly enforced, unless there was a pressure on space by reason of the arrival of a number of ships at the same time. Three days' later some of the jute was seriously damaged by a fire, the claim being settled by the plaintiff company with whom the consignee had effected an insurance against fire. The fire Underwriters then took up an assignment of the marine policy, and commenced an action to recover the amount of the loss from the defendants.

In the opinion of Mr. Justice Kennedy, supported by the Court of Appeal, the insured transit was not at an end when the fire happened. Construing the policy from a business point of view, the voyage was not to be considered at an end until the jute had been delivered to an export vessel, or at a wharf or warehouse within the limits of the port. In the view of the Court, the goods were in no different position than being temporarily placed upon the quay, and the marine Underwriters were liable.

That case was, of course, decided on the particular wording of the policy, and it was not until *John Martin of London, Ltd. v. Russell* [1960], that a similar problem had to be decided on the wording of the standard cargo clauses. The circumstances here were that consignments of American lard were being shipped from Great Lakes ports on landed terms ex-quay Liverpool. The custom at that port was to stow the goods in a transit shed opposite the discharge berth, and to treat the goods as being on the quay for the purposes of three days' free rent, and to charge special rent after that. In the case of one particular shipment of 7200 cartons, the lard was infested by an attack from copra beetles which had migrated from a cargo of copra stored in the transit shed on the floor above the lard. Costs were incurred in removing the lard for disinfestation by refrigeration, followed by reconditioning and repacking, also further storage. The question was, had the goods reached the "final warehouse" for the purpose of construing the insurance policy?

Mr. Justice Pearson ascertained that, in the majority of cases, the buyer would, by a delivery order, have allocated to him only part of the goods under one mark, and therefore there would at that stage be no appropriation of any particular part of the goods to the contract of sale. Accordingly the customer would not expect the property to pass to him until his vehicle came and collected his goods. If this procedure was not carried out within the three days' grace allowed by the Harbour Board, it was customary to remove the goods to the warehouse of the sellers' Liverpool Agents.

The learned judge, referring to the decision in the case of *Westminster Fire Office v. Reliance Marine Insurance Co.,* had little difficulty in concluding that the transit shed was essentially a shed in which goods were placed temporarily pending some further movement to another place. In this connection he was somewhat influenced by the fact that the Harbour Board treated the transit shed as a quay for rental purposes, or, to put it another way, goods in the transit shed counted as goods on the quay. He thought it was clear from the pertinent clause in the policy conditions that the mere putting of the goods on a quay did not terminate the insurance, since after the discharge there it was possible for the insurance to last for 60 days. In this case the plaintiffs still had an insurable interest at the time of the damage, and, as the transit shed could not be considered to be the final warehouse, the claim was allowed.

This decision earned the obvious displeasure of cargo Underwriters who took steps to revise the clause. In its present form (which is practically the same as it was in 1963) *the Transit Clause* reads:

8 8.1   This insurance attaches from the time the goods leave the warehouse or place of storage at the place named herein for the commencement of the transit, continues during the ordinary course of transit and terminates either

8.1.1   on delivery to the Consignees' or other final warehouse or place of storage at the destination named herein,

8.1.2   on delivery to any other warehouse or place of storage, whether prior to or at the destination named herein, which the Assured elect to use either

8.1.2.1   for storage other than in the ordinary course of transit or

8.1.2.2   for allocation or distribution,
or

8.1.3   on the expiry of 60 days after completion of discharge overside of the goods hereby insured from the oversea vessel at the final port of discharge, whichever shall first occur.

The effect of the clause is to treat any place used for the purposes of storage, or allocation or distribution, as the place where the insurance terminates. With regard to "storage", however, much will depend on the actions or intentions of the assured as to whether the goods can be regarded as being in the ordinary course of transit. If it is the practice of the consignees to leave the goods in store, or if they issue instructions for the goods to be stored, then obviously cover will cease immediately the goods enter the place of storage. If the assured clearly intend to take delivery from the wharf area, and they act with reasonable despatch, cover will continue until the goods reach the destination named in the policy even if delay occurs because of circumstances outside their control, such as a dock strike, or failure of the documents of title to arrive promptly. In any event, unless the assured make special arrangements with their Underwriters, the insurance will cease on the expiry of 60 days after completion of discharge, if delivery has not been previously effected. It must also be mentioned that if the goods are destined to a place inland but are insured only to the port of discharge, the warehouse in which the goods are deposited at the port to await transit to the inland destination must be regarded as the "final" warehouse.

Some thirty years ago a Marine Research Group of the Insurance Institute of Liverpool pointed out the standard clauses did not provide any clear indication as to where the risk terminated if the goods were simply insured to a transhipment port for on-carriage elsewhere, and summarised their own views as follows:

(1) With direct transhipment—the risk terminates on delivery of the goods to the on-carrying vessel.
(2) With transhipment by lighter—termination on delivery of the goods to the lighter.
(3) With goods being placed on shore—terminates on delivery to the transit or customs shed, or on being placed on the quay.

These views still seem appropriate today.

Clause 8.2 contemplates a situation where the final destination is voluntarily changed after the goods are landed at the port of discharge:

8.2 If, after discharge overside from the oversea vessel at the final port of discharge, but prior to termination of this insurance, the goods are to be forwarded to a destination other than that to which they are insured hereunder, this insurance, whilst remaining subject to termination as provided for above, shall not extend beyond the commencement of transit to such other destination.

The most common use of this clause occurs when the goods are sold before delivery to the original destination, and, in fact, reference was made to such a sale in previous versions of the clause. However, in *John Martin of London, Ltd. v. Russell*, Mr. Justice Pearson expressed difficulty in defining the word "sold" which he thought could refer to the making of the agreement to sell, or to the passing of the property, or even to what a reasonable business man would understand by the word. The present wording avoids this problem by simply confining itself to a change of destination, in which case the risk will cease on the commencement of the transit to the new destination. The clause, of course, operates only if the destination is changed before the expiry of the insurance in the normal way, as defined in Clause 8.

Another contingency for which Underwriters have provided is the case where the goods may have to end their voyage at a different port by reason of the termination of the contract of carriage, or the transit is otherwise terminated before its natural expiry, owing to circumstances beyond the control of the assured. This can happen if the destination port is strikebound or subject to political upheaval.

Clause 9, the *Termination of Contract of Carriage Clause*, actually had its origins in the Italo-Abyssinian dispute, following the application of "sanctions" against Italy by the League of Nations Assembly in 1935. Fearing that their vessels might have to terminate voyages at ports other than those described in the bills of lading in order to comply with the Assembly's instructions, shipowners took the precaution of protecting themselves by inserting a clause in their bills of lading giving themselves the liberty to do so. In their turn cargo Underwriters also undertook to protect the assured. The present clause reads as follows:

9   If owing to circumstances beyond the control of the Assured either the contract of carriage is terminated at a port or place other than the destination named therein or the transit is otherwise terminated before delivery of the goods as provided for in Clause 8 above, then this insurance shall also terminate *unless prompt notice is given to the Underwriters and continuation of cover is requested when the insurance shall remain in force, subject to an additional premium if required by the Underwriters*, either

9.1   until the goods are sold and delivered at such port or place, or, unless otherwise specially agreed, until the expiry of 60 days after arrival of the goods hereby insured at such port or place, whichever shall first occur,
or

9.2   if the goods are forwarded within the said period of 60 days (or any agreed extension thereof) to the destination named herein or to any other destination, until terminated in accordance with the provisions of Clause 8 above.

It must first of all be drawn to attention that when the carriage is terminated short of destination, the insurance will also terminate unless prompt arrangements are made with Underwriters to maintain it in force. When continuation of cover is granted, the policy can remain in force until the goods are sold and delivered at the port or place of termination, subject to this procedure being carried out within 60 days, or some other agreed period, after the arrival of the goods there. The mere sale of the goods — i.e. the passing of the property to another buyer, so that the assured lose their interest in the goods — does not necessarily end the cover. If the limitation period has not already operated to terminate the insurance, the cover ends when the goods are delivered to the purchaser. On the other hand, if the goods are forwarded to the original destination, or to a substituted destination, within the 60 days (or any agreed extension), cover will continue until terminating under the provisions of the *Transit Clause.*

A significant change from the previous version of this clause lies in the reference to the period after the *arrival* of the goods at the port or place, whereas under the old wording the period counted from the time *discharge* from the overseas vessel was completed. Evidently Underwriters had it in mind that, in some circumstances, such as when the carriers become insolvent and are unable to complete the voyage, the goods can remain in the ship for a considerable period before discharge. The revised wording ensures that an adequate premium can be charged for such delay.

Curiously enough, although Underwriters have defined the meaning of "arrival" in the Institute War Clauses (Cargo), they have not seen fit to adopt any such definition in the basic marine clauses. Possibly this is because the circumstances may be somewhat unusual, or the place where the transit is terminated may not be until after the goods are discharged, calling for a special appraisal of the facts.

A reader has written to enquire whether the extra forwarding charges are recoverable under the clauses in the event that the captain, on reaching the port of destination, finds there is delay due to congestion, and exercises the option in the contract of affreightment to discharge the cargo at a different port. Clause 12, however, informs us that the only occasions when such expenses can be recovered under the policy are when the costs arise as the result of an insured peril or in consequence of general average or salvage, the object being to ameliorate the effects of the operation of a risk covered by the insurance. In the absence of any threat of the goods being lost or damaged, or even to the completion of the adventure itself, the only "cause" which can be said to be relevant to the expenditure is the delay which was avoided. Such a cause is expressly excluded by Clause 4.5. Far from accepting liability for the extra costs concerned, therefore, it is open to the Underwriters to charge an additional premium to maintain the cover in force under the terms of Clause 9.

Chapter 20

DURATION OF THE RISK (3)

Concluding his series on the period of transit under the standard cargo clauses, the author explains some of the pitfalls which can result in lack of cover altogether.

Having looked at the application of the *Transit Clause* in some detail, and the provisions relating to the continuance of cover from the inception of the risk until termination at the final destination (or some alternative place as provided in the supporting clauses), it is worthwhile examining the circumstances under which the assured can find that the insurance has never attached in the first place.

The most obvious situation is where the commencement of the adventure is unreasonably delayed. In *De Wolf v. Archangel Maritime Insurance Co.* [1874] the risk was placed in mid-July, but the vessel did not arrive at Montreal, the loading port, until the end of August. It was held that the character of the voyage had changed from summer to winter conditions by reason of the delay, and the insurers were entitled to avoid the policy. Section 42 of the Marine Insurance Act has made it an implied condition that the voyage shall be commenced within a reasonable time.

This is, however, a situation which the assured can normally refer to Underwriters in order to maintain the cover in force. On other occasions the voyage may, for various reasons, be wrongly declared, and, in consequence, the assured will be unable to invoke any of the policy terms to remedy the defect.

Such a defect was brought to light in the case of *Simon, Israel and Co. v. Sedgwick and others* [1892]. Although this is an old case, it has more recently been echoed by the Judicial Committee of the Privy Council, and will, therefore, repay further study.

A shipper had been accustomed to forwarding some of his goods from a warehouse in Bradford to Liverpool for shipment, whence they were carried by sea to Seville, and from there overland to Madrid.

In March, 1892, having a similar consignment of goods, he declared the shipment under a floating policy which covered his interests "at and from the Mersey or London to any port in Portugal or Spain this side of Gibraltar, and thence by inland conveyances to any place in the interior of Spain or Portugal, including all risks whatever from the time of leaving the warehouse in the United Kingdom, and all risks of every kind until safely delivered at the warehouses of the consignee ..." There was also a marginal note to the effect that any deviation, change of voyage, or transhipment, not included in the policy, would be held covered at a premium to be arranged.

A few days after making the declaration, the shipper learned that the goods were being shipped by the *Lope de Viga*. Accordingly he instructed his broker to insert that name in the declaration, and to show the port of discharge as Seville, as on the previous shipments. In fact, the vessel did not intend to call at Seville, but only at Carril and Huelva on the west coast (this side) of Spain, and Cartagena and other ports on the east coast. She was lost on that part of the voyage which was common to vessels bound for either the Atlantic or Mediterranean ports, and when the bill of lading came to hand it was found the goods were due to be discharged at Cartagena, where they could be forwarded by rail to Madrid.

When the shipper discovered the mistake, he offered to pay the Underwriter an additional premium, relying on the "held covered" provision in the policy, but this was refused on the ground that the voyage to Cartagena was not covered. It was contended that the words "change of voyage" could only apply after the policy had once attached by the commencement of the voyage described; an initial declaration of insurance on a different voyage was outside the policy, and could not take effect.

In the Queen's Bench Division Mr. Justice Wright said: "The contention for the assured is that, when the goods left the warehouse, they being then intended by the consignors to proceed by a route covered by the policy, the declaration was rightly made, and the policy attached, and the clause applied, and the assured were entitled to change the voyage on the terms of paying extra premium to Cartagena, the amount of which is not in dispute. The point is a nice one, but I think that the contention of the Underwriters must prevail. If the substance of the policy is a maritime risk, I think that the character of the preliminary conveyance before the ship is reached must be determined by that of the voyage on which the goods were

146

actually shipped, and that the goods must, until shipment, be taken to have started for the voyage for which they were afterwards in fact shipped; and, if so, the voyage for which these goods were started was not a voyage for which they could be declared, and the policy and deviation clause never attached."

This decision was upheld in the Court of Appeal where the words of Lord Justice Bowen were significant: "... In the present case the goods started from Bradford and it has been contended that the moment they started from Bradford they were upon the insured voyage. If the goods had started the insured voyage, it seems to me the risk during the time that they were between Bradford and Liverpool would have been covered as incidental to and supplementary to the insured voyage. But we have here a conclusive fact that the goods never started upon the insured voyage. Accordingly, the risk between Bradford and Liverpool never could be incidental or supplementary to it. It is not necessary to decide what would have been the case supposing the goods, after having been specifically appropriated by a contract of carriage to the insured voyage, had been injured or lost during the transit between Bradford and Liverpool. It is not necessary to decide that case. In this case the facts here shew conclusively that the goods were never specifically appropriated to the insured voyage, because the person who had the control of the goods ... fixed the voyage outside the policy; and if that is so, the policy never attached ..."

Sections 43 and 44 of the Marine Insurance Act have since defined a "different voyage" as follows:

43. Where the place of departure is specified by the policy and the ship instead of sailing from that place sails from any other place, the risk does not attach.

44. Where the destination is specified in the policy, and the ship, instead of sailing for that destination, sails for any other destination, the risk does not attach.

A "change of voyage", on the other hand, is described by Section 45:

45.(1) Where, after the commencement of the risk, the destination of the ship is voluntarily changed from the destination contemplated by the policy, there is said to be a change of voyage.

(2) Unless the policy otherwise provides, where there is a change of voyage, the insurer is discharged from liability as from the time of change, that is to say, as from the time when the determination to change is manifested, and it is immaterial that the ship may not in fact have left the course of voyage contemplated by the policy when the loss occurs.

Underwriters have taken steps to protect the assured in cases of "change of voyage", by a clause of that description (No.10) reading:

Where, after attachment of this insurance, the destination is changed by the Assured, held covered at a premium and on conditions to be arranged subject to prompt notice being given to the Underwriters.

While this clause gives the assured discretion to change the destination of the ship once the risk has attached, it must be pointed out that the right to be "held covered" is dependent on prompt notice being given to Underwriters, and the *"Note"* at the foot of the clauses stresses that continuation of cover is dependent on compliance with that obligation. It is incumbent on the assured, therefore, to advise the Underwriters as soon as they elect to change the port of destination, otherwise the insurers can disclaim liability for any loss or damage occurring from that time.

It can readily be seen that the assured are in a vulnerable position if they declare the voyage wrongly, and the recent case of *Kallis (Manufacturers) Ltd. v. Success Insurance Ltd.* [1985] also shows that if the goods are shipped on a different vessel without their knowledge, they can become the innocent victims of a fraud.

Early in 1976, a firm manufacturing jeans in Cyprus agreed to buy a quantity of denim from suppliers in Hong Kong on c.i.f. terms to Limassol. This was to be in four parcels, and the suppliers arranged insurance on "all risks" terms by means of the Institute Cargo Clauses of 1.1.63 (which were in effect at that time) to cover the goods from their warehouse to the buyers' warehouse in Nicosia. Like the present clauses they made provision for the insurance to remain in force during any variation of the adventure arising from the exercise of a liberty granted to shipowners under the contract of affreightment.

The particular bales which were the subject of the dispute, were intended to be shipped on the *Oceania Maru* but that vessel was unable to accept the goods. Arrangements were then made through a shipping agent to forward the bales on the *Ta Shun* to Limassol. To this end the suppliers completed a shipping order instructing the master to receive the bales for shipment to Limassol, the space for transhipment being left blank. Printed at the bottom were the words "Other terms and conditions as per Carrier's Bill of Lading".

In due course a bill of lading was issued on a "receipt for shipment" form, this being dated and signed by the shipping agents. It also confirmed that the vessel was the *Ta Shun*, with the port of discharge as Limassol. Stamped on the bill of lading were the words "shipped on board 8th August 1976". The document contained an ill-assorted jumble of clauses which included a forwarding clause and a transhipment clause.

In fact, the goods were never shipped on board the *Ta Shun*, the vessel having apparently broken down before reaching Hong Kong, and on the date on which the goods were alleged to have been loaded they were still in the shipping agents' godown. The bill of lading had been fraudulently issued.

It later transpired that the goods had been included among a number of packages shipped on a vessel named *Ta Hung* on 16th August, 1976, and had been discharged at Keelung, in Taiwan, four days later. Here they remained until 16th November, when they were put on the *Intellect* for Cyprus. Regular enquiries by the buyers failed to elicit the truth. Some days later the vessel caught fire, and during the extinguishing operations the denim was damaged by water to such an extent that it was totally lost.

After the situation became known, the buyers were eventually obliged to assert a claim against the insurers, as any cause of action against the suppliers or the shipping agents had been rendered worthless by both firms going out of business. After all, the goods were lost by fire, and fire was an insured peril. But the insurers maintained that the insured adventure was the carriage of goods from Hong Kong to Limassol on *Ta Shun*, and since that voyage never took place the risk did not attach, so the goods were not on risk when actually lost.

The buyers argued, however, that the risk attached under the warehouse to warehouse clause in the policies, that the terms of the contract of affreightment concluded by the shipping agents included the bill of lading clauses referring to forwarding and transhipping, and since the goods were forwarded to Keelung, there to be transhipped to Limassol, the insured voyage to Limassol, performed in accordance with the liberties contained in the bill of lading, began when the goods left the suppliers' warehouse.

At first it was held that the buyers were entitled to succeed in their claim, but on appeal the Court of Appeal of Hong Kong reversed the decision. The dispute was then referred to the Judicial Committee of the Privy Council where the buyers sought to derive support from the case of *Simon, Israel and Co. v. Sedgwick*, but it was found that decision was against them when properly understood. It was not possible to look outside the bill of lading in order to ascertain the terms of the contract of affreightment, as the shipping note itself referred to the bill of lading terms, and, in any case, the only contract of affreightment to which the buyers were parties was that contained in or evidenced by the bill of lading itself. This contract was an "on board" bill of lading since the denim was stated, albeit untruthfully, to be on board the *Ta Shun* for carriage to Limassol. The clauses to which reference had been made could not operate inconsistently with an "on board" bill of lading, consequently there could not be any forwarding from, or transhipment from, a named ship going to a named destination when the goods in question had never been on board that ship bound for that destination.

Recalling the words of Lord Justice Bowen in the *Simon, Israel* case, Lord Roskill pointed out that here we had another situation where the goods had not been appropriated by a contract of carriage to the insured voyage, and added: "The opening paragraph of the warehouse to warehouse clause does not therefore help the appellants. Nor does the third paragraph of that clause for there was never the exercise of any liberty granted to the shipowners under the contracts of affreightment". Their Lordships were of the clear opinion that it was impossible to assert that the risk ever attached when the denim left the suppliers' warehouse in Hong Kong.

In the *Salem* case, which has frequently been mentioned in these pages, the cargo was also involved in a fraud, the vessel diverting to Durban after sailing from Mina al Ahmadi (Kuwait) instead of proceeding on her contractual voyage round the Cape to Italy. It will be recalled that after most of the cargo of oil had been discharged at Durban the vessel was scuttled off Senegal in an attempt to conceal the crime. In that case, of course, the cargo owners were completely innocent, but nevertheless the question did still arise as to whether the vessel had sailed for a different destination to the one specified in the policy, so that under Section 44 of the Marine Insurance Act it could be said that the risk had never attached. This question could have been difficult to answer because, although it was established that the shipowners and crew did not intend the vessel to reach Italy, it could be argued that the final and irrevocable decision was not taken until after she had sailed i.e. when it was established the circumstances were favourable, and the South African buyers had finally agreed to accept Kuwaiti oil rather than Saudi Arabian oil. Something might have happened between the loading at Mina and the discharge at Durban which would have prevented the conspirators from completing their plan fully, and might even have forced them to carry the oil, as they were contractually bound to do, to Europe.

The Court was saved from this dilemma by a curious turn of events. At the time the standard cargo clauses contained a *Change of Voyage Clause* reading: "Held covered at a premium to be arranged in case of change of voyage or of any omission or error in the description of the interest vessel or voyage", and the consignees, Shell International, might have tried to overcome the contention that the ship had sailed for Durban at the outset by relying on the "held covered" provision on the ground that in the policy there was an error in the description of the voyage and giving notice of it. But Shell never relied on the clause and never gave notice to the Underwriters, since, for tactical reasons, they did not want to concede that the vessel sailed for Durban, otherwise they could have been defeated by S.44. They preferred to contend that the vessel sailed for Europe and afterwards changed course for Durban.

Underwriters for their part were willing for the case to be determined on the basis that, by reason of the clause, the goods were on risk, even if it was for Durban and not Europe that the vessel had sailed. However, in the absence of any notice, they did not dispute the claim on that ground, neither did they seek to invoke S.44 of the Act, appreciating that a difficult question could arise, because the shippers and charterers intended the vessel to sail for Europe and the crew intended her to sail for Durban. These concessions enabled the case to be decided on the wording of the policy.

It is important to note that in the current *Change of Voyage Clause* there is no longer any reference to the assured being held covered in the event of any omission or error in the description of the interest vessel or voyage, as Underwriters decided they did not wish to be

151

obliged to maintain the cover in such circumstances. The new clause adheres closely to S.45(1) of the Marine Insurance Act.

The main issue in the *Salem* case was whether, under the restricted conditions applicable (F.P.A.), there was a "taking at sea", but the House of Lords decided that only on an "all risks" policy, or some other suitable form of cover, would the wrongful misappropriation of cargo by the shipowners be recoverable. Nevertheless, this decision was not reached until an interesting discourse had ensued in the Courts as to where the misappropriation had taken place. It was submitted on behalf of Underwriters that the proximate cause of the loss of the entire cargo, both of the bulk which was discharged at Durban and of the remainder which went down with the ship, was the fraudulent plan of the conspirators throughout, even before the loading of the cargo; or alternatively their procurement of the cargo at Mina, when the criminal plan and its subject matter, the cargo, came together.

Mr. Justice Mustill, in the High Court, was of the opinion that the moment must be identified by asking when the shipowners, through the agency of the master and crew, exercised control over the cargo for the benefit of themselves. This, he decided, occurred when the ship turned aside from the direct course to Europe and made for Durban. In the Court of Appeal, however, it was adjudged that there was no change of possession until the oil was pumped ashore at Durban. The House of Lords, having ruled that, in any event, the loss of the cargo discharged at Durban was not covered by the insured perils, nevertheless followed the view that, as the fraudulent conspiracy was not bound to succeed, the balance of the cargo was not lost until some overt act (in this case the sinking of the vessel) had sealed its fate.

A somewhat similar problem was considered in *Grundy (Teddington) Ltd. v. Fulton* [1983], which, oddly enough, ran concurrently with the *Salem* case. Here the plaintiffs were in the business of manufacturing beer casks, and for that purpose employed a number of lorry drivers to transport aluminium circles from their principle stores in Fulwell, to the main factory at Ashford. During a period of six months several loads to the value of £140,000 disappeared, having been stolen by the drivers who were able to take advantage of the haphazard system of checking on delivery at the factory, combined with the assistance of an employee at the factory who was able to cover up the shortages. The plaintiffs held a policy on their premises at Fulwell which was extended "to include goods in enclosed yards against the perils of burglary and theft" and the point at issue was whether the goods had been stolen from the yard, which was obviously "enclosed". Mr. Justice Stuart-Smith felt that, in the policy concerned, "theft" must be given the same meaning as in the criminal law, and turned to Section 1(1) of the Theft Act, 1968, which states:

> A person is guilty of theft if he dishonestly appropriates property belonging to another with the intention of permanently depriving the other of it.

As in the *Salem case*, it was necessary to decide when the loads were appropriated, and the learned judge concluded that, although it was fully intended to take the goods when the lorries were being loaded, there had to be some act, as opposed to a mere intention, which amounted to the assumption of rights as an owner, and no such act occurred until the drivers had deviated from their proper course. A layman would be more likely to say that the goods had been stolen in transit between the two premises, and the argument was advanced that, if the police had stopped the lorries before any deviation had taken place, they would have had great difficulty in bringing home any charges.

In the Court of Appeal it was agreed, on the particular facts, that the decisions to steal were not made until after leaving the yard, when the circumstances appeared favourable, accordingly there was no theft in the enclosed yard, and the claim failed. However, their Lordships were evidently of the opinion that, if it could be shown, on the balance of probabilities, the driver made his decision to steal a load in the yard, the misappropriation would have occurred when he started to put his lorry in motion.

This appears to leave it open for cargo Underwriters, in the right circumstances, to show that the theft of a consignment of goods in transit actually occurred before leaving the warehouse, if the lorry has been loaded inside, and the driver has already determined to make off with the goods.

Chapter 21

THE WATERBORNE AGREEMENT

Commencing an appraisal of the War Clauses, the author details in this article the development of the period of cover under the Transit Clause.

A study of the Institute War Clauses (Cargo) will reveal that many of the provisions are identical to those in the standard cargo clauses covering the marine risks under the designation (A), (B) and (C), while others, such as the *Both to Blame Collision Clause* and the *Strikes Exclusion Clause*, have been omitted because they have no bearing on loss or damage proximately caused by the perils detailed in the War Clauses. *The General Average Clause* is slightly modified so as to make it clear that general average and salvage charges are only recoverable if they are incurred in avoiding a loss from the particular perils covered by the War Clauses.

One of the most important differences will be found in the *Transit Clause* where the duration of the risk is significantly restricted. Originally, war risks cover could be obtained from warehouse to warehouse on the same basis as other perils, but with the advent of the Spanish Civil War in 1936, insurers became aware that the destructive powers of modern weapons, particularly bombs dropped from aircraft, could result in catastrophic losses to property on land, and it would not be possible to undertake the potential liabilities. Consequently an agreement was reached by insurers throughout the world to exclude cover for war risks on land.

Marine insurers for their part were also worried about the accumulation of cargoes at ports of loading, transhipment or discharge, which might be prone to congestion, but were more relaxed about goods whilst on voyage. As a result they negotiated the famous War Risk Waterborne Agreement of 1937 which reduced the period of war cover on cargoes to the time they were on board an oversea vessel.

Strangely enough, however, during the Second World War the Waterborne Agreement was modified to help the assured by including overland transit and delay at transhipping ports, thus providing continuity of cover, and overcoming the problem of congestion at such ports. In 1945 the cover was considerably extended by the inclusion of craft risk at the ports of shipment, transhipment, and discharge. Thus there was a continuous war risk from the time of being loaded into the craft or vessel, during transhipment (even if not customary) delay and overland risk during the voyage, until discharged from the vessel or craft at destination. No time limits were imposed at the transhipping port or at destination prior to discharge.

After the war concern was expressed by the International Union of Marine Insurance about the greater possibilities of catastrophic war losses in ports or on land, which could be brought about by the more powerful weaponry which had been produced. Accordingly, in 1949, time limits at ports of transhipment and discharge were introduced, while the risk in craft was limited to mines and derelict torpedoes. Unfortunately, the wording at that time still gave the impression that the goods could be fully covered during land transit from an intermediate port to another port during transhipment. It became apparent to Underwriters in 1970 that they were vulnerable to war losses on shipments being made to ports in the Mediterranean via Eilat (in the Gulf of Aqaba) and Ashdod (on the Mediterranean coast), mainly from East African and Australian ports. It was not intended that the cover should operate during overland transit through an area of warlike operations and in the following year the clauses were revised to show that the insurance continued in force only while the goods remained at the location where the goods were discharged. At that time it was also decided to exclude altogether any loss, damage, or expense arising from the hostile use of weapons of war employing atomic or nuclear fission, fusion or the like, although it was intimated that Underwriters were permitted to accept such risks by means of separate policies.

The period of cover is much the same today, having undergone little change except by way of clarification, but the *Transit Clause* in its entirety (Clause 5) looks rather complex, and is best understood by reference to its several features.

Basically the cover against the insured perils does not attach until any part of the cargo becomes waterborne on an oversea vessel (i.e. one carrying the cargo from one port to another which involves a sea passage), and ceases as any part is discharged from that vessel at destination. However, there is a time limit of 15 days in which to discharge the cargo, and if any remains on board on the expiry of that period, counting from midnight on the day of arrival, cover on that part will terminate then. Whether a ship has "arrived" or not has been considered in our Courts in cases involving disputes under charter-parties, and this has no doubt prompted Underwriters to insert a definition in the *Transit Clause*. Thus, a vessel is deemed to have "arrived" if the vessel is anchored, moored, or otherwise secured at a berth or other place within the Harbour Authority area, and if such a berth is not available the arrival is deemed to have occurred when the vessel first anchors, moors, or otherwise secures either at or off the intended port or place of discharge. This time limit serves to protect the insurers against delay and congestion at the point of discharge, and any extension of the limit is entirely at their discretion, as there is no provision under which the assured is "held covered".

The insurance against the risks of mines and derelict torpedoes is maintained whilst the goods are in craft during transit to or from the oversea vessel, but in no case will this period extend beyond 60 days after discharge from such vessel, unless the special agreement of Underwriters is obtained (Clause 5.4).

Unlike the marine clauses any deviation or variation of the adventure arising from the exercise of a liberty granted to shipowners or charterers under the contract of affreightment is not automatically held covered, and prompt notice must be given to the Underwriters if the insurance is to remain in force. This can attract an additional premium (see Clause 5.5)

There are a number of other situations which can also attract an additional premium, the first being when the vessel arrives but does not succeed in discharging the goods at the final port of discharge. If prompt notice is given to Underwriters they will be prepared to undertake the reattachment of the risk from the time the vessel sails from the original port of destination with the object of returning with the goods later, or taking them to a substituted port of destination. Thereafter the same provisions relating to discharge, craft risk and time limits apply (Clauses 5.1.3 and 5.1.4).

It can also happen that the voyage is terminated at a port other than that agreed, either because of a liberty contained in the contract of affreightment, the insolvency of the carriers, or when the voyage is necessarily abandoned at a port or refuge. In such circumstances it is indicated in Clause 5.3 that the insurance terminates at that place as if it were the final port of discharge. Nevertheless, if the goods are subsequently reshipped to the original or any other destination, here again Underwriters will be prepared (subject to an additional premium) to cover the goods to the final port, but it is emphasised that in such a case notice must be given to them before the *commencement of the further transit*. In the event that the goods have not been discharged from the oversea vessel the insurance will reattach when she sails again, but once the goods have been landed ashore it appears to be the intention to treat the reshipment as a new transit. This means that, although the clause only refers to the full war risk reattaching when any part of the goods is loaded on the on-carrying vessel for the voyage, under Clause 5.4 the risks of mines and derelict torpedoes will apply while the goods are being carried to the vessel in craft. However, some difficulty can be envisaged if the goods have been discharged into craft, and remain there pending reshipment. While Clause 5.4 refers to a 60 day limit of cover after discharge from the oversea vessel, it must be borne in mind that this is particularly related to a period *whilst in transit*, and not to storage. This is, therefore, a somewhat "grey area" and it would be advisable to seek the agreement of Underwriters to maintain the risks of mines and derelict torpedoes in force if desired.

The situation is a little different if the goods are discharged at an intermediate port, or a port of refuge, for the purpose of transhipment. Under Clause 5.2 full war risks cover continues for 15 days after the arrival of the oversea vessel, thus it is possible for such cover to apply while the goods are on land, and an additional premium may be required. However, as mentioned earlier, this concession is only available for goods remaining in the area where they have been discharged, and cover will be suspended on any part removed elsewhere, reattaching only if returned within the 15 day period.

If the goods are not reshipped until after the 15 day period has expired, full war risks cover does not come into operation again until they are loaded on to the on-carrying oversea vessel, but naturally the risks of mines and derelict torpedoes will still apply under Clause 5.4 if craft are employed. Once cover has recommenced the insurance will continue, subject to the terms of the *Transit Clause*, in the usual way.

The Clause takes care to cover the contingency of the goods being forwarded to destination by air instead by being on-carried by an oversea vessel. In such a case the current Institute War Clauses (Air Cargo) (excluding sendings by Post) are deemed to form part of the insurance so far as applicable to the air carriage. Under these clauses the risk attaches as any part of the goods is loaded on the aircraft and ceases as any part is discharged at destination, provided such discharge takes place within 15 days of the arrival of the aircraft.

Like the marine clauses, if the assured changes the destination after the attachment of the insurance, this can be held covered at a premium and on conditions to be arranged, subject to prompt notice being given to the Underwriters (Clause 6).

A *Clause Paramount* (Clause 7) states that if anything in the contract is inconsistent with the *Transit Clause* and the *Nuclear Exclusion Clause* (Clause 3.8) it shall, to the extent of such inconsistency, be null and void. This avoids any ambiguity with the terms of the marine clauses attached to the same policy, and ensures that the Waterborne Agreement is given strict priority.

In fact, since the outbreak of hostilities between Iraq and Iran, the agreement has come under pressure from some insurers, who feel that there is a case for change, in order to accommodate cargo owners in land locked countries, also shipowners who have a considerable investment in containers which are ashore. In particular, it has been stressed that because of Iraq's geographical location, and restricted access to the sea via the Persian Gulf, overland routes through Turkey and Syria have considerably increased the volume of cargo moving inland. It has been argued that a similar approach could be adopted to that of the non-marine market in insuring earthquake risks, provided the problem of accumulation can be controlled and contained within the capacity of the international market.

The first positive move came in 1982 when the Through Transport Club decided to protect its members from war risk losses on land in respect of containers and trailers, but the major trouble spots were excluded. Backed by a certain amount of reinsurance, however, the Club was able to include the Lebanon in the scope of the cover, and although some containers were confiscated by the Lebanese army, the claims were easily absorbed by the premium income. Continued encouraging results enabled the Club to increase the liability for each member to $1 million and to consider introducing cover in Iraq and Iran away from the immediate war zones.

Meanwhile, in April 1984, the Arab War Risk Insurance Syndicate launched a scheme to write war and strikes risks on land for Arab imports and exports carried on lorries, the clauses being modelled on similar lines to the Institute Clauses. The essential difference lies in the duration of the cover which, although basically following the English *Warehouse to Warehouse Clause*, defines "delivery" as "the time of signing of the delivery note (or similar document) or on the expiry of 24 hours after arrival at the point of destination named herein or at such time as the subject matter insured and as to any part as that part is loaded on/in any aircraft and/or any waterborne vessel or craft and/or any railway rolling stock, whichever is the earlier". Transit is deemed to include any waterborne crossing not exceeding 15 kilometres of any waterways, channels or straits en route provided such a crossing is not insured under any other policy.

Speaking at the International War Risks Insurance Conference in Baghdad in March 1986, Mr. Mowaffac Ridha, Chairman and General Manager of the National Insurance Co. of Iraq, pointed out that some waterborne risks currently insured carry liabilities in excess of $100 million and the technical reasons which had traditionally made cargo transported inland uninsurable against war risks had become of historical interest only. Referring to the AWRIS scheme he stated that the majority of cargo consignments were low in value, some 93% being below $200,000. The largest value which the syndicate had encountered on one truck amounted to $3.5 million, and, from their experience, it did not appear that the accumulation of liability at any one point would exceed $10 million. On this basis he did not consider there was any accumulation problem and said: "The fears which emanated in the traditional Waterborne Agreement do not seem to be apparent as far as this cover is concerned."

The theme is one which has been recurring at the conferences of the International Union of Marine Insurance in recent years, indicating that there is considerable interest in reviewing the Waterborne Agreement if war insurance on land can be strictly controlled. It remains to be seen whether insurers can come up with something in response to the growing demand.

Chapter 22

THE F. C. AND S. CLAUSE

Continuing with his series on the War Clauses, the author explains the difficulties brought about by the use of the "free of capture and seizure" warranty.

When the S.G. policy came into being in 1779 the method of insuring against war risks was comparatively simple, as such risks were included with the other perils in the body of the form, and were thus covered with the marine perils in one comprehensive document. These war risks were to be found under the words "men-of-war, enemies, letters of mart and countermart, surprisals, takings at sea, arrests, restraints, and detainments of all kings, princes, and people, of what nation, condition, or quality soever ..."

Letters of mart and countermart were sometimes described as "letters of marque and counter-marque", the expression probably being derived from a Spanish or French word, signifying the frontiers of a State. Letters of mart licensed the recipients to pass beyond the frontiers of another State, and were granted by the Crown to enable its subjects to act as privateers in retaliation against the subjects of other States who had seized their property. Letters of countermart were contrary letters granted in favour of those threatened by such reprisals, authorising them to resist the privateers furnished with letters of mart. This kind of private warfare, which prevailed between our Sovereign and the King of Spain, was abolished by the Treaty of Paris in 1856, and to that extent the perils became redundant.

When the effects of war became more far-reaching, a resolution was passed by the Members of Lloyd's to exclude war risks from the cover granted by the S.G. policy, and, in 1899, it was agreed to insert a warranty in all policies unless the contrary was written or printed in the slip or agreement for insurance. This form of warranty was originally attached as a special clause, but because of its established use it was eventually printed (in italics) in the policy form itself, being

160

known as the *Free of Capture and Seizure Clause* or, more briefly, as the *F.C. and S. Clause,* viz:

Warranted free of capture, seizure and detention, and the consequences thereof, or any attempt thereat, piracy excepted, and also from all consequences of hostilities or warlike operations, whether before or after declaration of war.

It was in this form that the clause appeared in the first Institute Cargo Clauses published in 1912.

It can be seen straight away that the excepted perils did not correspond with those in the original body of the policy, giving rise to much speculation as to whether the exclusions were wider than the cover provided in the first place. This subject was discussed in a case which concerned a consignment of gold bullion taken over by the Transvaal Government at the outbreak of the Boer War, when it was concluded that the purpose of the clause was to override all the perils in the policy where these were inconsistent. If it could be said that the risk was one covered by the body of the policy, it was necessarily excluded by the exception of "seizure". (*Robinson Gold Mining Co. v. Alliance Marine and General Insurance Co.Ltd.,* 1901).

Contemporary writers, however, did not anticipate any real difficulties about this strange situation. Templeman, in his early editions of *Marine Insurance*, was satisfied that "capture" was merely another way of describing "surprisals" and "takings at sea", while Gow, in his book similarly titled, considered that "capture" generally replaced "surprisals" (a term rarely heard in modern commerce) and "seizure" was modern commercial language for "takings at sea". The missing perils "arrests" and "restraints" were included in the clause in 1916 so that the opening words then read: "Warranted free of capture, seizure, arrest, restraint, or detainment ..."

In 1969, in the case of the *Mandarin Star,* the Court of Appeal (with Lord Denning presiding as Master of the Rolls) gave a new an unexpected meaning to the peril "takings at sea", when it was held that the words were wide enough to embrace a dishonest taking by the shipowner himself. This decision arose from a friendly action over a small sum disputed by Japanese insurers who had utilised the S.G. policy form, and, although the London market was not immediately involved, it was a case which came back to haunt them when the cargo on the *Salem* was misappropriated by the shipowners in 1979. Lord Denning was again in the chair in the Court of Appeal, but on this occasion he was persuaded that his earlier decision was wrong, and was prepared to risk the disfavour of the House of Lords by saying that the Appeal Court was not bound by its previous judgment. In the event, the House of Lords came to the conclusion that "takings at sea" meant capture or seizure by strangers to the adventure.

So it came about in the *Salem* case that the Courts finally managed to recognise that although the words in the exceptions clause did not mirror the war perils in the S.G. policy they covered the same ground in substance (per Kerr, L.J. in the Court of Appeal, 1982). But by then Underwriters had decided to abandon the S.G. policy and to express the cover for war risks in a more straightforward manner.

The desire to do this was because of the cumbersome method which had developed in providing positive cover for war risks when this was required. Deletion of the *F.C. and S. Clause* simply meant that the war risks specified in the body of the policy again formed part of the insurance. Thus it became customary to leave the *F.C. and S. Clause* in the conditions and to apply separate clauses for the attachment of war risks which expressed the intention to cover the risks excluded from the standard form of English marine policy by the *F.C. and S. Clause,* thereby making it necessary to repeat the wording of the clause all over again.

This system, although somewhat clumsy, worked reasonably well except for the problems caused by the use of the words "... all consequences of hostilities or warlike operations ..." In time of war vessels will naturally find that land-marks are not suitably lighted, and they themselves are obliged to sail without lights on occasions. They will also have to sail in convoy and zig-zag to confuse submarines, all adding to the hazards of navigation. During the first world war, therefore, much skill of argument was required in many cases to decide whether the circumstances giving rise to a casualty meant that the claim should be collected on the marine policy or against the war risks Underwriters, depending at what point the enhanced marine perils caused by wartime conditions could be regarded as the consequences of hostilities or warlike operations.

At first marine Underwriters were inclined to the opinion that where steps had been taken to prevent a "war" loss, such as by obscuring the lights, it was logical that any direct loss following on such steps should be considered as arising out of a "war" peril, and they were not keen to bear the increased risk in order to benefit the War Risks Underwriters.

In the case of the *Petersham* (*Britain S.S. Co. v. Rex,* 1919), however, the Court decided that although the risks of marine perils were increased on vessels engaged on peaceful missions in time of war, this fact did not convert them into war perils. Here the vessel was carrying a cargo of iron ore from Bilbao to Glasgow when she came into collision with the *Serra,* which was on her way from Swansea to Bilbao with a cargo of patent fuel. The *Petersham* was sunk, and the loss was admittedly due to the fact that neither vessel was exhibiting lights, no negligence being involved. In the circumstances of this case all the Courts up to the House of Lords held that the collision was neither the consequence of hostilities nor a warlike operation, the *Petersham* apparently being engaged on a non-warlike errand.

In 1918, whilst carrying a cargo of cotton from Egypt, the *Matiana* was in convoy with three other merchant ships under the command of the naval officer in charge of the escort vessels. The convoy had to traverse an area of the Mediterranean known to be infested with enemy submarines, and, in accordance with orders, the *Matiana* was steering a zig-zag course so as to avoid a possible attack at night. Whilst doing so she stranded on an unlighted reef, and some hours later was torpedoed forward while ashore. It was admitted that the ship was a total loss as a result of going on the reef, but in the Court of the first instance it was held that the loss was due to a war risk. In the Court of Appeal, however, that decision was reversed, and the House of Lords confirmed that the loss was not the proximate consequence of a warlike operation. (*British India v. Green,* 1919).

This judgment was followed in the case of *Inkonka (Harrison v. Shipping Controller,* 1920) which concerned a vessel laden with hospital stores for the British Government, and which also had on board a few British troops and officers whilst sailing from Salonica to Taranto. She arrived at Taranto at night time and in the ordinary way would not have attempted to enter the port, but was ordered by the escorting destroyer to follow a pilot vessel. During this operation the master lost sight of the pilot vessel's lights, and almost immediately the vessel ran ashore and was damaged. McCardie, J. decided that the presence of a few soldiers on board did not convert an otherwise peaceful mission into a warlike operation.

Where vessels were involved in the Gallipoli operation, the results were quite different. In *British and Foreign S.S. Co. v. The King* [1918] the *St. Oswald* was in collision with a French warship, but no blame was attached to either vessel, as they were both sailing without lights. The *St. Oswald* was engaged in removing troops from Gallipoli at the time, and on this occasion the Court held the loss to be a "war" loss, being the consequence of a warlike operation.

The *Geelong* came into collision with the *Bonvilston* in January 1916, when the latter was proceeding from Mudros to Alexandria, and was carrying ambulance wagons and other Government stores. Neither vessel was exhibiting lights, and there was no blame on either side. The Court noted that the evacuation of Gallipoli was proceeding at the time, and concluded that the carrying of ambulance wagons from one war base to another in time of war was a warlike operation. Consequently the *Geelong* was lost by a war risk (*Commonwealth Shipping Representative v. P. & O. Branch Service,* 1923).

The effect of the collision cases, therefore, was to treat a merchant ship on a wartime mission as if she were a warship, and if she came into collision with another ship on a peaceful voyage, the resultant loss would be classed as a war loss, except when the collision was caused solely by the peaceful ship. Thus, in the case of the *Clan Matheson (Clan Line Steamers, Ltd. v. Board of Trade,* 1929) the vessel was carrying a commercial cargo when there was a failure in her steering gear. As a result she was in collision with a vessel carrying munitions and sank. This loss was held to be due solely to the condition of the steering gear and not the consequence of a warlike operation.

Accordingly, after the first world war there was much conjecture as to whether the principles which had been applied to "merchant-warships" in collision cases would be extended to other perils, such as stranding, in the event of another conflagration. Despite this, no alteration of the *F.C. & S. Clause* was made until 1937, when the Spanish Civil War was in progress. It then read:

> Warranted free of capture, seizure, arrest, restraint or detainment, and the consequences thereof or of any attempt thereat; also from the consequences of hostilities or warlike operations, whether there be a declaration of war or not, civil war, revolution, rebellion, insurrection or civil strife arising therefrom, or piracy.

Comparison with the previous clause will show that at this point it was decided to exclude the risks of civil war and other forms of civil strife from the cover afforded by the marine policy. That was not to say that these risks were entirely covered in the first place, but Underwriters were alive to the possibility that some perils, e.g. fire, would be recoverable if brought about by civil war etc. in the absence of a suitable exclusion. The risk of "piracy" was also transferred from the marine to the war policy, presumably to avoid having to make any distinction between marauders who plundered at sea for personal gain, and those who acted from political motives.

At the outbreak of the second world war, however, Underwriters, being mindful of the exceptional amount of litigation which had arisen out of the wording in the 1914-1918 conflict, made some effort to try and amend the *F.C. & S. Clause,* but were unable to agree on a suitable format. It was not until the *Coxwold* case in 1942 that they were prodded into action.

It may be recalled in this case (*Yorkshire Dale Steamship Co.Ltd. v. Minister of War Transport,* 1942) that the vessel was carrying a cargo of petrol in tins from Greenock to Narvik in Norway, for the use of the British forces, and was thus admittedly taking part in a warlike operation. Although she was in convoy, visibility was poor, and the second officer was unable to take a bearing as the Neist Light was not being shown at full brilliancy. In addition it was difficult to follow the reflection in the water of the dimmed and shaded stern light of the vessel ahead. Despite this, and the fact that at one point a deviation was made for half an hour to avoid what was thought to be an enemy submarine, the *Coxwold* managed to follow the safe course set for the convoy accurately. Unfortunately, this was of no avail, as an unexpected and unexplained tidal set carried her some miles eastward, causing her to ground on the Isle of Skye. The House of Lords, however, looked at the whole story and were not prepared to find that the tidal set was the proximate cause of the stranding. Rather it was the consequence of the warlike operation in which she was engaged, this resulting in her being at the particular place and in the conditions prevailing at the time. The remarks of Lord Atkin were particularly significant: "If the warlike operation includes the direction of the war vessel through the water from one war starting point to another war destination, it seems to remain true that almost every casualty to a ship during such an operation will be the consequence of a war operation. Not all, for there may be circumstances of accident on board or the result of wind and wave that may not come within the definition ..."

Although the case removed any doubts as to whether strandings of merchant warships were to be considered any differently from collisions, where no negligence was involved, the judgment left Underwriters with the uneasy feeling that their normal function in supplying insurance against the recognised marine perils would be severely handicapped by the fact that vessels were committed to warlike operations. Somewhat remarkably, then, they now became anxious to provide cover for the enhanced risks brought about by wartime conditions, and rapidly altered the *F.C. & S. Clause* in order to restrict the meaning of the term "consequences of hostilities and warlike operations" and so maintain a realistic balance between marine and war risks.

In its new form in 1943, therefore, the *F.C. & S. Clause* did not exclude collision, contact with objects (other than mines or torpedoes), stranding, heavy weather, or fire unless caused directly by a hostile act by or against a belligerent power; the fact that the vessel might be on a warlike operation could be disregarded, and in the case of collision, this also applied to the colliding vessel.

The full version read as follows:

> Warranted free of capture, seizure, arrest, restraint or detainment, and the consequences thereof or of any attempt thereat; also from the consequences of hostilities or warlike operations, whether there be a declaration of war or not; but this warranty shall not exclude collision, contact with any fixed or floating object (other than a mine or torpedo), stranding, heavy weather or fire unless caused directly (and independently of the nature of the voyage or service which the vessel concerned or, in the case of a collision, any other vessel involved therein, is performing) by a hostile act by or against a belligerent power; and for the purpose of this warranty "power" includes any authority maintaining naval, military or air forces in association with a power.
>
> Further warranted free from the consequences of civil war, revolution, rebellion, insurrection, or civil strife arising therefrom, or piracy.

Nevertheless, although the revised wording gave Underwriters more opportunity to concentrate on the basic principles of proximate cause, the system of insuring war risks still came in for criticism, and caused Mr.Justice Mocatta, in the case of the *Anita* [1971], to say: "It cannot be beyond the wit of Underwriters and those who advise them in this age of law reform to devise more straightforward and easily comprehended terms of cover."

The decision to abandon the S.G. policy in 1982 enabled Underwriters to do precisely that, and in the succeeding articles we can look at an entirely new system to see how war risks cover is provided for cargo owners today.

Chapter 23

THE WAR PERILS (1)

In a series of four articles, the author examines the cover provided by the new war perils. Here he discusses the first group, with special emphasis on the meaning of "war".

In today's standard cargo clauses the *F. C. & S. Clause* has been superseded by the *War Exclusion Clause*, which, in the "A" Clauses reads:

6   In no case shall this insurance cover loss damage or expense caused by

6.1   war civil war revolution rebellion insurrection, or civil strife arising therefrom, or any hostile act by or against a belligerent power

6.2   capture seizure arrest restraint or detainment (piracy excepted), and the consequences thereof or any attempt thereat

6.3   derelict mines torpedoes bombs or other derelict weapons of war.

In the first group of perils it is to be observed that "war" is referred to for the first time, and with the retention of the words "any hostile act by or against a belligerent power", Underwriters have been able to dispense with the convoluted expression "the consequences of hostilities or warlike operations" which caused so much trouble in the two world wars.

It was established in *Pesquerias y Secaderos de Bacalao de Espana, S.A. v. Beer* [1949], a case centred round the Spanish Civil War, that the word "war" in a policy of insurance will be sufficient to embrace "civil war" unless the context makes it clear that a different meaning should be given to the word. Since "civil war" is specifically mentioned in the exclusion clause, it can be taken that the peril of "war" relates to a combat carried on by force of arms between nations.

In the case of *Pan American World Airways Inc. v. The Aetna Casualty and Surety Co.* [1975], Circuit Judge Hays, in the United States Court of Appeals, observed that English and American Courts have dealt with the insurance meaning of "war" in accordance with the international law definition, rather than by provisions in any national code. Thus it refers to and includes only hostilities carried on by entities that constitute governments, or at least have significant attributes of sovereignty.

In days gone by there was a certain code of conduct in commencing belligerent acts against the territory or property of other countries, as the absence of a formal declaration of war would make such acts barbarous. It was recognised that the difficulties of communication made some warning of impending hostilities desirable so as to protect the innocent. Even at sea, where it was quite an allowable stratagem to sail and chase under false colours, it was expected that a ship would fly her national flag immediately before engaging with the enemy. *Halleck's International Law* [1908] records the story of the French frigate, the *Sybille*, which in 1783 enticed the British man-of-war, the *Hussar*, by flying the British flag and pretending to be a distressed prize. When the *Hussar* approached to help, the *Sybille* immediately attacked her without hoisting the French flag, so that she was able to overpower and capture the British vessel. The commander of the *Hussar* publicly broke the sword of the captain of the *Sybille* whom he justly accused of perfidy, this form of treachery being strictly prohibited. It was considered that such acts could result in the loss of lives of persons, who, had they been made aware of the real character of the vessel, might not have resisted.

Nevertheless, in these enlightened times, wars do not break out without some previous build up of tension or formal discussion on grievances, and, with international awareness that hostilities might commence, no great importance is attached to the lack of any formal declaration of war.

However, unless a formal declaration of war is made, it can be difficult to establish whether a state of war exists between two countries, in particular whether "trading with the enemy" is involved, and whether the validity of contracts is affected. In some cases the matter can be resolved by obtaining a certificate from the Secretary of State to show when a state of war came into existence, but much will depend upon the circumstances.

In the case of *Kawasaki Kisen Kabushiki Kaisya v. Bantham Steamship Company* [1939], for instance, the owners and charterers of a vessel had the option of cancelling the charter-party if war broke out involving Japan, and following the undertaking of military operations by both China and Japan, the owners gave notice to the charterers on September 18, 1937, informing them of their intention to withdraw their steamship. In the dispute over breach of contract which followed the Foreign Office stated that the situation in China on that date was indeterminate and anomalous, and that His Majesty's Government were not prepared to say that in their view a state of war existed. The matter proceeded to the Court of Appeal where it was confirmed that, in construing the cancellation clause in the charter-party, it could be considered that war had broken out involving Japan, and the owners were entitled to cancel.

The difficulty of establishing whether a state of war exists between two foreign countries was also illustrated by the case of *Dalmia Dairy Industries Ltd. v. National Bank of Pakistan* [1978]. While this was also not an insurance case, it is interesting to see how the Courts approached the subject of the validity of an Arbitration Clause.

The plaintiffs were a firm carrying on business in India who agreed to sell two cement factories in West Pakistan to a Pakistani resident of Karachi. Payment was to be made by deliveries of cement from the factories over a period of three years at two places on the India/Pakistan border. The transaction had the approval of both the Governments of India and Pakistan. Payment was guaranteed by the defendants on 30th September, 1964, with a provision that any dispute would be settled by a sole arbitrator, and on the same day ownership of the factories passed to the buyer.

Dalmia gave the first of their delivery instructions on 19th December, 1964, but no cement was ever received. Accordingly, in January, 1966, Dalmia presented a demand to the bank for payment of the purchaser's obligation.

Unfortunately the matter became somewhat complicated by the fact that relations between India and Pakistan had become strained over Kashmir. In August, 1965, Pakistani guerillas infiltrated the territory, and on the 1st September Pakistani troops crossed the ceasefire lines in Kashmir, causing armed hostilities to break out a few days later. Although a ceasefire agreement was reached on 23rd September, the situation remained confused, and the bank denied liability on the grounds that the contract became abrogated by illegality because Dalmia and the bank remained "enemies" as a result of the conflict. Nevertheless, two arbitrations were carried out in Geneva with the knowledge and consent of both governments, although the bank made it clear that they were conducted without prejudice to its contention that the arbitrator had no jurisdiction. On both occasions an award was made in favour of Dalmia. In the meantime another armed conflict occurred between the two countries in December, 1971, and the action was finally brought to this country as the bank had a branch and assets here.

This posed something of a dilemma, as the bank's case depended on establishing the existence of "war" in some sense of the word, or, at least, "external aggression", whatever that meant in the law of the two countries. As Mr. Justice Kerr observed in the High Court: "... it would be quite wrong for an English judge to decide whether a state of war exists or existed ... between two friendly foreign states [that is, friendly to this country] without seeking to obtain the views of Her Majesty's Government and, in the unusual circumstances of the present case, also of the governments of the states concerned, if their views can be ascertained through Her Majesty's Government". In order to avoid a good deal of time being spent on further enquiries, therefore, both parties were agreeable to the judge deciding the case on the most favourable assumptions towards the bank on its contentions, i.e. that at the material times a state of war existed between the countries according to (a) Indian Law, (b) Pakistan Law, (c) International Law, or (d) English Law. This meant that if Dalmia were to succeed on other grounds, it would, subject to any appeal, be the end of the matter. If, on the other hand, the bank won on this hypothetical basis, it would not be the final victory for the bank, for Dalmia could then go back for hearing of evidence and argument on the issue of "war".

As it happened it was not necessary to institute further enquiries. The arbitration agreement made it clear that Indian law should be applied, and since the Indian Government had given permission for the transaction to be carried out before the commencement of hostilities, there was no illegal act in that respect. In addition, by consenting to the arbitration, the Indian Government had endorsed their maintenance of the guarantee — abrogation would merely confer benefits on persons in Pakistan who might be regarded as "enemies" by Indian law. On the other hand it also had to be borne in mind that the government of Pakistan, as the sovereign of the bank, had in effect permitted the bank to have commercial intercourse with an "enemy" by allowing it to take part in the arbitrations. The Court found that there was no difference in English common law where trading with the enemy is not unlawful if it is permitted by licence from the Crown, and neither the guarantee nor the arbitration agreement were abrogated. This decision was upheld in the Court of Appeal and the arbitrator's award confirmed. Even if there was war between India and Pakistan, the judges were far from satisfied that an arbitration clause between "enemies" would be abrogated on the outbreak of war if the main contract in which it was contained was not abrogated, and if no dispute requiring arbitration had then arisen.

In the above case much reliance was placed on the classic and oft-cited statement of Mr. Justice Willes in *Esposito v. Bowden* [1857] when he said: "The force of a declaration of war is equal to that of an Act of Parliament prohibiting intercourse with the enemy except by the Queen's licence. As an act of State, done by virtue of the Prerogative exclusively belonging to the Crown such a declaration carries with it all the force of law."

The main benefit of a declaration of war, therefore, is that it brings more certainty to the relations between the contestants. In this country it is illegal for contracts of insurance to be issued on the property of an alien enemy, the position being aptly stated by Lord Alvanley in the case of *Furtado v. Rogers* [1802] when he said: "The question is whether it be competent to an English underwriter to indemnify persons who are engaged in war with his own sovereign, from the consequences of that war ; and we are all of opinion that, on the principles of English law, it is not competent to any subject to enter into a contract to do anything which may be detrimental to the interests of his own country; and that such contract is as much prohibited as if it had been expressly forbidden by Act of Parliament."

As can be surmised the position is largely governed by the principle of public policy, and even if the contract were valid at the inception of the risk, any loss after the outbreak of war would not be recoverable (*Gamba v. Le Mesurier*, 1803).

In *Janson v. Driefontein Consolidated Mines* [1901], however, Underwriters sought to extend the principle. Before the outbreak of the Boer War was officially recognised in 1899, there was a period of tension between the South African Republic and the British Government, during which a consignment of gold in transit to the

United Kingdom was seized by order of the Republican Government. The gold was the property of a company incorporated in the Republic, and the insurers in this country sought to avoid the policy, which covered the loss, on the grounds that the contract was illegal because the property has been seized by a prospective alien Government, and it was not possible to indemnify one of its own subjects. The House of Lords, nevertheless, were of the opinion that expected wars did not render a contract illegal between parties of two nations between whom war was anticipated, and upheld the majority opinion of the Court of Appeal that, at the time of the seizure, the two countries were still at peace, and the assured could recover the loss. The case was somewhat unusual in that the trial took place during the war when the Courts are normally closed to enemy aliens, any right of action being suspended until peace is restored. In this instance the parties had agreed that no dilatory plea should be set up, and much discussion took place as to whether the Courts should give effect to such an agreement.

It is commonly accepted that the object of waging maritime war on an enemy is to create havoc with his trade, so as to weaken his determination to carry on with the struggle. Once war has been declared it is recognised that a belligerent nation has the right to interfere with the trading rights of neutral countries where this involves assistance to the opposing side which will sustain his effort and so prolong the war. While a neutral merchant can legitimately trade with a belligerent, this does mean that contraband goods can also lawfully be captured and condemned, and when such goods are insured, it is important that the Underwriter should be fully informed of the nature of the shipment, also the circumstances connected with the voyage, otherwise liability can be avoided on the grounds of concealment of material facts. Attention can also be drawn to Section 41 of the Marine Insurance Act, which states:

> There is an implied warranty that the adventure insured is a lawful one, and that, so far as the assured can control the matter, the adventure shall be carried out in a lawful manner.

Of course, it is always open to the Underwriter to stipulate that the goods are "warranted neutral", and, in that case, Section 36(1) will apply:

Where insurable property, whether ship or goods, is expressly warranted neutral, there is an implied condition that the property shall have a neutral character at the commencement of the risk, and that, so far as the assured can control the matter, its neutral character shall be preserved during the risk.

It is to be observed that the *War Exclusion Clause* does not merely relate to "war", but also to "any hostile act by or against a belligerent power". In the old *F.C. & S. Clause* the word "hostilities" connoted the idea of belligerent nations at war with one another, and so included operations of an offensive, defensive, or protective nature involving such nations (per Lord Atkinson in the *Petersham* and *Matiana cases*).

In this connection it is perhaps useful to refer to the case of the *Tennyson (Atlantic Mutual Insurance Co. v. King,* 1919), in which a loss was caused by a bomb planted in the hold of the ship at Bahia during the First World War, by a German national domiciled in Brazil. The Court was of the opinion that it was an act carried out in furtherance of his country's objectives in the sense that he was behaving as an agent for his own Government; thus, despite the lack of proof of any official appointment, the act could fall within the meaning of "hostilities" as used at the time.

It is submitted, however, that in the context of the current wording, only one belligerent power need be involved, and therefore acts of a hostile nature committed by individuals or groups of persons exercising their own initiative in opposition to the aims of a nation at war would equally be excluded by the clause.

The United States Courts had occasion to consider the words in the case of *International Dairy Engineering Co. v. American Home Assurance Co.* [1973] when the plaintiff's stock of box material, which was stored in a warehouse at Thu Duc Village, South Vietnam, was destroyed by a fire set when an aerial parachute flare deployed by American forces fell on the warehouse. The Court viewed the Vietcong to be a "belligerent", and held that the loss was not covered by a fire policy excluding losses caused "by a hostile act by or against a belligerent power." The loss was at the site of hostilities, it was caused by a warlike agency, and the lost property belonged to a belligerent national.

Continuing with Clause 6.1, this also excludes any loss, damage or expense caused by certain types of civil disorder in an ascending scale of unrest ranging from "insurrection" to "civil war".

"Insurrection" was defined in the *Pan Am* case as a "violent uprising by a group or movement acting for the specific purpose of overthrowing the constituted government and seizing its powers." Reference was made to an incident in 1950 in which buildings were burned in the town of Jayuya as part of an uprising staged by a small band of extremists calling themselves the Nationalist Party of Puerto Rico, and it was observed that the revolutionary purpose need not be objectively reasonable. Any intent to overthrow, no matter how quixotic, is sufficient to bring the violence within the term "insurrection".

A similar conclusion was reached by Mr. Justice Mustill in *Spinney's [1948] Ltd. v. Royal Insurance Co. Ltd.* [1980]. when he also decided that a "rebellion" was a more organised and serious effort to supplant the existing rulers of a country, or at least to deprive them of authority over part of their territory. It is interesting to note that a "rebellion" describes a rising which fails; a successful attempt comes within the description of "revolution".

In the same case the learned judge considered that the words "civil war" did not simply denote a violent internal conflict on a large scale, but a war which had the special character of being internal rather than external. This special characteristic meant that certain features of an international war were absent, nevertheless a civil war was still a war. He did not attempt any general definition of a civil war, but it seemed to him that the conflict had to be between combatants who formed "sides" clearly identifiable by reference to a community of objective, leadership and administration. He was not convinced that where the term was used in ordinary speech, the only motive which could ever put the contestants into a state of civil war was a desire to seize or retain the reins of state; there could still be a civil war if the objective was not to seize complete political power, but perhaps to force changes in the way in which power was exercised without fundamentally changing the political structure. Again, the participants could be activated by tribal, racial or ethnic animosities. Another consideration was the character and scale of the conflict, and its effect on public order and on the life of the inhabitants.

He agreed that a small body of men, occupying a modest amount of ground could be engaged in civil war, if united by an explicit purpose to produce far reaching political changes, possessed of a high degree of discipline skill and weaponry, and backed by substantial popular support. Such a situation arose in *Curtis v. Mathews* [1918] which involved damage to property in Dublin in April 1916, during what became to be known as the "Easter Rebellion". Various persons set up a Provisional Government, and claimed the support of the "gallant allies in Europe" — i.e. the Central Powers, then at war with the United Kingdom. Armed rebels, estimated to number 2000 men, occupied several buildings in the city, including the General Post Office, which was shelled by the military forces of the Crown with 18 pound guns. The rising collapsed after five days of house and street fighting. Although it was not necessary to discuss the meaning of "civil war" in that case, it was agreed that there was civil strife amounting to "warfare", consequently subsequent Courts supported the view that this was the type of situation capable of amounting to a civil war.

In the *Spinney's* case, Mr. Justice Mustill, who had cause to deliberate on events in the Lebanon in 1976, stressed that the difficulty is to interpret what is happening, and to apply the facts to the ordinary business meaning of the words "civil war" in a policy of insurance. In this instance he was reluctant to invite any opinion from the Secretary of State, which would be based on the term used in Public International Law, rather than in the context of a policy, since it was not practical to define the latter with sufficient precision to enable the Secretary of State to adopt the same interpretation.

Fortunately the perils of civil war, revolution, rebellion and insurrection can usually be related to a state of organised and active opposition or resistance to established authority with the object of forcibly overthrowing the government or regime in power, thus rendering any precise classification superfluous. The situation is also assisted by the use of the generic expression "or civil strife arising therefrom", which is sufficient to widen the scope of a loss, although it must still be connected with the enumerated perils.

At this juncture it is as well to emphasise that while the *War Exclusion Clause* serves to eliminate all loss, damage or expense caused by the specified perils during the whole period of the transit, the *Institute War Clauses (Cargo)* only cover such perils in terms of the Waterborne Agreement. It will be recalled that the insurance on land is restricted to the area where goods are discharged for transhipment, and is subject to a limitation of 15 days after arrival of the oversea vessel.

Chapter 24

THE WAR PERILS (2)

In the second of this series of four articles, attention is now directed to the perils of "capture" and "seizure", especially the problems connected with the latter.

Having drawn attention in the previous article to the fact that the Institute War Clauses (Cargo) only serve to reinstate the exclusions in the marine clauses to a limited degree, it is now appropriate to study the next section of the *War Exclusion Clause* where the difference between the excepted perils and the cover provided by the War Clauses is even more marked.

In the "A" Clauses the exceptions preclude any claims being made against insurers in respect of the following causes:

> 6.2 capture seizure arrest restraint or detainment (piracy excepted), and the consequences thereof or any attempt thereat

whereas the War Clauses merely provide positive cover for such perils when they arise from the risks discussed in the last article. Thus the War Clauses will include claims for loss of or damage to the cargo caused by:

> capture seizure arrest restraint or detainment, arising from
> war civil war revolution rebellion insurrection, or civil strife
> arising therefrom, or any hostile act by or against a
> belligerent power
> and the consequences thereof or any attempt thereat.

"Capture" is normally associated with the rights of belligerents to seize enemy goods or ships at sea, such rights being extended to contraband of war being carried under a neutral flag, and to ships breaking a blockade or resisting visit and search.

The capture is considered to be complete when the vessel submits to the will of the captor, but it would appear that an act of taking possession is not indispensably necessary to make a capture; it is sufficient if there is obedience to a hostile attack or to a force known to be hostile (*La Esperanza*, 1822). However, there is no change in the right of property in the ship or cargo until it is brought into port and condemned as prize by a court of competent jurisdiction, at which time the owner's interest is deemed to have ceased on the date of capture (*Anderson v. Marten*, 1908).

Capture in neutral waters is distinctly frowned upon. During the First World War, for instance, several German ships sailing near the Dutch coast were hailed by a British warship. They lowered their flags, not because they were submitting to the will of the captor, but as a *ruse de guerre* to avoid being fired upon. By changing their course towards the land, and with assistance from the wind and tide, they managed to drift inside Dutch territorial waters before being boarded and taken possession of by the prize crews. The English Prize Court decided that the captures were invalid (the *Pellworm and other ships*, 1922).

An important case bearing on the meaning of "capture" in insurance policies is that of *Becker Gray and Co. v London Assurance Corporation* (1918), which concerned one of a number of British cargoes being carried in a German vessel to an enemy port at the outbreak of war. Many such vessels at sea, being unable to reach German ports, immediately (if possible) made for neutral ports, where the masters decided to remain. In August, 1914, the *Kattenturm*, a German vessel, was carrying 800 bales of jute from Calcutta to Hamburg, this cargo having been sold by British owners to a firm of German merchants. Fearing capture by the French and English fleets the master put into the Mediterranean port of Messina with the intention of abandoning the voyage. In the subsequent action against the insurers it was argued that the adventure was lost due to a "war" peril, on the grounds that if the voyage had been continued the vessel would have been captured, or, alternatively, that the continuation of the voyage was illegal. The Court held that the latter plea was invalid as it would not have been illegal for the master to carry on to Hamburg, as he, being a German, was not within the jurisdiction of the English law. It was also decided that the *causa proxima* of the destruction or abandonment of the voyage was the voluntary act of the master, who merely acted as any other intelligent person in his place would, under the circumstances, have done. Being safe from capture is not the same thing as being in danger of being captured, and it was reasoned that here there was merely a fear of encountering the peril, rather than a loss from the operation of the peril itself. As Lord Sumner said in the House of Lords: "I should have been a good deal surprised (and may I say, disappointed) if the vessel had gone on her way and escaped capture; but when or where that fate would have overtaken her, no one can tell ... she might have avoided capture for many days, and for all that we know, she might have been lost by fire or stranding, or some cause unconnected with hostilities, before ever any enemy hove in sight."

In similar circumstances in the Second World War, however, different results ensued after complex litigation had arisen out of three test cases in which the events concerning ships of German ownership under the control of German masters on the outbreak of war were considered. Acting on the orders of the German Government, one of the ships managed to reach Hamburg with her cargo; the other two were scuttled at sea and lost with their cargoes. The House of Lords upheld the decision in the Court of Appeal that the cargo-owners could recover under the war risk cover, it being stressed again and again that in all that they did the masters were acting as agents of the German Government alone. One of the many passages succinctly summarising the decision on this point occurred in the speech of Lord Wright in the *Minden* in which he said: "Here there was a capture or seizure of the goods by the German Government acting through the master, and the seizure or capture continued until the ship was scuttled." It was concluded there was a "restraint" by the German Government as soon as the master ceased to hold the goods as carrier, i.e. when he effected a change of possession by taking them and controlling them as agent for the German Government. (*Forestal Land, Timber and Railways Company v. Rickards* (1942) and other cases).

What is the difference between "capture" and "seizure"? In search of such an explanation lawyers will invariably turn to the words of Lord Fitzgerald from the case of *Cory v. Burr* (1883), which have often been quoted with approval by our Courts. In considering the *Free of Capture and Seizure warranty* in that particular case he had occasion to express the following distinction between the two terms: "In the construction of this warranty it is observable that 'capture' and 'seizure' do not mean the same thing. 'Capture' would seem

179

properly to include every act of seizing or taking by an enemy or belligerent; 'seizure' seems to be a larger term than 'capture', and goes beyond it, and may reasonably be interpreted to embrace every act of taking forcible possession either by a lawful authority or by overpowering force." The case is, therefore, useful authority for the proposition that all types of seizure (whether by a belligerent nation, governmental power, revenue or sanitary authorities, or simply a group of individuals acting for their own ends), can be avoided by marine insurers under the *War Exclusion Clause.*

The case also affords an excellent example of the effect of an exceptions clause. The master of the ship had on board a shipment of tobacco, and, disregarding his obligations to the shipowners, had arranged to smuggle it into Spain in order to avoid payment of the duty. While awaiting the arrival of the smugglers' boats off the coast, the vessel was sighted by a Spanish revenue cutter and ordered to proceed to port for examination. Finding their suspicions justified the governmental authorities seized the vessel with a view to confiscation, but agreed to release her on payment of a fine when the shipowners had convinced them that they were not responsible for the behaviour of the master, who had acted barratrously. As the policy provided cover against the risk of "barratry" the shipowners sought to recover from the Underwriters the amount they had paid. It was held, however, that the effective cause of the expense was the seizure by the Spanish authorities, and since "seizure" was excluded by the *F.C. & S. Clause,* the Underwriters were not liable, notwithstanding that the seizure was the result of barratry.

This brings us to a closer study of "seizure" in relation to other insured perils, particularly piratical and barratrous seizures. In *Naylor v. Palmer* [1854], where coolie emigrants murdered the captain and some of the crew, subsequently making off with the ship and the remaining crew, the mutinous act was held to be "piracy". Effect was given to this decision by the Marine Insurance Act, 1906, where it is stated in Rule 8 for the Construction of the Policy that the term "pirates" includes passengers who mutiny. But in a similar case, that of *Kleinwort v. Shepard* [1859], in which coolie passengers also took control of a ship and made off with her, the policy contained the exception of "seizure" and the Underwriters were held not to be liable despite the loss falling to be considered as "piracy". An alternative plea of "barratry" also failed on the basis that the passengers owed no duty of loyalty to the shipowner, and were, therefore, incapable of committing barratry. Underwriters did not wish to exclude piratical seizure from the scope of the cover provided by the "A" Clauses, hence it is specifically stated in section 6.2 of the *War Exclusion Clause* that the exceptions do not apply to the risk of "piracy". The risk of "piracy" is only appropriate to the "A" Clauses, accordingly no similar dispensation has been made in the *War Exclusion Clause* in the "B" and "C" Clauses.

A more difficult point arises with regard to barratrous seizures. In the same case of *Kleinwort v. Shepard* it was suggested by Counsel for the assured that "seizure" within the exclusion had to come from without and could not be applied to the coolie passengers. In order to counter this suggestion the Court enquired, argumentatively: "If the crew, intending to turn pirates, were to murder the captain and to run away with the ship, would not this be a loss by seizure?"

While the English Courts have not yet had cause to pronounce on this problem, the American Courts have responded most emphatically, reaching the conclusion that the insurance meaning of the word "seizure" is not so broad as its popular meaning. Accordingly they have adopted the attitude that it is to be understood in a restricted and limited sense.

This attitude is founded on the celebrated and widely cited opinion of Chief Justice Bigelow in *Greene v. Pacific Mutual Life Insurance Company* [1864] in which he gave an immediate answer to the above question. This case concerned a whaling ship taken from the command of the officers and the possession of the owner by a mutinous crew. The master and third officer were killed, the first and second officers were badly wounded, and the ship and its equipment were so badly damaged that the voyage was necessarily abandoned. Although the policy protected the assured against "barratry of master or mariners" the company defended the claim on the ground that the evidence showed a "seizure" of the vessel by the mutinous acts of the crew, and was thus caught by the exclusion of that peril. The Court, however, entered judgment for the assured.

Bigelow, C.J., speaking for the whole Court, said: "Inasmuch as barratry is one of the risks assumed by the assured (sic), unless particular acts are clearly excepted in terms which leave no doubt as to their meaning, the general words of the policy must have full operation ... But we do not deem it necessary to put the decision of this point on so narrow a ground. Upon careful consideration, we are of the opinion that the exception of a loss by seizure does not include the risk of mutiny of the mariners and the forcible taking of the ship from the control of the officers; or in other words, that it does not properly exclude from the operation of the policy a loss by barratry. Certainly the word 'seizure' cannot be applied to any barratrous act of the master. He has by law possession and control of the ship. He may, it is true, take her out of her course, or convert her to his own use in violation of his duty to the owners. But he cannot be justly said to seize that which is already in his own keeping. The same is true to a certain extent of the mariners. While in the discharge of their duty they have a qualified possession of the vessel. Subject to the order of the master, it is in their care and custody. If they violate their duty and disobey the master, displace him from command and assume entire control of the vessel, it is a breach of trust rather than a seizure."

For many years after that it was generally recognised by text-book writers, marine insurers and their technical advisers — at least, in America — that the term "seizure" did not include a violent taking of possession of the ship by a mutinous crew. It was not until 1957 that the position was challenged in the case of the "*Hai Hsuan*" and six other Chinese vessels (*Republic of China v. National Union Fire Insurance Company of Pittsburgh*).

The origins of the case can be related to the growth of the Chinese communist movement which, until 1937, was relatively unimportant. At that time it became active in organising resistance to Japan in northern China, and after the Second World War communist armies dominated the countryside as far south as the Yangtse. Early in 1949 the communist armies started driving southwards, and a state of civil war existed on April 19th. Thereafter the Nationalist Government was forced to move its capital on several occasions, until settling at Taipei, on the island of Taiwan, on December 9, 1949. By that time nearly the whole of the Chinese mainland was under the control of communist forces, acting for the rival *de facto* government which had proclaimed the People's Republic of China on October 1st.

The seven Liberty ships which became involved in the litigation had been sold by the United States to the Nationalist Government in 1946-7, subject to preferred ship mortgages in favour of the United States, and were operated by an agency of the Nationalist Government which had its head office in Shanghai until May 1949; after that date it was transferred to Taipei.

The operators also maintained a branch office in Hongkong, and in January 1950 six of the vessels remained at the island, while the masters, officers and crew ignored many messages from the head office to take the vessels to Taiwan or sail to Japan. It did not appear that the ship's personnel, or the employees of the Hong Kong office, had any real loyalty to either the Nationalist or the Communist Government, but, after many discussions, they eventually ran up the red flag and held the ships at the disposal of the Communist Government, feeling that it would be best for them and their families, many of whom were living on the mainland.

The remaining vessel, the *Hai Hsuan,* was on the high seas bound for Japan with a cargo of salt from Spain, when the officers and crew learned from the radio that the Hongkong vessels and the branch office had defected. They wanted to go to Hongkong, but, as the master had already received orders from head office not to go there, he tried to persuade them to proceed to Taiwan. However, the brewing trouble in the next few days caused him to be sick with fear, and he was obliged to take to his bed. The Chief Officer, contrary to instructions, then took the vessel into Singapore where the master was admitted into hospital. Two days later the Nationalist flag was replaced by a Chinese Communist flag provided by some communist agent or sympathiser at the port, and thereafter the wages of the officers and crew were paid by the Hongkong office on behalf of the Communist Government. It was common ground that there was a constructive total loss of each ship when the flags were changed.

The issue before the Court was whether any claim could be recovered under the marine or war policies and, if so, which. The marine policy covered losses due to barratry of the master or mariners, but under the *F.C. & S. Clause* excluded claims resulting from capture and seizure, or from the consequences of civil war. The war policy covered only those risks which would have been recoverable under the marine policy but were excluded by the *F.C. & S. warranty,* and further provided cover against the risk of civil war. However, there was a specific exclusion of capture and seizure even under the war policy, because Underwriters were aware that the progress of the communist armies down the coast of China exposed the vessels to capture by communist gunboats or sampans. If the vessels were held to be "seized", therefore, there would be no recovery at all.

In the District Court of Maryland Chief Judge Thomsen concluded there was no seizure of the six Hongkong vessels. Here he was influenced by the fact that there was no show of force or threat of violence by anybody, and also by the decision in *Greene v. Pacific Mutual Life Insurance Company* to the effect that "seizure" could not be applied to any barratrous act of the master. The losses therefore fell to be considered as due to "barratry" but were still excluded from the marine policy because they were the consequence of civil war. Being excluded from the marine policy by the *F.C. & S. warranty* the peril of "barratry" was covered by the war policy, which was intended to be complementary to the marine policy; in any event the war policy also provided cover against "civil war".

In respect of the *Hai Hsuan* he decided that, bearing in mind the question raised in *Kleinwort v. Shepard,* barratry of the mariners alone, who threatened violence to the captain, expressly or impliedly, and took the ship from his custody and control by the use of threat of superior force, amounted to a seizure. The loss was excluded by the exception in both the marine and war policies. He noted that even in *Greene v. Pacific Mutual Life Insurance Company* there was recognition of the distinction between the "possession and control" of the ship by the master, and the "qualified possession" by the mariners.

The case went to the United States Court of Appeals where the decision on the six Hongkong vessels was upheld. In the view of the Court, however, the law was clearly established in *Greene,* and the Appeal judges were satisfied that the term "seizure" did not include a violent taking of possession of the ship by a mutinous crew. The decision on the *Hai Hsuan* was reversed, and the result was the same as with the other six vessels.

It would appear from the review of previous case history in the judgments that American law has not progressed past the stage of relating "seizure" to the action of a government or its authorised representatives in taking possession of a ship or its cargo, or of goods on land, by the use or threat of a superior force. This is because most of the early American cases turned on the question whether the Confederacy, established at the time of their civil war, was a *de facto* government.

There is, therefore, a distinct difference between English and American law on the subject of "seizure", since under the former it is generally accepted, on the authority of *Cory v. Burr,* that action by a governmental authority is not a necessary element. Whether a modern Court would hold that a dispossession by a barratrous master or crew would amount to "seizure" is, nevertheless, a matter of some conjecture.

The *Hai Hsuan* judgment did provoke considerable comment in the London market, however, where there was some sympathy with the idea that one ought to distinguish between seizure by the master and members of the crew, and seizure by other parties whose acts to the prejudice of the shipowner can in no circumstances constitute "barratry". It was felt that such action on the part of the ship's personnel should also be recoverable as a loss by "barratry" under English policies, notwithstanding the exclusion of "seizure".

It is significant, therefore, that under the standard hull clauses, in which "barratry" and "piracy" are specified perils, provision is made in the *War Exclusion Clause* for neither to be defeated by the exception of "seizure". UNCTAD, in their deliberations over standard international wordings for hull and cargo insurance have gone a step further by suggesting that clarity will be achieved by indicating that the exclusion of "seizure" refers only to acts of governments or organisations claiming governmental powers.

Of course, it can be argued that the master or mariners cannot commit barratry against the cargo, since, by definition in Rule for Construction No.11 in the Marine Insurance Act, there is no "barratry" unless the wrongful act wilfully committed by the ship's personnel results in prejudice to the shipowner or charterer. This is only true to a certain extent, as the shipowner or demise charterer may also own the cargo, and, in any case, some action to the prejudice of the shipowner or charterer whether they own the cargo or not, can still result in loss or damage to the cargo.

An illustration of this is the case of *Goldschmidt v. Whitmore* [1811], in which the master of the *Anna Catherina,* having goods on board which were the joint property of the plaintiff and certain Hamburg merchants, barratrously sailed for a blockaded port in Holland. After being taken by an English cruiser, the goods were seized and condemned as enemy property. The policy, in fact, actually covered the goods against capture, seizure, or detention by any power whatsoever, nevertheless the Court ruled that the loss by condemnation for trading with the enemy was allowable as a loss by "barratry".

The most serious deficiency under the present arrangements arises from the fact that the cover provided by the War Clauses is no longer "back to back" with the exclusions in the Institute Cargo Clauses (A).

The exclusion of "seizure" makes it possible for insurers to argue that the hijacking of containers or lorries by gangs of thieves on land is not covered by the marine clauses, whereas the protection afforded by the War Clauses for "seizure" is confined to war, civil war and the associated types of risk illustrated by the clausing shown at the beginning of this article. In any case land risks are virtually eliminated by the terms of the Waterborne Agreement.

Finally, it is appropriate to comment on the effect of the words "the consequences thereof or any attempt thereat". Since it is recognised that the word "consequences" only refers to direct consequences operating on the subject-matter insured, it was debated whether to drop the expression "the consequences thereof" during the redrafting of the clauses, on the basis that the words were merely surplusage and did not add anything to the perils enumerated. It is an area where the application of *causa proxima* plays an important part, for obviously there are times when the resulting losses must be considered to be too remote from the operation of the perils.

On the other hand it was deemed necessary to retain the words "any attempt thereat" because they serve to qualify the stated perils. Thus any loss or damage caused by attempted capture or seizure would equally be recoverable as a claim for capture or seizure itself. Indeed, an excellent illustration of such a situation was given by Chief Justice Erle in the famous *Hatteras Light* case (*Ionides v. Universal Marine Insurance Co.,* 1863) when he took the example of a ship which, in order to avoid being captured by a hostile cruiser, seeks refuge in a bay where she remains trapped. Due to the lack of an anchorage she is driven ashore by the weather, and is lost. The loss came about because she could not escape from the situation in which she found herself, and was thus caused by an attempt at capture, i.e. by a war peril.

As it happened, Underwriters opted to retain the time-honoured phrase in its entirety.

Chapter 25

THE WAR PERILS (3)

To what extent do insurers provide cover against "arrest restraint or detainment" of cargo under the present War Clauses? This is the third of four articles in which the author looks at the war perils

With the revision of the Institute War Clauses (Cargo) in January, 1982, and the disappearance of the S.G. policy form, there is no longer any qualification that the perils of "arrest, restraint or detainment" are related to the actions of "all kings, princes, and people, of what nation, condition or quality soever ..." Consequently little regard can now be paid to Rule for Construction No.10 in the Marine Insurance Act, which describes losses falling under that description as those emanating from political or executive acts, although most situations involving the perils will continue to arise from such acts. In fact, under the new clauses, as previously stressed, Underwriters have taken the opportunity to confine their liability to the occasions when the arrest, restraint or detainment flows from "war civil war revolution rebellion insurrection, or civil strife arising therefrom, or any hostile act by or against a belligerent power ..."

Earlier writers have had some difficulty in distinguishing between the terms, as it seemed they tended to be synonymous — an arrest could be a restraint, while a restraint could result in a detainment. In the fullness of time, however, the Courts have managed to pronounce on most of the circumstances involving an unusual interference with the adventure, with the result that Underwriters have gradually modified the cover originally provided, so that the main source of claims in normal trading conditions will occur when the carrying vessel is trapped in an area where nations are involved in a dispute.

In order to elaborate on this subject reference can first be made to the case of *Rodocanachi v. Elliot* [1874] in which Mr. Justice Brett defined "arrest" as a "taking with intent ultimately to restore to the owner". Arrests are usually made for the purpose of enforcing a debt, or to inflict a fine for an infringement of customs or trading regulations; as such they come under the heading of "ordinary judicial process". It was never the intention of Underwriters to accept responsibility for loss or damage to goods arrested in the normal course of litigation, and since only a temporary detention is envisaged it is unlikely a constructive total loss will develop from that cause.*

A "restraint", on the other hand, contemplates a situation where an owner of goods finds himself deprived of the free use and disposal of his property, or unable to complete the voyage, usually by reason of a governmental order or municipal law coming into effect after the risk has commenced. Such situations can arise when trading with the enemy becomes prohibited on the outbreak of war, ports become blockaded, or embargoes are laid on the movement of certain goods. They can also occur from the application of sanctions, or powers given to local health authorities. It is not necessary for force to be employed, it is sufficient if there is power to enforce the restraint or to impose some penalty for non-compliance. However, under present conditions, Underwriters are freed from many claims which might arise from "restraint".

In the first place care has to be taken to distinguish between losses proximately caused by "restraint" and those caused by a mere apprehension of the peril.

For instance, in *Lubbock v. Rowcroft* [1803], a cargo was in course of shipment to Messina, but on arrival of the ship at Port Mahon, Minorca, it was learned that Messina was under blockade by the French, and the voyage was abandoned. The Court declined to allow a total loss under the policy since it was not occasioned by a peril acting upon the goods immediately. Again, in the case of *Forster v. Christie* [1809], it was held that the cargo Underwriters were not liable, although the further prosecution of the adventure was rendered impossible. Here a British ship was carrying goods to St. Petersburg when she was detained in the Baltic by the commander of a British convoy in anticipation of a hostile Russian embargo. In fact, if she had proceeded she might have completed the adventure before the embargo was laid on. A different verdict was reached in *Aubert v. Gray* [1862], however, when the Spanish Government, being in need of vessels to prosecute a dispute with Morocco, laid an embargo on

* See, however, the case of the *Morning Star* [1987] 1 Lloyd's Rep.401

ships in Corunna. The cargo in one of the ships, which belonged to a Spanish subject but was insured in this country, was damaged during the enforced unloading. This was held to be recoverable from Underwriters.

While English law is clear on the point that the mere inaccessibility of the destination port does not give rise to a constructive total loss of the cargo, it must be remembered that, without specific provision, a cargo policy does cover a loss of the adventure when there is some restraining influence on the cargo itself. This has been made abundantly clear by two classic cases which are frequently quoted.

The first case, *Miller v. Law Accident Insurance Co.* [1903], illustrates a "restraint" by local authorities, and concerned a shipment of cattle destined for Buenos Aires. On arrival there the Argentine Ministry ordered them to be removed from the port without landing because it was thought they were suffering from a contagious disease. It became necessary to tranship them and sell them at Montevideo for a substantial loss. The Court of Appeal was unable to draw any distinction between a restraint by a blockading force and a restraint arising under the operation of a sanitary law, and held that the loss was caused by the intervention of the Argentine Government. As Lord Justice Mathew said: "If actual force was not used it was because there was no opposition. The master submitted to the orders of the administration. The result was the same as if force had been used."

The other case, that of *Sanday v. British and Foreign Marine Insurance Company Ltd.* [1916], had the most far-reaching effects, however, as it involved many cargoes on British ships which were destined to enemy ports on the outbreak of war with Germany in August, 1914. Sanday and Co. were a firm of merchants who had arranged shipments of linseed and wheat by the steamers *St.Andrew* and *Orthia* from the River Plate to Hamburg in July, 1914. Both vessels were still at sea when trading with the enemy became illegal by the declaration of war. The *St. Andrew*, when off the Lizard, was challenged by a French cruiser, and instructed to proceed to Falmouth. At that port further instructions were received from the naval authorities for the vessel to sail to Liverpool, where the cargo was discharged. The *Orthia* called at St. Vincent for orders and was instructed to go to Glasgow by the owners, following a suggestion from the Admiralty, and this cargo was also discharged on arrival. Both cargoes were eventually sold.

The merchants brought an action against their Underwriters for a total loss in each case, but it was argued that the linseed and wheat were still in existence, and the loss which resulted was due entirely to the difference in the market prices at the time of sale in this country as compared with the values in Hamburg. The House of Lords reached a unanimous verdict that an insurance on cargo provided not only cover against loss by insured perils but also by frustration of the voyage, and held that as the declaration of war restrained the merchants from delivering the cargo at destination, the adventure was destroyed. The Underwriters were obliged to pay a total loss and become the owners of the cargo. It was immaterial whether the restraint was that exercised by force of an enemy or by lawful obedience of a subject to an act or proclamation issued by his government.

The decision was one which caused great concern to Underwriters as they were faced with many claims which were in the nature of loss of market rather than loss or damage to the goods themselves. The question might have come into even greater prominence during the war, but apparently in ordinary circumstances where the government diverted cargo, they paid for the incidental expenses incurred; also at an early stage of the war Underwriters introduced the *British and Allies, etc., Capture Clause* which contained the warranty: "... free of any claim arising from capture, seizure, arrest, restraint, or detainment, except by the enemies of Great Britain or by the enemies of the country to which the Assured or the ship belongs." In July, 1919, however, they went a step further by introducing the *Frustration Clause* into the standard clauses, reading as follows:

> Warranted free of any claim based upon loss of, or frustration of, the insured voyage, or adventure, caused by arrests, restraints or detainments of kings, princes or peoples.

On the 22nd September, 1939, immediately after the outbreak of the Second World War, insurers took the precaution of publishing a revised edition of the *British and Allies, etc., Capture Clause*, this being known as the *United Kingdom and Allies Clause*, viz:

> This policy is warranted free of any claim arising from capture seizure arrest restraint or detainment by the Government of the United Kingdom or of any of its Allies. Warranted also that the cargo insured is not, at any time during the voyage, the property

of any government or of any person firm or corporation (including those domiciled in neutral territory) who are alien enemies of the United Kingdom or its Allies.

This clause was incorporated into all war risks policies, and, combined with the *Frustration Clause*, made it clear that Underwriters were fully protected against trading with the enemy, or the actions of allied governments.

Nevertheless, the *Frustration Clause* was put to a severe test during the Second World War, when, in the circumstances already referred to in *Forestal Land, Timber and Railways Company v. Rickards* [1942], and other cases, ships of German ownership, on the commencement of hostilities, were instructed by the German Government to try and reach Germany, and to scuttle themselves if capture became unavoidable. Numerous British cargoes were lost by their owners in this way. Based on the findings in the case of *Sanday*, Underwriters refused to meet the claims on the grounds that the adventure was, in each case, frustrated by "restraint of princes", and they were relieved from liability by the *Frustration Clause*. This argument found favour with Mr. Justice Hilbery in the High Court, but the House of Lords affirmed the decision of the Court of Appeal to the effect that the clause did not operate to exclude a claim for loss of or damage to the goods themselves, which was notionally severable from a claim for loss of the adventure, and therefore there was a claim for "restraint of princes".

Viscount Maugham put it this way: "... the policy in its essence is a contract by the Underwriters to indemnify the assured either for losses (total or partial) of the goods themselves, or for losses he may sustain by reason of the goods not arriving in safety at their destination, though the goods themselves are in safety and uninjured, and in either case as a direct consequence of one of the perils insured against ... I am quite unable to see why the respondents in the present case should not be able to claim indemnity simply on the basis of loss of goods, and as if the doctrine of loss of adventure had never been accepted as part of our maritime law."

The true meaning of the *Frustration Clause*, according to the Law Lords, was that it operates when, and only when, the claim is based entirely on the loss of the insured voyage by frustration of the adventure.

In today's Institute War Clauses (Cargo) the *Frustration Clause* has been somewhat simplified, and appears among the general exclusions where, under Section 3.7, provision is made to exclude cover for:

> any claim based upon loss of or frustration of the voyage or adventure.

It is also to be observed that this exclusion is made of paramount importance by Clause 7, which stipulates that anything contained in the contract which is inconsistent with the *Frustration Clause* shall, to the extent of such inconsistency, be null and void.

Of course, if the assured wishes to claim for a constructive total loss of his goods by reason of being deprived of his property due to a restraint arising from an insured peril, it is incumbent on him to show that it is reasonable to abandon the subject-matter insured on account of its actual total loss appearing to be unavoidable, or that it is unlikely he can recover it, these conditions being expressed in Section 60 of the Marine Insurance Act. It has since been held, in the case of *Polurrian Steamship Co. Ltd. v. Young* [1913], that the test which should be applied is whether it is unlikely that the assured can recover his property "within a reasonable time", a construction which has been followed by subsequent Courts.

The question of what should be considered to be a reasonable time came up for discussion in the case of the *Bamburi*, which was trapped in the Shatt-al-Arab on the outbreak of the Iraq-Iran dispute in September 1980. In this case the vessel had arrived at her berth and commenced discharging her cargo of cement on the day that Iraq invaded Iran. Subsequently all movements of merchant shipping were prohibited. Although the ship remained undamaged by any hostilities in the vicinity, and there was no known navigational obstruction to the vessel sailing from the port of discharge, nevertheless despite repeated requests, it proved impossible to obtain permission to leave. Notice of abandonment was tendered to the hull Underwriters on both 30 September 1981, and 14 October 1981.

Neither the Iraqi nor the Iranian Governments asserted any rights to the vessel, and there was no Iraqi presence on board which would have interfered with the day-to-day life on the ship, consequently Underwriters had some reservations as to whether it could be said that the owners had been deprived of possession of their property on the dates of the notices of abandonment. However, as the issue was one which affected many vessels insured against War Risks in the London market, Underwriters arranged an arbitration to obtain authoritive guidance on such claims. Mr. Justice Staughton heard the evidence and argument in November and December 1981 in his capacity as sole arbitrator, and found that the ship was a constructive total loss by restraint of princes, an insured peril.

In his reasons for the award, he stated it was clear beyond dispute that the initial order not to sail emanated from an executive organ of the government of Iraq, and previous case history showed that it was unnecessary for actual force to be used. He was disposed to favour the concept, applied by earlier authorities, of whether the assured had lost the "free use and disposal" of the vessel, and concluded there was no special reason for confining the cover against restraints and detainments to cases where the master and crew were expelled from the vessel; therefore, there was a loss of possession within the meaning of the policy. He also concluded that it was unlikely that the owners would recover possession of their vessel within 12 months from the notice of abandonment, which he judged to be a reasonable period.

Since then hull insurers have adopted a more liberal approach and it will be found in the standard War and Strikes Clauses used for the insurance of vessels that:

> In the event that the Vessel shall have been the subject of capture, seizure, arrest, restraint, detainment, confiscation, or appropriation, and the Assured shall thereby have lost the free use and disposal of the Vessel for a continuous period of 12 months then for the purpose of ascertaining whether the vessel is a constructive total loss the Assured shall be deemed to have been deprived of the possession of the Vessel without any liklihood of recovery.

In the absence of a similar provision in the cargo clauses each claim will, naturally, have to be decided on the merits of the case, but there would seem to be no reason why cargo insurers should not also consider 12 months to be a reasonable limit for an assured to be deprived of the possession of his goods when these are trapped in the carrying vessel.

In some cases no direct restraint is put upon the subject-matter insured, the ship or goods simply become trapped and detained by the operation of hostilities. In June 1967, during the Arab-Israeli War, it was the blockage of the Suez Canal which provided difficulties for

Underwriters and assureds, for it was on that occasion that 14 ships forming a north-bound convoy were trapped in the Great Bitter Lake, while the American vessel *Observer*, which was southward bound, was confined to Lake Timsah, having been delayed by fire. As time went on, and the canal remained closed to navigation, Underwriters came under severe pressure to pay claims for constructive total loss, eventually yielding to a commercial response, despite having doubts about their legal liability. London Underwriters had a massive interest in the cargoes on board the vessels, and, by way of subrogation, hoped that, eventually, something would be recovered to offset the payments to cargo owners, especially on the disposal of valuable metals which, naturally, tended to appreciate in value. The Canal was, in fact, reopened 8 years later, when some of the vessels, quite remarkably, were still able to proceed under their own power — a tribute to the maintenance of the crews who had remained on board. Not only had the vessels and cargoes been detained all that time, but many people were also surprised to receive mail which had been delayed on board.

The difficulty of deciding whether it is likely that cargo will be detained for an unreasonable period is one which gained prominence in the previously mentioned case of *Rodocanachi v.Elliot* [1874]. This case arose from the Franco-Prussian War of 1870, when silk goods were insured from Shanghai to London, including transit by land from Marseilles to Boulogne. The goods arrived safely in Paris, but before they could be further despatched on their journey, that city was besieged by the Prussian armies so that all communication with any other place was prevented.

The owners of the goods abandoned them to the Underwriters and claimed a total loss, but the claim was declined, as there was no detainment or restraint actually operating on the goods themselves. The owners thereupon issued a writ, and persisted with their claim, although by the time the trial commenced the Prussians had already left Paris so that the goods had arrived safely in London.

The Court, however, was obliged to deal with the matter on the facts as they existed at the time of the issue of the writ, and not as they subsequently appeared. On this basis it was decided that the detention appeared unlikely to cease within a reasonable time, accordingly the assured could recover for a constructive total loss by restraint or detainment of princes. It was held that the goods were detained just as much as if the Prussians had exercised a forcible control over them.

Such a claim would, of course, now be barred by reason of the operation of the Waterborne Agreement, which excludes risks occurring during overland transit.

Claims for arrest, restraint or detainment which are not related to war, civil war, etc., are likewise not recoverable under the terms of the clauses, and this fact will effectively exclude those falling within the term "ordinary judicial process", or those caused by the operation of local sanitary laws. The *Frustration Clause* will prevent the recovery of any claim depending entirely on the loss of the adventure when the goods are still within the control of the assured, and, in any event, when delivery at the destination port is denied, either by blockade, embargo or sanctions, such factors do not consistute a "restraint" within the meaning of the peril. Also ruled out would be any arrest, restraint or detainment on political grounds alone, i.e. where a foreign Court acts on the instructions of its politicians to interfere with the cargo, knowingly exceeding its powers.

It must be stressed that if the destination is changed by the assured after attachment of the insurance (Clause 6), or if there is any deviation or variation of the adventure arising from the exercise of a liberty granted to shipowners or charterers under the contract of affreightment Clause 5.5), it is essential to give prompt notice to Underwriters to maintain the cover in force, and to arrange payment of any additional premium.

Unlike the marine clauses the Institute War Clauses (Cargo) do not specifically include a *Forwarding Charges Clause* under which the Underwriters undertake to pay the extra expenses incurred in forwarding the goods to destination if, by reason of the operation of an insured peril, the transit is terminated at a different port. However, under the *Duty of Assured Clause*, the assured are bound to take reasonable measures to avert or minimise any loss recoverable under the terms of the insurance, and Underwriters will reimburse them for any charges properly and reasonably incurred for that purpose.

Since there will be some occasions when the assured will be unable to recover additional expenses incurred in consequence of War Risks, Underwriters offer special facilities by means of the Institute Additional Expenses Clauses (Cargo—War Risks), issued on 1st July 1985. These clauses set out to indemnify the assured for any extra charges (which cannot be recovered under the standard marine or war clauses) incurred by reason of the interruption or frustration of the adventure by arrests, restraints, detainment or acts of kings, princes and peoples in prosecution of hostilities, or by blockades or other warlike operations. They also extend to cover the exercise by the carrier of any liberty granted by any "War Risk" clause in the contract of affreightment. Thus, where goods are discharged at a port other than the specified port of destination, Underwriters will normally pay the landing and warehouse charges, and the cost of transhipment to the original destination. Alternatively they might agree to pay for returning the goods to the point of origin of shipment, or for transhipping them to a substituted destination, depending on the economics of such action. The additional expenses will include marine and war risks premiums, also any duty.

The actions of local health authorities in frustrating the adventure, and perhaps requiring the destruction of goods not meeting the required standards, has resulted in the growth of special policies covering "Rejection Risks". Often the cause of rejection can be a pre-existing condition on shipment, but in other cases the authorities may be over-cautious. At a conference held in London in March 1985, Mr. Michael Pyer of Perfect, Lambert and Company quoted a case involving a cargo of corn in the Caribbean which had suffered minor water damage. The local health department was persuaded not to dump the entire cargo at sea, but afterwards unconfirmed reports gave the impression that aflatoxin was present. This being a carcino-genic substance apparently resulting from moulds on grain, the department then reversed its decision.

Chapter 26

THE WAR PERILS (4)

In the concluding part of this series the author looks at the cover provided against mines, torpedoes, bombs and other weapons of war.

In the ordinary course of events the risks of loss or damage to the subject-matter insured, by mines, torpedoes, bombs or other weapons of war, will be covered under Clause 1.1 of the Institute War Clauses (Cargo) by the perils of war, civil war, revolution, rebellion, insurrection (or civil strife arising therefrom), or any hostile act by or against a belligerent power; provided, of course, that such perils operate whilst carriage is being effected in an oversea vessel according to the terms of the *Transit Clause*, or during the short period that the property may be insured on land whilst in the process of being transhipped.

As we are all aware, however, claims from these sources are not confined to the actual areas of hostilities, or even to the time when hostilities are in operation, and it is interesting to recall that in a report issued by the American Cargo War Risk Reinsurance Exchange in 1958 it was recorded that 446 vessels had been damaged or sunk as a result of mine explosions since the end of World War Two, and that, in the previous two years, almost 250 floating mines had been specifically reported by ships at sea or by shore stations. Whilst the greatest concentration of reports had come from the waters around the British Isles, a number of mines had been sighted in the Gulf of Mexico and the United States Atlantic coastwise shiplanes, as far north as Cape Cod and south to the Florida Strait.

Even today sightings are still being made around our shores, causing vessels to be warned to navigate with extreme caution. It is assumed the mines have been torn from where they have been laid or planted, many years before, by severe storms. Also occasionally reported from the sea-lanes of the world are stray or derelict torpe-does, aerial bombs, or depth charges.

When loss or damage occurs from explosive objects in unexpected quarters of the sea, this can give rise to difficulties as to whether a claim can be made under the particular policy conditions. In *Stoomvaart Maatschappij "Sophie H". v. Merchants' Marine Insurance Co.* [1919], for instance, the vessel sank after striking three mines in the Gulf of Finland, which had drifted some 30 miles from a Russian minefield. In an action under the marine policy it was held by the House of Lords that the Underwriters were protected by the *F.C. & S. Clause* then in operation, such loss being the consequence of hostilities. This suggests that, in similar circumstances today, there is no reason why a claim should not be settled either under the heading of "war" or as being caused by the hostile act of a belligerent power, if the war clauses are applicable.

Naturally, it is much more of an open question whether a loss caused by a mine, torpedo, bomb or the like, long after the cessation of hostilities, would constitute a claim as a war peril, since it might be regarded as being too remote from the operations of war. Indeed, in the case of the *Nassau Bay* [1978], the vessel dredged up some shells which had been dumped in the waters of Mauritius after the cessation of hostilities, and subsequently sank from the explosion which followed. Mr. Justice Walton was of the opinion that the dumping could not be classified as a warlike operation, but was rather in the nature of an act of pacification, like beating swords into ploughshares. He was unable to accept the view that the loss was the "consequences of hostilities or warlike operations."

Underwriters, being aware that losses could arise from many years to come, despite the intensive mine-sweeping operations carried out, habitually included the risk of mines in their war policies after the First World War, together with those of torpedoes and bombs, so as to avoid any dispute on the point.

As can be appreciated from the case just quoted, dredgers are particularly prone to such risks, one exceptionally tragic occurrence taking place in Marseilles harbour in September 1958, when the Dutch bucket dredger *H.A.M. No. 110*, which was working in the harbour, dredged up a large mine which exploded. This caused damage to nearby quays, wharf sheds, vehicles and buildings on shore, as well as seven other vessels. Four people were killed.

In April 1980, a cutter suction dredger, the *Asakura Maru No. 12*, was working in a widened part of the Suez Canal away from the navigable channel, when she sucked a torpedo into her pump-room, and sank following an explosion. She was later declared a constructive total loss. Apparently the accident occurred on one of the few occasions when the steel anti-bomb grill, normally laid on the canal bed prior to the commencement of dredging, was not placed in position.

In the same month, the sand suction dredger *Bowherald*, while operating off the East Coast of England, suffered an explosion in her dredge pump machinery space and started taking water. However, she was able to move under her own power to an anchorage for inspection, and was then towed to another anchorage where temporary repairs could be effected. Following this she was able to make her way up the Thames for permanent repairs to be carried out. Bomb fragments discovered after the explosion were identified as parts of a British 500 lb. medium capacity bomb. The claim was settled as a war loss.

In a similar incident in August, 1986, while dredging off Great Yarmouth, the sand suction dredger *Arco Tees* picked up an explosive device in her suction pipe, believed to be a bomb from World War II. The explosion which followed damaged her watertight doors, allowing water to enter, but firemen were able to contain the flooding while the vessel rested on a sandbank. Pumping assistance was rendered by a sistership which had been dredging nearby and she was then towed to Lowestoft. However, she was subsequently considered to be a war constructive total loss.

Prior to 1982 the war clauses provided specific cover against "mines, torpedoes, bombs or other engines of war" without qualification, but under the present conditions this has been restricted to *derelict* mines, torpedoes, bombs, or other *derelict* weapons of war (Clause 1.3). This is a significant alteration which can affect whether a loss is recoverable under the marine or war clauses, and, in particular, whether some claims will be caught by the exclusions contained in the "B" and "C" Clauses.

The alteration appears to have been adopted in lieu of a *Pollution Hazard Clause* which was introduced in the hull market in 1973 to cover loss or damage to a vessel directly caused by any governmental authority acting under the powers invested in them to prevent or mitigate a pollution hazard, provided such action was in consequence of the operation of an insured peril. The clause owes its origins to the disaster to the tanker *Torrey Canyon*, which went aground near the Scilly Isles on 18th March 1967. As a result of the grounding many of the cargo tanks had become damaged and it was estimated that, by 20th March, some 30,000 tons of oil had escaped to the sea. Subsequent strong winds and high seas broke the back of the vessel, so that by 27th March a further 30,000 tons had been released, with a likelihood of even more escaping later. Thus, in order to avoid serious pollution to the Cornish coast, the government ordered the wreck to be bombed, so as to destroy any remaining oil by fire. The actions of the United Kingdom Government in doing this were contrary to international law at the time and, indeed, were described in some quarters as piracy, but they did lead to a general review of the problems of pollution at sea, and resulted in the *1969 Convention on Intervention on the High Seas in Cases of Oil Pollution Casualties.*

In drafting up the new clauses, however, cargo Underwriters did not consider there was any need for a specific *Pollution Hazard Clause*, since such losses would, in many cases, form a claim under the marine clauses in the absence of any exclusion to the contrary. In examining the question of liability, therefore, close attention must be paid to the scope of the insured perils in the marine clauses, whether there is an exception in the particular circumstances, and, if so, what recovery may be possible under the war clauses, or even the strikes clauses.

As regards the Institute Cargo Clauses (A), which are basically on "all risks" conditions, the deliberate destruction of a cargo by bombs, to avert pollution, would certainly be a "risk" within the meaning of the term. The loss could, in no way, be said to have been caused by war, civil war etc. and would therefore not be caught by that exclusion in Clause 6.1. Neither would the exclusion of *derelict* bombs in Clause 6.3. operate.

In the "B" and "C" Clauses there is cover for loss or damage to the cargo which can be reasonably attributed to fire or explosion, but in any event, when the danger of pollution emanates from the stranding of the vessel, the subsequent destruction of the cargo can be viewed as being reasonably attributable to the stranding—another contingency for which the clauses provide. Although there is an exclusion of deliberate damage or deliberate destruction (Clause 4.7) this is only applicable when carried out by the wrongful act of some person. The other exclusions, mentioned above, are also not applicable and, accordingly, settlement should be sought under the marine clauses.

As an alternative, where a hazardous cargo is involved, and the vessel is a danger to navigation, the authorities may simply take her out to sea and sink her. This expedient was adopted in the case of the *Cavo Cambanos*, a Greek products tanker, which, in April 1981, whilst carrying 18,000 tons of volatile naphtha, sustained a fire in her engine room and was abandoned by her crew. Half submerged, she drifted in the Mediterranean for three months until the French authorities decided to remove the obstacle and the threat of pollution. The vessel was towed about 150 kilometres off Corsica where frogmen placed explosives under the hull and set off charges to sink her. The naphtha cargo was expected to evaporate in the explosion, but several naval vessels stood by on pollution control duty.

In circumstances like these, the owners of cargo insured under the "B" and "C" Clauses would not only have protection from losses reasonably attributable to fire or explosion, but would also have the option of claiming that the loss was reasonably attributable to the vessel being sunk. In the "A" Clauses there would be no difficulty, and in no case under the three sets of clauses would the exclusions apply.

In the main the exclusions will also not apply to accidents occurring when bombs or missiles are being used during military training exercises in peace-time, or being tested, since they will be neither "derelict" nor being employed for hostile purposes. A recent example of such an occurrence was that of the tanker *Western Sun* which was struck by a Sidewinder air-to-air missile whilst laden with oil off the coast of Norfolk, Virginia, in July 1986, this having been fired by a U.S. Navy F-14 jet aircraft during manoeuvres. The missile, which was unarmed, made a 2½ ft. hole in the vessel's hospital area and caused a fire. Fortunately, most of the crew were in the mess at the time and were able to put out the fire within 30 minutes, using extinguishers and seawater pumps. It would appear that the vessel was not fully aware of the area of the manoeuvres, which included heavily used shipping lanes.

However, in the case of weapons of war employing atomic or nuclear fission or fusion, or the like, there is a specific exclusion in the marine clauses relieving Underwriters from liability for any loss, damage, or expense arising from that source, whatever the reason. In the war clauses the exception also appears but here it is limited to the *hostile* use of such weapons. This seems to leave open the possibility of an accidental detonation being caused by the operations of a war, civil war, etc.. which could affect cargoes at sea.

Although such a possibility is no doubt remote, we have already experienced the results of the explosion which happened at the Chernobyl nuclear reactor in the Soviet Union in 1986. Cargo Underwriters in the London market were involved in only a small way, but it was realised the impact could have been much worse had the weather conditions been less favourable. Some concern has therefore been expressed over the fact that the exclusion in the marine clauses is confined to nuclear weapons of war, and consideration is being given to the question of introducing a wider exclusion clause so as to avoid the potential effects of a more serious radioactive fall-out from a power station or reasearch establishment.

Explosive devices, which cause damage to cargoes, may not always be "derelict" or set by a belligerent power as a hostile act; many such occurrences are now the work of terrorists or persons acting from a political motive. As such, they are properly recoverable under the Institute Strikes Clauses (Cargo). Naturally, it can sometimes be difficult to identify the source of the device, and so determine which particular peril has operated.

Indicative of this difficulty was the damage caused to the Norwegian-owned tanker *Iver Chaser* in 1984, following the deployment of mines in the Nicaraguan port of Corinto. It was later acknowledged that the placement of the mines carried the approval of the U.S. Government against whom redress was sought by the Norwegian war insurers. In the action in the Federal Court, however, Judge Tenney had to concede he had no jurisdiction over the executive branch of the government, and the Court was incapable of assessing the underlying military and diplomatic considerations which resulted in the decision to place the mines without warning to innocent third party vessels.*

Another example of secret mining operations came to light as the result of damage to up to 20 ships in the Gulf of Suez and the Red Sea by mysterious explosions in the latter part of 1984. At first they were ascribed to explosive materials used in the offshore search for oil; however, from the descriptions of the incidents, experts soon decided that they were the results of mines planted for some sinister purpose. This view appeared to be confirmed by a member of the

*Upheld by the Supreme Court in January, 1988.

"Jihad" (Holy War) organisation who claimed that his group had placed 190 mines in the area in a campaign against Western interests. An international task force undertook an extensive search combined with mine-sweeping operations, but no definite evidence was found before the shipping lanes were thought to be clear. Accusations and denials of involvement abounded, but the source of the mines remained unexplained.

Fortunately, so far as cargo assureds are concerned, the Institute War Clauses (Cargo) and the Institute Strikes Clauses (Cargo) are complementary on this subject, and no practical difficulty should arise if they should find themselves burdened with claims of this nature.

However, there is one curious feature in the war clauses relating to goods whilst in craft in the course of transit to or from the oversea vessel, where protection is strictly limited to "the risks of mines and derelict torpedoes, floating or submerged" (Clause 5.4). It would seem that the intention is to cover loss or damage from mines during such transit, whether they are derelict or related to a hostile act by or against a belligerent power, but it can be argued that the wording does not achieve that result without some direct reference to the peril of "derelict mines". It could bring us back to the point mentioned earlier, i.e. whether a loss caused by a mine, long after the cessation of hostilities, can be classed as a loss by war, civil war, or any of the perils stated in Clause 1.1.

Chapter 27

THE STRIKES CLAUSES (1)

This is the first of two parts of a study of the Institute Strikes Clauses (Cargo). In this part the author discusses the distinction between the war and strikes risks, and their relationship with the Institute Malicious Damage Clause.

In studying the effects of the revised Institute Strikes Clauses (Cargo) it is probably useful to commence with a comparison of the present insured perils with those in operation prior to 1982. Basically the *Risks Clause* in the 1982 conditions covers loss of or damage to the subject-matter insured caused by

    1.1   strikers, locked-out workmen, or persons taking part in labour disturbances, riots or civil commotions

    1.2   any terrorist or any person acting from a political motive.

If reference is made to the previous clauses it will be seen that the risk of "persons acting maliciously" has disappeared completely, to be replaced by those of terrorism or politically motivated persons. This is not intended to qualify acts carried out in a malicious manner, but reflects a shift in attitude on the part of Underwriters towards violence, whereby certain types of deliberate damage will be retained under the marine clauses.

In practice, when the old strikes clauses were utilised, it was quite common to add the risks of vandalism and sabotage to that of malicious damage, but it will be remembered that all these forms of damage are now available under the special *Institute Malicious Damage Clause* for use with the "B" and "C" Clauses. Clearly then, there has been a fundamental change by switching claims from such sources over to the marine cover, and we shall return to this subject a little later in this article.

In order to study the overall position more closely it will be as well to look at the cover provided by the marine clauses, and to see to what extent the strikes clauses are complementary, careful attention being paid to the exclusion clauses.

The first point to notice is that the *Transit Clause* in the Institute Strikes Clauses (Cargo) is on the same terms as that in the standard marine clauses, so that the cargo is insured from warehouse to warehouse, subject to the time limit of 60 days after completion of discharge from the oversea vessel. This is an important consideration, since, unlike the war clauses, protection is afforded whilst the goods are on land, where they can be vulnerable to acts of terrorism, apart from the civil disorders stipulated.

Under the "all risks" terms of the "A" clauses, of course, any physical loss or damage is recoverable, whether it arises from accidental or violent means, unless there is a specific exclusion. The *Strikes Exclusion Clause*, in particular, reads:

7   In no case shall this insurance cover loss damage or expense
7.1   caused by strikers, locked-out workmen, or persons taking part in labour disturbances, riots or civil commotions
7.2   resulting from strikes, lock-outs, labour disturbances, riots or civil commotions
7.3   caused by any terrorist or any person acting from a political motive.

The essential difference from the *Risks Clause* in the Institute Strikes Clauses (Cargo) is that the exclusion refers to "expense" as well as to loss or damage, especially when *resulting from* strikes, lock-outs, labour disturbances, riots or civil commotions (Clause 7.2).

The most common expense resulting from strikes and similar risks is the extra cost of forwarding goods to the original destination, when the carrier exercises the liberty in the contract of carriage to discharge the goods at another port in order to avoid trouble and delay at a port of destination beset with labour problems. It became a popular misconception that the additional expenditure would be payable by cargo Underwriters and the wordings have been tightened up considerably to dispel any such notions on this subject.

In the first place it will be observed that the wording of the *Risk Clause* makes it clear that only physical loss or damage to the cargo is covered. Of course, there may be attendant expenses relating to the loss or damage, but these will often be recoverable in the nature of "Minimising Losses" (Clause 11), or when required to quantify the loss. Special provision is made for general average and salvage charges under Clause 2, when these are incurred in connection with the avoidance of loss from a risk covered under the strikes clauses.

Next, if reference is made to the *General Exclusions Clause* in the strikes clauses it will be observed that under Clause 3.7 there is no cover for:

> loss damage or expense arising from the absence shortage or withholding of labour of any description whatsoever resulting from any strike, lockout, labour disturbance, riot or civil commotion.

This clause echoes the exclusion in the marine clauses and serves to emphasise that Underwriters are not liable for claims of a consequential nature caused by delay. It is also made clear in Clauses 3.4 and 3.5 that the cover does not embrace losses or expenses proximately caused by delay, or by inherent vice, thus relieving them from deterioration of goods held up by civil disorders, or for claims arising from loss of market.

Just in case the argument is advanced that the policy would protect the assured from a loss of the adventure if the goods are detained in a strike-bound port, Underwriters have now taken the precaution of including a *Frustration Clause*, and in no case will they pay for:

> 3.8   any claim based upon loss of or frustration of the voyage or adventure.

Usually, however, civil disturbances do not last very long, and the question of whether the assured has been deprived of his goods, so as to constitute a constructive total loss under Section 60(2)(1), of the Marine Insurance Act, is unlikely to arise.

However, the assured needs to bear in mind certain relevant features of the clauses. While the *Transit Clause* extends the period of transit during any delay beyond his control, thus covering loss or damage to the goods from insured perils which may occur during that delay, there are some limitations. If the 60 day limit after discharge is likely to be exceeded, an extension of the cover should be sought from the insurers. Similarly, if the goods are discharged at another port under the option expressed in the contract of carriage, it is stipulated in the clause that the insurance will terminate at the port unless prompt notice is given to the Underwriters to keep the insurance in force, this being subject to an additional premium if required.

All the expenses of storing the goods and reshipping them to destination, plus the cost of extra insurance under the marine, war, and strikes clauses, can add up to a lot of money, which the innocent assured will have the burden of paying. For that reason there is available in the market a special insurance to cover "strike-diversion expenses" which may be expressed in something like the following terms:

> This insurance is to pay (only) any additional expenditure incurred by the assured by reason of the exercise by the shipowners or charterers of any liberty granted by the contract of affreightment whereby solely in consequence of strikes, riots, civil commotions, lock-outs or labour disturbances, the within mentioned goods are over-carried or discharged at a port other than the ultimate port of discharge named in the contract of affreightment, such expenditure being payable irrespective of any other loss whether total or partial recoverable under the terms of any other insurance upon the interest.
>
> Basis of valuation: As in marine policy but limit of Underwriters' liability hereunder shall be 20 per cent. of such value.

It may also be stipulated that the assured shall bear 10 per cent. of any claim, which amount must remain uninsured and at his own risk.

It should, of course, be pointed out that, if a strike is imminent, Underwriters will be most reluctant to provide cover against additional costs, and such insurance is normally on a long term basis, possibly utilising a 12 months' policy incorporating all the assured's shipments.

Another factor which the assured should bear in mind is the danger of an accumulation of goods at a strike-bound port. Regular cargo shipments are customarily insured under an open cover embracing all the assured's sendings for one year. This will invariably contain a *Location Clause* under which the insurers limit their liability to a stipulated sum for any one accident or series of accidents arising from the same event in any one location. The assured is, therefore, well advised to make sure he is adequately covered.

Past experience has shown that congestion of cargo brings an increased number of claims. There are difficulties over security when storage facilities become full, which tends to encourage theft and pilferage. Goods may also be left in the open, at the mercy of the elements. Damage can result from the use of unskilled labour, often employed to move perishable goods during an emergency. Ever present, however, is the threat of a catastrophic loss, such as by fire.

The assured is, of course, expected to act as if uninsured, and to minimise the risk of congestion where this is possible. If the strike is at the port of shipment one effective way is not to send the goods forward, unless normal transit can be foreseen.

When goods are insured on limited conditions, such as the "B" and "C" Clauses, without any specific reference to coverage for strikes and similar risks, there is another popular misconception that Underwriters have no liability for loss or damage arising from those causes. Why, it is asked, should it be necessary to exclude losses from such perils when they are not included in the first place? The short answer is that under those clauses, the insurers are responsible for loss or damage reasonably attributable to various named perils which can result from the action of strikers or other persons taking part in civil disorders. Thus, without some qualification, the insurers would be obliged to pay for damage caused to goods by fire or explosion, or any of the other risks stated, although such damage is intended to be covered under the strikes clauses for a separate premium.

While the "B" and "C" Clauses contain an exception for all deliberate damage occasioned by the wrongful acts of any persons (Clause 4.7), a glance at the *Institute Malicious Damage Clause* will reveal that the terms on which the exclusion is deleted continue to make deliberate damage subject to the other exclusions contained in the insurance, viz:

> In consideration of an additional premium, it is hereby agreed that the exclusion "deliberate damage to or deliberate destruction of the subject-matter insured or any part thereof by the wrongful act of any person or persons" is deemed to be deleted and further that this insurance covers loss of or damage to the subject-matter insured caused by malicious acts vandalism or sabotage, subject always to the other exclusions contained in this insurance.

Thus, there can still be some conflict between the perils envisaged by the *Institute Malicious Damage Clause* and the exclusions of war and strikes (Clauses 6 and 7), where some overlapping can occur, depending on the motives behind "malicious acts, vandalism or sabotage".

To understand the application of this clause it will be convenient to take "malicious acts" as an example. In the case of *Nishina Trading Company Ltd. v. Chiyoda Fire and Marine Insurance Co. Ltd.* [1969] it was found in the Court of Appeal by Lord Denning and Lord Justice Davies that, in a policy of insurance, the word "maliciously" involved an element of spite or ill-will, a definition which was repeated in the *Salem* case in 1981 and 1982, during its progress to the House of Lords.

Since malicious damage can be inflicted by strikers, rioters or persons taking part in civil commotions, it is readily apparent that claims arising from such sources are recoverable under the strikes clauses, even if they occur on land. On the other hand if, during a civil war, rebel troops maliciously damage goods in the course of transit on land, Underwriters will be protected by the *War Exclusion Clause* in the marine clauses, and will also be able to disclaim liability under the war clauses which, by reason of the Waterborne Agreement, do not cover the property during overland transit.

Where there is loss or damage caused deliberately, therefore, the prime consideration is whether the exclusions of the war and strikes perils apply. If not, claims under the *Institute Malicious Damage Clause* will be appropriate in respect of:

      (1)   malicious acts, vandalism or sabotage,

or (2)   other wrongful, deliberate acts which result in loss or damage reasonably attributable to fire, explosion, or any other peril specified in the "B" and "C" Clauses.

In practice, of course, it is not always straightforward to identify loss or damage in terms of the insured perils, because it is a feature of civil disorder and political upheaval that intelligence services and communications are reduced, and may even cease entirely. On such occasions it can prove difficult to ascertain whether the scale of unrest or violent activity has developed beyond a riot or civil commotion (insured under the strikes clauses) to the proportions of an insurrection, or worse (insured under the war clauses, subject to the terms of the Waterborne Agreement). On top of that there is the added complication that individuals, who are not connected with the disturbance, will take advantage of the confused situation to indulge in theft or pilferage, giving rise to a claim under the "all risks" conditions of the "A" Clauses. It is at times like these when the lack of information causes Underwriters to deal with losses on the balance of probabilities, and they will tend to treat each claim on its merits.

In trying to determine the borderline between the disturbances mentioned in the strikes clauses and those detailed in the war clauses, it may be helpful to refer back the comments made in the first part of the study of the war perils, where it was established that "insurrection" involves a group or movement in a violent uprising with the object of overthrowing the constituted government, and that "rebellion", "revolution", and "civil war" are stages in this process. The broad distinction between those perils, and the perils in the strikes clauses, is that riots, labour disturbances, and civil commotions can be classed as disorders in the nature of public demonstrations of *protest* against the existence of certain conditions, and lack the element of organised opposition to established authority which marks an insurrection.

Even so, some grasp of the meaning of "riots" and "civil commotions" is desirable since the layman's ideas on these subjects can differ materially from the legal definitions employed in this country. These will be discussed in the second part of this article.

Chapter 28

THE STRIKES CLAUSES (2)

In the concluding part of this appraisal of the Institute Strikes Clauses (Cargo), the perils of "riots" and "civil commotions" are examined closely. The author also raises a debate on the extent of cover provided against terrorism and politically motivated acts.

The natural commencing point in understanding what constitutes a "riot" is the case of *Field and Others v. The Receiver of Metropolitan Police* [1907] in which a legal definition was first laid down. This concerned an incident which took place in Canning Town, London, on a night in October, 1906, when seven or eight youths, of varying ages between 14 and 18, congregated on the pavement outside a particular property shouting and using bad language. At this spot the pavement adjoined a nine-inch wall of considerable length, which enclosed a yard and was toothed into a house. Some of the youths were standing with their backs to the wall, and others were running against them, or against the wall, with their hands extended. Not unnaturally, after the wall had suffered this form of abuse for about a quarter of an hour, part of it fell down. The noise brought the caretaker into the street, whereupon the youths dispersed in different directions.

In the subsequent action to determine whether the police were liable to provide compensation for the damage under the Riot (Damages) Act, 1886, it was necessary to show that property had been injured by "persons riotously and tumultuously assembled together". It was deduced from the existing criminal law that there are five necessary elements of a riot:

1. Number of persons, three at least.
2. A common purpose.
3. Execution or inception of the common purpose.
4. An intent to help one another, by force if necessary, against

any person who may oppose them in the execution of their common purpose.

5. Force or violence not merely used in demolishing, but displayed in such a manner as to alarm at least one person of reasonable firmness and courage.

The Court found that there was no reason to suppose that the youths would have resisted had the caretaker come forward earlier and required them to desist. Nor was the conduct of the youths such as would be calculated to alarm persons of reasonable firmness and courage. In the absence of elements four and five, therefore, the claim failed.

It is noticeable that there is no mention of a "tumultuous disturbance" being one of the essential ingredients of a riot, a situation which subsequent Courts have not seen fit to alter.

In *Bolands Ltd. v. London and Lancashire Fire Insurance Co.Ltd.* [1924] four armed men entered a bakery, held up the employees with revolvers and took away cash of £1250. The policy provided cover against loss of the cash by burglary, housebreaking and theft, but there was proviso which excluded loss directly or indirectly caused by, or happening through, or in consequence of riots. It was found in the House of Lords that the circumstances in which the money was stolen constituted a" riot" within the legal definition of the word, and the argument was not accepted that the exception did not apply because the riot was in truth the theft itself under another name. Lord Sumner agreed that the uninstructed layman would probably not think of the word "riot" in such circumstances, he would probably think of something more noisy. "But", he said, "there is no warrant here for saying that when the proviso uses a word which is emphatically a term of art it is to be confined in the interpretation of the policy to circumstances which are within popular notions of the subject and are not within the technical meaning of the word."

Again, in May 1962, four hooded men entered a jeweller's shop in the East End of London, armed with iron bars or coshes. After threatening the occupants they removed some of the property and made a successful escape. The Court held that, although there was only "bustle" and the whole activity was on too small a scale to be properly described as a "tumult", nevertheless the four men were riotously assembled, and the hold-up which had occurred, during which the property was stolen, constituted a riot, since all the classic

212

elements laid down in the *Field* case were present (*Dwyer Ltd. v. Receiver for the Metropolitan Police District*, 1967).

More recently, in the case of the *Andreas Lemos* [1982], Mr. Justice Staughton was able to adopt the definition of a riot provided in the *Field* case, and apply it to a marine policy. In June, 1977, the vessel was anchored in the Chittagong Roads, some 2.8 miles from the land, but within the port limits, when she was boarded at night by six or seven men armed with long knives, who stealthily proceeded to remove some of the ship's mooring lines. When they were discovered by a sailor on watch, they threatened him as he was running away to obtain assistance, and when more of the officers and crew arrived, threatened to stop them, before making their escape by jumping into the sea.

The learned judge commented that the word "riot" in its current and popular sense would mean the sort of civil disturbances that had recently occurred in Brixton, Bristol or Wormwood Scrubs. But he accepted the view that in construing an archaic expression still to be found in a policy of insurance, one cannot go by its ordinary meaning in our language today, but must treat it as a term of art, and interpret it in accordance with its original meaning. However, although he determined that a riot did occur, it was not complete until after the loss; thus the loss was not caused by a riot. "Clandestine thieves, who use or threaten violence in order to escape, after the theft had been committed, do not give rise to a loss by riots ...".

The definition of a "riot", followed by the English Courts so faithfully for over eighty years, has, however, not been supported in America, where, in the case of *Pan American World Airways Inc. v. The Aetna Casualty and Surety Co. and Others* [1975], the United States Court of Appeals expressed some criticism of English jurisprudence, and concluded that the meaning of the term should be in accord with the popular and usual meaning intended by the parties. Under this formula, a riot occurs when some multitude of individuals gathers and creates a tumult. This is the definition they found to be most in accord with common sense, feeling it was unlikely that the parties to the policies expected their dealings to be governed by an artificial and technical definition of a riot.

It can be recalled that in this case a Boeing 747 aircraft, while on a scheduled flight from Brussels to New York, was hijacked by two men working for the Popular Front for the Liberation of Palestine. The aircraft was ordered to Beirut where it was loaded with explosives, and then flown to Cairo where it was blown up and destroyed.

Although there were times,while it was on the ground, when there were more than two members of the Popular Front on board, the Court could not accept the notion of a flying riot in geographic instalments being squeezed into the ancient formula for a riot, which they saw to be a local disturbance, normally by a mob, not a complex, travelling conspiracy of the kind they were faced with. But at least they did agree that a riot required an assembly of at least three "actors", thereby achieving a little harmony with English law.*

In the same case it was held that a "civil commotion" was essentially a kind of domestic disturbance which can occur among fellow citizens of one community. Here the agents causing the disorder must gather together and cause a disturbance and tumult.

It can be seen that, in American eyes, the distinction between a "riot" and a "civil commotion" depends largely on the form of the disturbance. Much the same conclusion has been reached in the English Courts, but not without some difficulty caused by the famous Lord Mansfield in a case concerning the Gordon Riots heard in 1780.

In the case in question, *Langdale v. Mason*, a distillery owned by Langdale, a Catholic, was set on fire by a mob in London during the "no popery" riot led by Lord George Gordon, who resented the withdrawal of certain restrictions on the Roman Catholics. The distillery was covered by a fire policy issued by the Sun Fire Office, but this excluded losses caused by "civil commotion" and "military or usurped power".

In his summing up to the jury Lord Mansfield described a "civil commotion" as "an insurrection of the people for general purposes, though it may not amount to a rebellion where there is usurped power". In due course the jury decided that there had been a "civil commotion", although it could scarcely be said that there had been an insurrection within the usual meaning of that term. The Gordon Riots, which began as a rising against Roman Catholics, eventually degenerated into mere destruction and plunder, and there was never any attempt to overthrow the Government of the country.

Nevertheless, one might be justified in saying that it would require the wisdom of a Solomon to differentiate between a civil commotion and an insurrection when the words of Lord Mansfield have been quoted as authority on the meaning of "civil commotion" for the best part of two centuries. Fortunately, a judge of that name,

* For the effect of the Public Order Act, 1986, see the postscript at the end of this chapter.

Mr. Justice Solomon, assisted in that process in the South African Courts in the case of *Lindsay and Pirie v. The General Accident Fire and Life Assurance Corporation Ltd.* [1914]. After observing that there was no express exclusion of "insurrection" in the policy with which Lord Mansfield had to deal, he went onto say: "... I do not think we are justified in supposing that Lord Mansfield intended in his summing up to the jury to give an exhaustive definition of the term "civil commotion", but rather that he was explaining the words in reference to the facts of the particular case which he was trying ... Even if we accept his definition as an exhaustive one, I do not think that he could possibly have used the word insurrection in its ordinary sense of a rising of the people in open resistance against established authority with the object of supplanting that authority. On the contrary it would appear from the rest of his language that he used the word in its strictly etymological sense of 'rising', and that the effect of his direction to the jury was that a rising of the people (by which I presume he meant a considerable number of the population), for purposes of general mischief amounted to civil commotion within the sense of the exception to the insurance policy."

When Mr. Justice Mustill had cause to consider the situation in Beirut in January, 1976, in the case of *Spinney's [1948] Ltd.v. Royal Insurance Co. Ltd.* [1980], he found the above judgment most helpful, and decided there was nothing in the authorities compelling the Court to hold that a civil commotion must involve a revolt against the government, although the disturbances must have sufficient cohesion to prevent them from being the work of a mindless mob. In his opinion Lord Mansfield's summing up as a whole in the *Langdale* case was concerned with explaining to the jury that if there had been a rebellion or insurrection (perils not specifically excepted in the policy sued upon) the events would have fallen within the exception of usurped power; but that the jury need not concern themselves with this, because "civil commotion" was a wider exception, of which rebellion was not an ingredient. As Mustill, J. pointed out, the Gordon rioters were not seeking to take over power, but were intent on forcing the redress of a particular grievance.

Confusing as the cases may have been in the past there is, thus, in law, now a distinct borderline between the types of disorders insured under the strikes clauses as compared with those covered by the war clauses.

Perhaps not quite so distinct is the boundary between terrorism or politically motivated acts which fall under the war clauses rather than the strikes clauses. Although Clause 1.2 of the strikes clauses provides positive cover against such risks, it has to be borne in mind that, under Clause 3.10 in the *General Exclusions Clause*, the Underwriters are not liable for

> loss damage or expense caused by war civil war revolution rebellion insurrection, or civil strife arising therefrom, or any hostile act by or against a belligerent power.

Accordingly, there would seem to be occasions when it is apt to describe loss or damage arising from a political motive as being caused by a hostile act against a belligerent power; as, for instance, in the circumstances described in *Atlantic Mutual Insurance Co. v. King* [1919] in the first part of our study on the war perils. If the war perils apply there is, of course, no cover during land transit.

It is interesting to speculate how the present clauses would have applied if cargo had been damaged in transit during the ill-fated "Jameson Raid" which took place in the Transvaal in 1895. After Cape Colony had passed into British hands, the Boer descendants of the Dutch colonists trekked northwards to settle in the territory of the Transvaal, and considerable friction with the British remained. This was followed by the battle of Majuba Hill in 1881, in which the British were defeated, leading to the Transvaal being given self-government in internal affairs; external affairs remained under the guardianship of Great Britain. When gold was discovered, the "outsiders" who flooded into the territory by their thousands were subject to oppression or denial of political rights under the administration of President Kruger, and, naturally, further bitterness ensued.

In 1895, Dr. Leander S. Jameson, acting without the sanction of the British Government, but supported by his friend Cecil Rhodes, who was Prime Minister of Cape Colony at that time, organised an armed incursion into the Boer republic with a small party of men, with the object of aiding the outsiders against the oppressive measures of the president. This only made matters worse, for Dr. Jameson was taken prisoner, and, when Rhodes' connection with this armed attack on a friendly state was proved, he was forced to resign the premiership.

Although this action appears to have sown the seeds of the three year Boer War in 1899, it is clear that neither the republic nor the invading band could be described as a "belligerent power" at the time of the incident. Since it was also unauthorised by the British Government, there was also no act of war in the international sense, consequently there would be no reason for applying the war perils on those grounds. However, there was no doubt that the raiders were acting from a political motive, thereby bringing any claim for damage to cargo within the ambit of the strikes clauses. Of course, it might be argued that the raid was part of an insurrection planned by the outsiders, but, in the absence of sufficient proof to that effect Underwriters would be unable to bring themselves within the *War Exclusion Clause* expressed in section 3.10 of the strikes clauses.

The same sort of problem arises with acts of sabotage. In its most popular sense "sabotage" is related to deliberate damage carried out clandestinely in order to disrupt the economic or military resources of an enemy. Thus, an act of sabotage might be concerned with the waging of war, civil war, revolution, rebellion or insurrection, or simply constitute a hostile act against a belligerent power. On the other hand it may only be the means by which terrorists express a protest of a political nature. The word does not appear to have been defined in law, but the English Oxford Dictionary includes a variety of meanings, one of which is the malicious damaging or destruction of an employers' property by workmen during a strike. The motives which prompt the action are, therefore, clearly important when it comes to establishing whether the war clauses apply, so as to exclude loss or damage to goods occurring during land transit. Since most claims for sabotage will fall under the war or strikes clauses, it may well be asked what cover is provided by that specific peril when the *Institute Malicious Damage Clause* is employed in conjunction with the "B" and "C" Clauses, as its appearance there seems to imply a much wider meaning of the word "sabotage". Here it might be necessary to draw on a more general interpretation provided by the dictionary, which would tend to suggest that it could be applied to any indirect means employed to ruin, destroy or disable property deliberately and maliciously. The difference between "malicious acts", "vandalism" and "sabotage" is probably only distinguishable by the way the damage is inflicted.

UNCTAD have endeavoured to avoid this problem in their own composite text of "all risks" clauses by the exclusion of the following risks:

sabotage or terrorism committed with a political motive; detonation of an explosive caused by any person acting maliciously or from a political motive.

Finally, it will serve as a useful exercise to recall an incident which took place on the *Achille Lauro* in October, 1985, shortly after the eventful cruise during which the vessel was hijacked off Egypt by Palestinian commandos, and an American passenger was killed.

While the vessel was cruising off Piraeus the vessel's owners were informed that explosives had been placed in a car and in a container taken on board at Cairo. Although no cars or containers had been loaded at that port, the crew searched the ship, and, as a precaution, dumped part of a cargo of slot machines into the sea. As it happened, the alarm turned out to be false.

If the cargo had been insured on English conditions, it is quite possible that Underwriters would reject a claim under the war and strikes clauses on the basis that, whatever the motive might have been, no real peril existed, and there was merely the fear of an explosion, rather than any loss from an explosion itself (see *Becker Gray and Co. v. London Assurance Corporation*, 1918).

The unexpected dumping of the cargo would, however, clearly be a risk covered by the "A" Clauses, but to what extent would such a loss be recoverable under the "B" and "C" Clauses? Both sets cover loss or damage directly caused by "jettison", which is not necessarily confined to situations where goods are thrown overboard to release a ship from the grip of a strand, or to relieve her from the stress of bad weather (e.g. *Butler v. Wildman*, 1820 — money thrown overboard to avoid it falling into enemy hands; *Symington and Co. v. Union Insurance Society of Canton*, 1928 — goods thrown off a loading quay to avoid the spread of fire). Nevertheless, jettison of cargo, which is not a general average act, would come under the category of deliberate damage, and would thus be excluded under Clause 4.7 of the "B" and "C" Clauses if the destruction were to be treated as a wrongful act.

It just shows that, to be on the safe side, one should try and stick to the "A" Clauses ...

— — — — — — —

Postscript

The first part of the Public Order Act, 1986, has now come into effect, redefining the meaning of "riot". Instead of the requirement of 3 or more persons as hitherto, this has been increased to 12 as follows:

1.(1)   *Where 12 or more persons who are present together use or threaten unlawful violence for a common purpose and the conduct of them (taken together) is such as would cause a person of reasonable firmness present at the scene to fear for his personal safety, each of the persons using unlawful violence for the common purpose is guilty of riot.*

According to Section 10(2) the references in the Marine Insurance Act to "rioters" and "riot" in the Rules for Construction (Nos. 8 and 10) shall be construed in accordance with the above section on all policies taking effect on or after 1st April, 1987, unless a different intention appears.

There is a new offence of "violent disorder" which is similar to "riot", but only 3 or more persons need to be present together. There is, however, no requirement of a common purpose.

Appendix A

MARINE INSURANCE ACT, 1906

CHAPTER 41
(6 EDW. 7)

AN Act to codify the Law relating to Marine Insurance. (21st December 1906.)

BE it enacted by the King's most Excellent Majesty, by and with the advice and consent of the Lords Spiritual and Temporal, and Commons, in this present Parliament assembled, and by the authority of the same, as follows—

MARINE INSURANCE

Marine insurance defined

1. A contract of marine insurance is a contract whereby the insurer undertakes to indemnify the assured, in manner and to the extent thereby agreed, against marine losses, that is to say, the losses incident to marine adventure.

Mixed sea and land risks

2.—(1) A contract of marine insurance may, by its express terms, or by usage of trade, be extended so as to protect the assured against losses on inland waters or on any land risk which may be incidental to any sea voyage.

(2) Where a ship in course of building, or the launch of a ship, or any adventure analogous to a marine adventure, is covered by a policy in the form of a marine policy, the provisions of this Act, in so far as applicable, shall apply thereto; but, except as by this section provided, nothing in this Act. shall alter or affect any rule of law applicable to any contract of insurance other than a contract of marine insurance as by this Act defined.

Marine adventures and maritime perils defined

3.—(1) Subject to the provisions of this Act, every lawful marine adventure may be the subject of a contract of marine insurance.

(2) In particular there is a marine adventure where—

  (a) Any ship goods or other moveables are exposed to maritime perils. Such property is in this Act referred to as " insurable property ";
  (b) The earning or acquisition of any freight, passage money, commission, profit, or other pecuniary benefit, or the security for any advances, loan, or disbursements, is endangered by the exposure of insurable property to maritime perils:
  (c) Any liability to a third party may be incurred by the owner of, or other person interested in, or responsible for, insurable property, by reason of maritime perils.

" Maritime perils " means the perils consequent on, or incidental to, the navigation of the sea, that is to say, perils of the seas, fire, war perils, pirates, rovers, thieves, captures, seizures, restraints, and detainments of princes and peoples, jettisons, barratry, and any other perils, either of the like kind or which may be designated by the policy.

INSURABLE INTEREST

Avoiding of wagering or gaming contracts

4.—(1) Every contract of marine insurance by way of gaming or wagering is void.

(2) A contract of marine insurance is deemed to be a gaming or wagering contract—

(a) Where the assured has not an insurable interest as defined by this Act, and the contract is entered into with no expectation of acquiring such an interest; or

(b) Where the policy is made " interest or no interest," or " without further proof of interest than the policy itself," or " without benefit of salvage to the insurer," or subject to any other like term:

Provided that, where there is no possibility of salvage, a policy may be effected without benefit of salvage to the insurer.

Insurable interest defined

5.—(1) Subject to the provisions of this Act, every person has an insurable interest who is interested in a marine adventure.

(2) In particular, a person is interested in a marine adventure where he stands in any legal or equitable relation to the adventure or to any insurable property at risk therein, in consequence of which he may benefit by the safety or due arrival of insurable property, or may be prejudiced by its loss, or by damage thereto, or by the detention thereof, or may incur liability in respect thereof.

When interest must attach

6.—(1) The assured must be interested in the subject-matter insured at the time of the loss though he need not be interested when the insurance is effected:

Provided that where the subject-matter is insured " lost or not lost," the assured may recover although he may not have acquired his interest until after the loss, unless at the time of effecting the contract of insurance the assured was aware of the loss, and the insurer was not.

(2) Where the assured has no interest at the time of the loss he cannot acquire interest by any act or election after he is aware of the loss.

Defeasible or contingent interest

7.—(1) A defeasible interest is insurable, as also is a contingent interest.

(2) In particular, where the buyer of goods has insured them, he has an insurable interest, notwithstanding that he might, at his election, have rejected the goods, or have treated them as at the seller's risk, by reason of the latter's delay in making delivery or otherwise.

Partial interest

8. A partial interest of any nature is insurable.

Re-insurance

9.—(1) The insurer under a contract of marine insurance has an insurable interest in his risk, and may re-insure in respect of it.

(2) Unless the policy otherwise provides, the original assured has no right or interest in respect of such re-insurance.

Bottomry

10. The lender of money on bottomry or respondentia has an insurable interest in respect of the loan.

Master's and seamen's wages

11. The master or any member of the crew of a ship has an insurable interest in respect of his wages.

Advance freight

12. In the case of advance freight, the person advancing the freight has an insurable interest, in so far as such freight is not repayable in case of loss.

Charges of insurance

13. The assured has an insurable interest in the charges of any insurance which he may effect.

Quantum of interest

14.—(1) Where the subject-matter insured is mortgaged, the mortgagor has an insurable interest in the full value thereof, and the mortgagee has an insurable interest in respect of any sum due or to become due under the mortgage.

(2) A mortgagee, consignee, or other person having an interest in the subject-matter insured may insure on behalf and for the benefit of other persons interested as well as for his own benefit.

(3) The owner of insurable property has an insurable interest in respect of the full value thereof, notwithstanding that some third person may have agreed, or be liable, to indemnify him in case of loss.

Assignment of interest

15. Where the assured assigns or otherwise parts with his interest in the subject-matter insured, he does not thereby transfer to the assignee his rights under the contract of insurance, unless there be an express or implied agreement with the assignee to that effect.

But the provisions of this section do not affect a transmission of interest by operation of law.

INSURABLE VALUE

Measure of insurable value

16. Subject to any express provision or valuation in the policy, the insurable value of the subject-matter insured must be ascertained as follows—

(1) In insurance on ship, the insurable value is the value at the commencement of the risk, of the ship, including her outfit, provisions and stores for the officers and crew, money advanced for seamen's wages, and other disbursements (if any) incurred to make the ship fit for the voyage or adventure contemplated by the policy, plus the charges of insurance upon the whole:

The insurable value, in the case of a steamship, includes also the machinery, boilers, and coals and engine stores if owned by the assured, and, in the case of a ship engaged in a special trade, the ordinary fittings requisite for that trade:

(2) In insurance on freight, whether paid in advance or otherwise, the insurable value is the gross amount of the freight at the risk of the assured, plus the charges of insurance:

(3) In insurance on goods or merchandise, the insurable value is the prime cost of the property insured, plus the expenses of and incidental to shipping and the charges of insurance upon the whole:

(4) In insurance or any other subject-matter, the insurable value is the amount at the risk of the assured when the policy attaches, plus the charges of insurance.

Insurance is uberrimae fidei

17. A contract of marine insurance is a contract based upon the utmost good faith, and, if the utmost good faith be not observed by either party, the contract may be avoided by the other party.

Disclosure by assured

18.—(1) Subject to the provisions of this section, the assured must disclose to the insurer, before the contract is concluded, every material circumstance which is known to the assured, and the assured is deemed to know every circumstance which, in the ordinary course of business, ought to be known by him. If the assured fails to make such disclosure, the insurer may avoid the contract.

(2) Every circumstance is material which would influence the judgment of a prudent insurer in fixing the premium, or determining whether he will take the risk.

(3) In the absence of inquiry the following circumstances need not be disclosed, namely—

(a) Any circumstance which diminishes the risk;

(b) Any circumstance which is known or presumed to be known to the insurer. The insurer is presumed to know matters of common notoriety or knowledge, and matters which an insurer in the ordinary course of his business, as such, ought to know;

(c) Any circumstance as to which information is waived by the insurer;

(d) Any circumstance which it is superfluous to disclose by reason of any express or implied warranty.

(4) Whether any particular circumstance, which is not disclosed, be material or not is, in each case, a question of fact.

(5) The term "circumstance" includes any communication made to, or information received by, the assured.

Disclosure by agent effecting insurance

19. Subject to the provisions of the preceding section as to circumstances which need not be disclosed, where an insurance is effected for the assured by an agent, the agent must disclose to the insurer—

(a) Every material circumstance which is known to himself, and an agent to insure is deemed to know every circumstance which in the ordinary course of business ought to be known by, or to have been communicated to, him; and

(b) Every material circumstance which the assured is bound to disclose, unless it come to his knowledge too late to communicate it to the agent.

Representations pending negotiation of contract

20.—(1) Every material representation made by the assured or his agent to the insurer during the negotiations for the contract, and before the contract is concluded, must be true. If it be untrue the insurer may avoid the contract.

(2) A representation is material which would influence the judgment of a prudent insurer in fixing the premium, or determining whether he will take the risk.

(3) A representation may be either a representation as to a matter of fact, or as to a matter of expectation or belief.

(4) A representation as to a matter of fact is true, if it be substantially

223

correct, that is to say, if the difference between what is represented and what is actually correct would not be considered material by a prudent insurer.

(5) A representation as to a matter of expectation or belief is true if it be made in good faith.

(6) A representation may be withdrawn or corrected before the contract is concluded.

(7) Whether a particular representation be material or not is, in each case, a question of fact.

When contract is deemed to be concluded

21. A contract of marine insurance is deemed to be concluded when the proposal of the assured is accepted by the insurer, whether the policy be then issued or not; and for the purpose of showing when the proposal was accepted, reference may be made to the slip or covering note or other customary memorandum of the contract, *although it be unstamped.**

THE POLICY

Contract must be embodied in policy

22. Subject to the provisions of any statute, a contract of marine insurance is inadmissible in evidence unless it is embodied in a marine policy in accordance with this Act. The policy may be executed and issued either at the time when the contract is concluded, or afterwards.

What policy must specify†

23. A marine policy must specify—
    (1) The name of the assured, or of some person who effects the insurance on his behalf:
    (2) The subject-matter insured and the risk insured against:
    (3) The voyage, or period of time, or both, as the case may be, covered by the insurance:
    (4) The sum or sums insured:
    (5) The name or names of the insurers.

Signature of insurer

24.—(1) A marine policy must be signed by or on behalf of the insurer, provided that in the case of a corporation the corporate seal may be sufficient, but nothing in this section shall be construed as requiring the subscription of a corporation to be under seal.

(2) Where a policy is subscribed by or on behalf of two or more insurers, each subscription, unless the contrary be expressed, constitutes a distinct contract with the assured.

Voyage and time policies

25.—(1) Where the contract is to insure the subject-matter at and from, or from one place to another or others, the policy is called a "voyage policy," and where the contract is to insure the subject-matter for a definite period of time the policy is called a "time policy." A contract for both voyage and time may be included in the same policy.

‡ (2) Subject to the provisions of section eleven of the Finance Act, 1901, a time policy which is made for any time exceeding twelve months is invalid.

* The words italicised were repealed by the Finance Act, 1959.
† Sub-sections (2) to (5) inclusive were repealed by the Finance Act, 1959.
‡ This sub-section (2) was repealed by the Finance Act, 1959.

Designation of subject-matter

26.—(1) The subject-matter insured must be designated in a marine policy with reasonable certainty.

(2) The nature and extent of the interest of the assured in the subject-matter insured need not be specified in the policy.

(3) Where the policy designates the subject-matter insured in general terms, it shall be construed to apply to the interest intended by the assured to be covered.

(4) In the application of this section regard shall be had to any usage regulating the designation of the subject-matter insured.

Valued policy

27.—(1) A policy may be either valued or unvalued.

(2) A valued policy is a policy which specifies the agreed value of the subject-matter insured.

(3) Subject to the provisions of this Act, and in the absence of fraud, the value fixed by the policy is, as between the insurer and assured, conclusive of the insurable value of the subject intended to be insured, whether the loss be total or partial.

(4) Unless the policy otherwise provides, the value fixed by the policy is not conclusive for the purpose of determining whether there has been a constructive total loss.

Unvalued policy

28. An unvalued policy is a policy which does not specify the value of the subject-matter insured, but, subject to the limit of the sum insured, leaves the insurable value to be subsequently ascertained, in the manner hereinbefore specified.

Floating policy by ship or ships

29.—(1) A floating policy is a policy which describes the insurance in general terms, and leaves the name of the ship or ships and other particulars to be defined by subsequent declaration.

(2) The subsequent declaration or declarations may be made by indorsement on the policy, or in other customary manner.

(3) Unless the policy otherwise provides, the declarations must be made in the order of dispatch or shipment. They must, in the case of goods, comprise all consignments within the terms of the policy, and the value of the goods or other property must be honestly stated, but an omission or erroneous declaration may be rectified even after loss or arrival, provided the omission or declaration was made in good faith.

(4) Unless the policy otherwise provides, where a declaration of value is not made until after notice of loss or arrival, the policy must be treated as an unvalued policy as regards the subject-matter of that declaration.

Construction of terms in policy

30.—(1) A policy may be in the form in the First Schedule to this Act.

(2) Subject to the provisions of this Act, and unless the context of the policy otherwise requires, the terms and expressions mentioned in the First Schedule to this Act shall be construed as having the scope and meaning in that schedule assigned to them.

Premium to be arranged

31.—(1) Where an insurance is effected at a premium to be arranged, and no arrangement is made, a reasonable premium is payable.

(2) Where an insurance is effected on the terms that an additional premium

is to be arranged in a given event, and that event happens but no arrangement is made, then a reasonable additional premium is payable.

Double insurance
32.—(1) Where two or more policies are effected by or on behalf of the assured on the same adventure and interest or any part thereof, and the sums insured exceed the indemnity allowed by this Act, the assured is said to be over-insured by double insurance.

(2) Where the assured is over-insured by double insurance—

(a) The assured, unless the policy otherwise provides, may claim payment from the insurers in such order as he may think fit, provided that he is not entitled to receive any sum in excess of the indemnity allowed by this Act;

(b) Where the policy under which the assured claims is a valued policy, the assured must give credit as against the valuation for any sum received by him under any other policy without regard to the actual value of the subject-matter insured;

(c) Where the policy under which the assured claims is an unvalued policy he must give credit, as against the full insurable value, for any sum received by him under any other policy;

(d) Where the assured receives any sum in excess of the indemnity allowed by this Act, he is deemed to hold such sum in trust for the insurers according to their right of contribution among themselves.

Nature of warranty
33.—(1) A warranty, in the following sections relating to warranties, means a promissory warranty, that is to say, a warranty by which the assured undertakes that some particular thing shall or shall not be done, or that some condition shall be fulfilled, or whereby he affirms or negatives the existence of a particular state of facts.

(2) A warranty may be express or implied.

(3) A warranty, as above defined, is a condition which must be exactly complied with, whether it be material to the risk or not. If it be not so complied with, then, subject to any express provision in the policy, the insurer is discharged from liability as from the date of the breach of warranty, but without prejudice to any liability incurred by him before that date.

When breach of warranty excused
34.—(1) Non-compliance with a warranty is excused when, by reason of a change of circumstances, the warranty ceases to be applicable to the circumstances of the contract, or when compliance with the warranty is rendered unlawful by any subsequent law.

(2) Where a warranty is broken, the assured cannot avail himself of the defence that the breach has been remedied, and the warranty complied with, before loss.

(3) A breach of warranty may be waived by the insurer.

Express warranties
35.—(1) An express warranty may be in any form of words from which the intention to warrant is to be inferred.

(2) An express warranty must be included in, or written upon, the policy, or must be contained in some document incorporated by reference into the policy.

(3) An express warranty does not exclude an implied warranty, unless it be inconsistent therewith.

Warranty of neutrality

36.—(1) Where insurable property, whether ship or goods, is expressly warranted neutral, there is an implied condition that the property shall have a neutral character at the commencement of the risk and that, so far as the assured can control the matter, its neutral character shall be preserved during the risk.

(2) Where a ship is expressly warranted " neutral " there is also an implied condition that, so far as the assured can control the matter, she shall be properly documented, that is to say, that she shall carry the necessary papers to establish her neutrality, and that she shall not falsify or suppress her papers, or use simulated papers. If any loss occurs through breach of this condition, the insurer may avoid the contract.

No implied warranty of nationality

37. There is no implied warranty as to the nationality of a ship, or that her nationality shall not be changed during the risk.

Warranty of good safety

38. Where the subject-matter insured is warranted " well " or " in good safety " on a particular day, it is sufficient if it be safe at any time during that day.

Warranty of seaworthiness of ship

39.—(1) In a voyage policy, there is an implied warranty that at the commencement of the voyage the ship shall be seaworthy for the purpose of the particular adventure insured.

(2) Where the policy attaches while the ship is in port, there is also an implied warranty that she shall, at the commencement of the risk, be reasonably fit to encounter the ordinary perils of the port.

(3) Where the policy relates to a voyage which is performed in different stages, during which the ship requires different kinds of further preparation or equipment, there is an implied warranty that at the commencement of each stage the ship is seaworthy in respect of such preparation or equipment for the purpose of that stage.

(4) A ship is deemed to be seaworthy when she is reasonably fit in all respects to encounter the ordinary perils of the seas of the adventure insured.

(5) In a time policy there is no implied warranty that the ship shall be seaworthy at any stage of the adventure, but where, with the privity of the assured, the ship is sent to sea in an unseaworthy state, the insurer is not liable for any loss attributable to unseaworthiness.

No implied warranty that goods are seaworthy

40.—(1) In a policy on goods or other moveables there is no implied warranty that the goods or moveables are seaworthy.

(2) In a voyage policy on goods or other moveables there is an implied warranty that at the commencement of the voyage the ship is not only seaworthy as a ship, but also that she is reasonably fit to carry the goods or other moveables to the destination contemplated by the policy.

Warranty of legality

41. There is an implied warranty that the adventure insured is a lawful

one, and that, so far as the assured can control the matter, the adventure shall be carried out in a lawful manner.

THE VOYAGE

Implied condition as to commencement of risk

42.—(1) Where the subject-matter is insured by a voyage policy as " at and from " or " from " a particular place, it is not necessary that the ship should be at that place when the contract is concluded, but there is an implied condition that the adventure shall be commenced within a reasonable time, and that if the adventure be not so commenced the insurer may avoid the contract.

(2) The implied condition may be negatived by showing that the delay was caused by circumstances known to the insurer before the contract was concluded, or by showing that he waived the condition.

Alteration of port of departure

43. Where the place of departure is specified by the policy, and the ship instead of sailing from that place sails from any other place, the risk does not attach.

Sailing for different destination

44. Where the destination is specified in the policy, and the ship, instead of sailing for that destination, sails for any other destination, the risk does not attach.

Change of voyage

45.—(1) Where, after the commencement of the risk, the destination of the ship is voluntarily changed from the destination contemplated by the policy, there is said to be a change of voyage.

(2) Unless the policy otherwise provides, where there is a change of voyage, the insurer is discharged from liability as from the time of change, that is to say, as from the time when the determination to change it is manifested; and it is immaterial that the ship may not in fact have left the course of voyage contemplated by the policy when the loss occurs.

Deviation

46.—(1) Where a ship, without lawful excuse, deviates from the voyage contemplated by the policy, the insurer is discharged from liability as from the time of deviation, and it is immaterial that the ship may have regained her route before any loss occurs.

(2) There is a deviation from the voyage contemplated by the policy—

    (*a*) Where the course of the voyage is specifically designated by the policy, and that course is departed from; or

    (*b*) Where the course of the voyage is not specifically designated by the policy, but the usual and customary course is departed from.

(3) The intention to deviate is immaterial; there must be a deviation in fact to discharge the insurer from his liability under the contract.

Several ports of discharge

47.—(1) Where several ports of discharge are specified by the policy, the ship may proceed to all or any of them, but, in the absence of any usage or sufficient cause to the contrary, she must proceed to them, or such of them as she goes to, in the order designated by the policy. If she does not there is a deviation.

(2) Where the policy is to " ports of discharge," within a given area, which are not named, the ship must, in the absence of any usage or sufficient cause

to the contrary, proceed to them, or such of them as she goes to, in their geographical order. If she does not there is a deviation.

Delay in voyage
48. In the case of a voyage policy, the adventure insured must be prosecuted throughout its course with reasonable despatch, and, if without lawful excuse it is not so prosecuted, the insurer is discharged from liability as from the time when the delay became unreasonable.

Excuses for deviation or delay
49.—(1) Deviation or delay in prosecuting the voyage contemplated by the policy is excused—
    (*a*) Where authorised by any special term in the policy; or
    (*b*) Where caused by circumstances beyond the control of the master and his employer; or
    (*c*) Where reasonably necessary in order to comply with an express or implied warranty; or
    (*d*) Where reasonably necessary for the safety of the ship or subject-matter insured; or
    (*e*) For the purpose of saving human life, or aiding a ship in distress where human life may be in danger; or
    (*f*) Where reasonably necessary for the purpose of obtaining medical or surgical aid for any person on board the ship; or
    (*g*) Where caused by the barratrous conduct of the master or crew, if barratry be one of the perils insured against.
(2) When the cause excusing the deviation or delay ceases to operate, the ship must resume her course, and prosecute her voyage with reasonable despatch.

ASSIGNMENT OF POLICY
When and how policy is assignable
50.—(1) A marine policy is assignable unless it contains terms expressly prohibiting assignment. It may be assigned either before or after loss.
(2) Where a marine policy has been assigned so as to pass the beneficial interest in such policy, the assignee of the policy is entitled to sue thereon in his own name; and the defendant is entitled to make any defence arising out of the contract which he would have been entitled to make if the action had been brought in the name of the person by or on behalf of whom the policy was effected.
(3) A marine policy may be assigned by indorsement thereon or in other customary manner.

Assured who has no interest cannot assign
51. Where the assured has parted with or lost his interest in the subject-matter insured, and has not, before or at the time of so doing expressly or impliedly agreed to assign the policy, any subsequent assignment of the policy is inoperative:
Provided that nothing in this section affects the assignment of a policy after loss.

THE PREMIUM
When premium payable
52. Unless otherwise agreed, the duty of the assured or his agent to pay the premium, and the duty of the insurer to issue the policy to the assured

or his agent, are concurrent conditions, and the insurer is not bound to issue the policy until payment or tender of the premium.

Policy effected through broker

53.—(1) Unless otherwise agreed, where a marine policy is effected on behalf of the assured by a broker, the broker is directly responsible to the insurer for the premium, and the insurer is directly responsible to the assured for the amount which may be payable in respect of losses, or in respect of returnable premium.

(2) Unless otherwise agreed, the broker has, as against the assured, a lien upon the policy for the amount of the premium and his charges in respect of effecting the policy; and, where he has dealt with the person who employs him as a principal, he has also a lien on the policy in respect of any balance on any insurance account which may be due to him from such person, unless when the debt was incurred he had reason to believe that such person was only an agent.

Effect of receipt on policy

54. Where a marine policy effected on behalf of the assured by a broker acknowledges the receipt of the premium, such acknowledgment is, in the absence of fraud, conclusive as between the insurer and the assured, but not as between the insurer and broker.

LOSS AND ABANDONMENT

Included and excluded losses

55.—(1) Subject to the provisions of this act, and unless the policy otherwise provides, the insurer is liable for any loss proximately caused by a peril insured against, but, subject as aforesaid, he is not liable for any loss which is not proximately caused by a peril insured against.

(2) In particular—
- (a) The insurer is not liable for any loss attributable to the wilful misconduct of the assured, but unless the policy otherwise provides, he is liable for any loss proximately caused by a peril insured against, even though the loss would not have happened but for the misconduct or negligence of the master or crew;
- (b) Unless the policy otherwise provides, the insurer on ship or goods is not liable for any loss proximately caused by delay, although the delay be caused by a peril insured against;
- (c) Unless the policy otherwise provides, the insurer is not liable for ordinary wear and tear, ordinary leakage and breakage, inherent vice or nature of the subject-matter insured, or for any loss proximately caused by rats or vermin, or for any injury to machinery not proximately caused by maritime perils.

Partial and total loss

56.—(1) A loss may be either total or partial. Any loss other than a total loss, as hereinafter defined, is a partial loss.

(2) A total loss may be either an actual total loss, or a constructive total loss.

(3) Unless a different intention appears from the terms of the policy, an insurance against total loss includes a constructive, as well as an actual, total loss.

(4) Where the assured brings an action for a total loss and the evidence proves only a partial loss, he may, unless the policy otherwise provides. recover for a partial loss.

(5) Where goods reach their destination in specie, but by reason of obliteration of marks, or otherwise, they are incapable of identification, the loss, if any, is partial, and not total.

Actual total loss

57.—(1) Where the subject-matter insured is destroyed, or so damaged as to cease to be a thing of the kind insured, or where the assured is irretrievably deprived thereof, there is an actual total loss.

(2) In the case of an actual total loss no notice of abandonment need be given.

Missing ship

58. Where the ship concerned in the adventure is missing, and after the lapse of a reasonable time no news of her has been received, an actual total loss may be presumed.

Effect of transhipment, etc.

59. Where, by a peril insured against, the voyage is interrupted at an intermediate port or place, under such circumstances as, apart from any special stipulation in the contract of affreightment, to justify the master in landing and reshipping the goods or other moveables, or in transhipping them, and sending them on to their destination, the liability of the insurer continues, notwithstanding the landing or transhipment.

Constructive total loss defined

60.—(1) Subject to any express provision in the policy, there is a constructive total loss where the subject-matter insured is reasonably abandoned on account of its actual total loss appearing to be unavoidable, or because it could not be preserved from actual total loss without an expenditure which would exceed its value when the expenditure had been incurred.

(2) In particular, there is a constructive total loss—
  (i) Where the assured is deprived of the possession of his ship or goods by a peril insured against, and (*a*) it is unlikely that he can recover the ship or goods, as the case may be, or (*b*) the cost of recovering the ship or goods, as the case may be, would exceed their value when recovered; or
  (ii) In the case of damage to a ship, where she is so damaged by a peril insured against that the cost of repairing the damage would exceed the value of the ship when repaired.
       In estimating the cost of repairs, no deduction is to be made in respect of general average contributions to those repairs payable by other interests, but account is to be taken of the expense of future salvage operations and of any future general average contribution to which the ship would be liable if repaired; or
  (iii) In the case of damage to goods, where the cost of repairing the damage and forwarding the goods to their destination would exceed their value on arrival.

Effect of constructive total loss

61. Where there is a constructive total loss the assured may either treat the loss as a partial loss, or abandon the subject-matter insured to the insurer and treat the loss as if it were an actual total loss.

Notice of abandonment

62.—(1) Subject to the provisions of this section, where the assured elects to abandon the subject-matter insured to the insurer, he must give notice of abandonment. If he fails to do so the loss can only be treated as a partial loss.

(2) Notice of abandonment may be given in writing, or by word of mouth, or partly in writing and partly by word of mouth, and may be given in any terms which indicate the intention of the assured to abandon his insured interest in the subject-matter insured unconditionally to the insurer.

(3) Notice of abandonment must be given with reasonable diligence after the receipt of reliable information of the loss, but where the information is of a doubtful character the assured is entitled to a reasonable time to make inquiry.

(4) Where notice of abandonment is properly given, the rights of the assured are not prejudiced by the fact that the insurer refuses to accept the abandonment.

(5) The acceptance of an abandonment may be either express or implied from the conduct of the insurer. The mere silence of the insurer after notice is not an acceptance.

(6) Where notice of abandonment is accepted the abandonment is irrevocable. The acceptance of the notice conclusively admits liability for the loss and the sufficiency of the notice.

(7) Notice of abandonment is unnecessary where, at the time when the assured receives information of the loss, there would be no possibility of benefit to the insurer if notice were given to him.

(8) Notice of abandonment may be waived by the insurer.

(9) Where an insurer has re-insured his risk, no notice of abandonment need be given by him.

Effect of abandonment

63.—(1) Where there is a valid abandonment the insurer is entitled to take over the interest of the assured in whatever may remain of the subject-matter insured, and all proprietary rights incidental thereto.

(2) Upon the abandonment of a ship, the insurer thereof is entitled to any freight in course of being earned, and which is earned by her subsequent to the casualty causing the loss, less the expenses of earning it incurred after the casualty; and where the ship is carrying the owner's goods, the insurer is entitled to a reasonable remuneration for the carriage of them subsequent to the casualty causing the loss.

PARTIAL LOSSES (INCLUDING SALVAGE AND GENERAL AVERAGE AND PARTICULAR CHARGES)

Particular average loss

64.—(1) A particular average loss is a partial loss of the subject-matter insured, caused by a peril insured against, and which is not a general average loss.

(2) Expenses incurred by or on behalf of the assured for the safety or preservation of the subject-matter insured, other than general average and salvage charges, are called particular charges. Particular charges are not included in particular average.

Salvage charges

65.—(1) Subject to any express provision in the policy salvage charges incurred in preventing a loss by perils insured against may be recovered as a loss by those perils.

(2) " Salvage charges " means the charges recoverable under maritime law by a salvor independently of contract. They do not include the expenses of services in the nature of salvage rendered by the assured or his agents, or

any person employed for hire by them, for the purpose of averting a peril insured against. Such expenses, where properly incurred, may be recovered as particular charges or as a general average loss, according to the circumstances under which they were incurred.

General average loss

66.—(1) A general average loss is a loss caused by or directly consequential on a general average act. It includes a general average expenditure as well as a general average sacrifice.

(2) There is a general average act where any extraordinary sacrifice or expenditure is voluntarily and reasonably made or incurred in time of peril for the purpose of preserving the property imperilled in the common adventure.

(3) Where there is a general average loss, the party on whom it falls is entitled, subject to the conditions imposed by maritime law, to a rateable contribution from the other parties interested, and such contribution is called a general average contribution.

(4) Subject to any express provision in the policy, where the assured has incurred a general average expenditure, he may recover from the insurer in respect of the proportion of the loss which falls upon him; and, in the case of a general average sacrifice, he may recover from the insurer in respect of the whole loss without having enforced his right of contribution from the other parties liable to contribute.

(5) Subject to any express provision in the policy, where the assured has paid, or is liable to pay, a general average contribution in respect of the subject insured, he may recover therefor from the insurer.

(6) In the absence of express stipulation, the insurer is not liable for any general average loss or contribution where the loss was not incurred for the purpose of avoiding, or in connexion with the avoidance of, a peril insured against.

(7) Where ship, freight, and cargo, or any two of those interests, are owned by the same assured, the liability of the insurer in respect of general average losses or contributions is to be determined as if those subjects were owned by different persons.

MEASURE OF INDEMNITY

Extent of liability of insurer for loss

67.—(1) The sum which the assured can recover in respect of a loss on a policy by which he is insured, in the case of an unvalued policy to the full extent of the insurable value, or, in the case of a valued policy to the full extent of the value fixed by the policy, is called the measure of indemnity.

(2) Where there is a loss recoverable under the policy, the insurer, or each insurer if there be more than one, is liable for such proportion of the measure of indemnity as the amount of his subscription bears to the value fixed by the policy in the case of a valued policy, or to the insurable value in the case of an unvalued policy.

Total loss

68. Subject to the provisions of this Act and to any express provisions in the policy, where there is a total loss of the subject-matter insured—

(1) If the policy be a valued policy, the measure of indemnity is the sum fixed by the policy:

(2) If the policy be an unvalued policy, the measure of indemnity is the insurable value of the subject-matter insured.

233

Partial loss of ship
69. Where a ship is damaged, but is not totally lost, the measure of indemnity, subject to any express provision in the policy, is as follows—

(1) Where the ship has been repaired, the assured is entitled to the reasonable cost of the repairs, less the customary deductions, but not exceeding the sum insured in respect of any one casualty:

(2) Where the ship has been only partially repaired, the assured is entitled to the reasonable cost of such repairs, computed as above, and also to be indemnified for the reasonable depreciation, if any, arising from the unrepaired damage, provided that the aggregate amount shall not exceed the cost of repairing the whole damage, computed as above:

(3) Where the ship has not been repaired, and has not been sold in her damaged state during the risk, the assured is entitled to be indemnified for the reasonable depreciation arising from the unrepaired damage, but not exceeding the reasonable cost of repairing such damage, computed as above.

Partial loss of freight
70. Subject to any express provision in the policy, where there is a partial loss of freight, the measure of indemnity is such proportion of the sum fixed by the policy in the case of a valued policy, or of the insurable value in the case of an unvalued policy, as the proportion of freight lost by the assured bears to the whole freight at the risk of the assured under the policy.

Partial loss of goods, merchandise, etc.
71. Where there is a partial loss of goods, merchandise, or other moveables, the measure of indemnity, subject to any express provision in the policy, is as follows—

(1) Where part of the goods, merchandise or other moveables insured by a valued policy is totally lost, the measure of indemnity is such proportion of the sum fixed by the policy as the insurable value of the part lost bears to the insurable value of the whole, ascertained as in the case of an unvalued policy:

(2) Where part of the goods, merchandise or other moveables insured by an unvalued policy is totally lost, the measure of indemnity is the insurable value of the part lost, ascertained as in case of total loss:

(3) Where the whole or any part of the goods or merchandise insured has been delivered damaged at its destination, the measure of indemnity is such proportion of the sum fixed by the policy in the case of a valued policy, or of the insurable value in the case of an unvalued policy, as the difference between the gross sound and damaged values at the place of arrival bears to the gross sound value:

(4) " Gross value " means the wholesale price or, if there be no such price, the estimated value, with, in either case, freight, landing charges, duty paid beforehand; provided that, in the case of goods or merchandise customarily sold in bond, the bonded price is deemed to be the gross value. " Gross proceeds " means the actual price obtained at a sale where all charges on sale are paid by the sellers.

234

Apportionment of valuation

72.—(1) Where different species of property are insured under a single valuation, the valuation must be apportioned over the different species in proportion to their respective insurable values, as in the case of an unvalued policy. The insured value of any part of a species is such proportion of the total insured value of the same as the insurable value of the part bears to the insurable value of the whole, ascertained in both cases as provided by this Act.

(2) Where a valuation has to be apportioned, and particulars of the prime cost of each separate species, quality, or description of goods cannot be ascertained, the division of the valuation may be made over the net arrived sound values of the different species, qualities, or descriptions of goods.

General average contributions and salvage charges

73.—(1) Subject to any express provision in the policy, where the assured has paid, or is liable for, any general average contribution, the measure of indemnity is the full amount of such contribution, if the subject-matter liable to contribution is insured for its full contributory value; but, if such subject-matter be not insured for its full contributory value, or if only part of it be insured, the indemnity payable by the insurer must be reduced in proportion to the under-insurance, and where there has been a particular average loss which constitutes a deduction from the contributory value, and for which the insurer is liable, that amount must be deducted from the insured value in order to ascertain what the insurer is liable to contribute.

(2) Where the insurer is liable for salvage charges the extent of his liability must be determined on the like principle.

Liabilities to third parties

74. Where the assured has effected an insurance in express terms against any liability to a third party, the measure of indemnity, subject to any express provision in the policy, is the amount paid or payable by him to such third party in respect of such liability.

General provisions as to measure of indemnity

75.—(1) Where there has been a loss in respect of any subject-matter not expressly provided for in the foregoing provisions of this Act, the measure of indemnity shall be ascertained, as nearly as may be, in accordance with those provisions, in so far as applicable to the particular case.

(2) Nothing in the provisions of this Act relating to the measure of indemnity shall affect the rules relating to double insurance, or prohibit the insurer from disproving interest wholly or in part, or from showing that at the time of the loss the whole or any part of the subject-matter insured was not at risk under the policy.

Particular average warranties

76.—(1) Where the subject-matter insured is warranted free from particular average, the assured cannot recover for a loss of part, other than a loss incurred by a general average sacrifice, unless the contract contained in the policy be apportionable; but, if the contract be apportionable, the assured may recover for a total loss of any apportionable part.

(2) Where the subject-matter insured is warranted free from particular average, either wholly or under a certain percentage, the insurer is nevertheless liable for salvage charges, and for particular charges and other expenses properly incurred pursuant to the provisions of the suing and labouring clause in order to avert a loss insured against.

235

(3) Unless the policy otherwise provides, where the subject-matter insured is warranted free from particular average under a specified percentage, a general average loss cannot be added to a particular average loss to make up the specified percentage.

(4) For the purpose of ascertaining whether the specified percentage has been reached, regard shall be had only to the actual loss suffered by the subject-matter insured. Particular charges and the expenses of and incidental to ascertaining and proving the loss must be excluded.

Successive losses

77.—(1) Unless the policy otherwise provides, and subject to the provisions of this Act, the insurer is liable for successive losses, even though the total amount of such losses may exceed the sum insured.

(2) Where, under the same policy, a partial loss, which has not been repaired or otherwise made good, is followed by a total loss, the assured can only recover in respect of the total loss.

Provided that nothing in this section shall affect the liability of the insurer under the suing and labouring clause.

Suing and labouring clause

78.—(1) Where the policy contains a suing and labouring clause, the engagement thereby entered into is deemed to be supplementary to the contract of insurance, and the assured may recover from the insurer any expenses properly incurred pursuant to the clause, notwithstanding that the insurer may have paid for a total loss, or that the subject-matter may have been warranted free from particular average, either wholly or under a certain percentage.

(2) General average losses and contributions and salvage charges, as defined by this Act, are not recoverable under the suing and labouring clause.

(3) Expenses incurred for the purpose of averting or diminishing any loss not covered by the policy are not recoverable under the suing and labouring clause.

(4) It is the duty of the assured and his agents, in all cases, to take such measures as may be reasonable for the purpose of averting or minimising a loss.

Right of subrogation

79.—(1) Where the insurer pays for a total loss, either of the whole, or in the case of goods of any apportionable part, of the subject-matter insured, he thereupon becomes entitled to take over the interest of the assured in whatever may remain of the subject-matter so paid for, and he is thereby subrogated to all the rights and remedies of the assured in and in respect of that subject-matter as from the time of the casualty causing the loss.

(2) Subject to the foregoing provisions, where the insurer pays for a partial loss, he acquires no title to the subject-matter insured, or such part of it as may remain, but he is thereupon subrogated to all rights and remedies of the assured in and in respect of the subject-matter insured as from the time of the casualty causing the loss, in so far as the assured has been indemnified, according to this Act, by such payment for the loss.

Right of contribution

80.—(1) Where the assured is over-insured by double insurance, each insurer is bound, as between himself and the other insurers, to contribute rateably to the loss in proportion to the amount for which he is liable under his contract.

(2) If any insurer pays more than his proportion of the loss he is entitled to maintain an action for contribution against the other insurers, and is entitled to the like remedies as a surety who has paid more than his proportion of the debt.

Effect of under-insurance

81. Where the assured is insured for an amount less than the insurable value or, in the case of a valued policy, for an amount less than the policy valuation, he is deemed to be his own insurer in respect of the uninsured balance.

RETURN OF PREMIUM

Enforcement of return

82. Where the premium, or a proportionate part thereof is, by this Act, declared to be returnable : —

> (a) If already paid, it may be recovered by the assured from the insurer; and
>
> (b) If unpaid, it may be retained by the assured or his agent.

Return by agreement

83. Where the policy contains a stipulation for the return of the premium, or a proportionate part thereof, on the happening of a certain event, and that event happens, the premium, or, as the case may be, the proportionate part thereof, is thereupon returnable to the assured.

Return for failure of consideration

84.—(1) Where the consideration for the payment of the premium totally fails, and there has been no fraud or illegality on the part of the assured or his agents, the premium is thereupon returnable to the assured.

(2) Where the consideration for the payment of the premium is apportionable and there is a total failure of any apportionable part of the consideration, a proportionable part of the premiums is, under the like conditions, thereupon returnable to the assured.

(3) In particular : —

> (a) Where the policy is void, or is avoided by the insurer as from the commencement of the risk, the premium is returnable, provided that there has been no fraud or illegality on the part of the assured; but if the risk is not apportionable, and has once attached, the premium is not returnable;
>
> (b) Where the subject-matter insured, or part thereof, has never been imperilled, the premium, or as the case may be, a proportionate part thereof, is returnable:
>> Provided that where the subject-matter has been insured " lost or not lost " and has arrived in safety at the time when the contract is concluded, the premium is not returnable unless, at such time, the insurer knew of the safe arrival;
>
> (c) Where the assured has no insurable interest throughout the currency of the risk, the premium is returnable, provided that this rule does not apply to a policy effected by way of gaming or wagering;
>
> (d) Where the assured has a defeasible interest which is terminated during the currency of the risk, the premium is not returnable;

(e) Where the assured has over-insured under an unvalued policy, a proportionate part of the premium is returnable;

(f) Subject to the foregoing provisions, where the assured has over-insured by double insurance, a proportionate part of the several premiums is returnable:

Provided that, if the policies are effected at different times, and any earlier policy has at any time borne the entire risk, or if a claim has been paid on the policy in respect of the full sum insured thereby, no premium is returnable in respect of that policy, and when the double insurance is effected knowingly by the assured no premium is returnable.

MUTUAL INSURANCE

Modification of Act in case of mutual insurance

85.—(1) Where two or more persons mutually agree to insure each other against marine losses there is said to be a mutual insurance.

(2) The provisions of this Act relating to the premium do not apply to mutual insurance, but a guarantee, or such other arrangement as may be agreed upon, may be substituted for the premium.

(3) The provisions of this Act, in so far as they may be modified by the agreement of the parties, may in the case of mutual insurance be modified by the terms of the policies issued by the association, or by the rules and regulations of the association.

(4) Subject to the exceptions mentioned in this section, the provisions of this Act apply to a mutual insurance.

SUPPLEMENTAL

Ratification is assured

86. Where a contract of marine insurance is in good faith effected by one person on behalf of another, the person on whose behalf it is effected may ratify the contract even after he is aware of a loss.

Implied obligations varied by agreement of usage

87.—(1) Where any right, duty, or liability would arise under a contract of marine insurance by implication of law, it may be negatived or varied by express agreement, or by usage, if the usage be such as to bind both parties to the contract.

(2) The provisions of this section extend to any right, duty or liability declared by this Act which may be lawfully modified by agreement.

Reasonable time, etc., a question of fact

88. Where by this Act any reference is made to reasonable time, reasonable premium, or reasonable diligence, the question of what is reasonable is a question of fact.

Slip as evidence

89. Where there is a duly stamped policy, reference may be made, as heretofore, to the slip or covering note, in any legal proceeding.

Interpretation of terms

90. In this Act, unless the context or subject-matter otherwise requires:—

" Action " includes counter-claim and set off:

" Freight " includes the profit derivable by a shipowner from the employment of his ship to carry his own goods or moveables, as well as freight payable by a third party, but does not include passage money :

"Moveables" means any moveable tangible property, other than the ship, and includes money, valuable securities, and other documents:

"Policy" means a marine policy.

Savings

91.—(1) Nothing in this Act, or any repeal effected thereby, shall affect—

(a) The provisions of the Stamp Act, 1891, or any enactment for the time being in force relating to the revenue;

(b) The provisions of the Companies Act, 1862, or any enactment amending or substituted for the same;

(c) The provisions of any statute not expressly repealed by this Act.

(2) The rules of the common law including the law merchant, save in so far as they are inconsistent with the express provisions of this Act, shall continue to apply to contracts of marine insurance.

Repeals

92. The enactments mentioned in the Second Schedule to this Act are hereby repealed to the extent specified in that schedule.

Commencement

93. This Act shall come into operation on the first day of January one thousand nine hundred and seven.

Short title

94. This Act may be cited as the Marine Insurance Act, 1906.

SCHEDULES

FIRST SCHEDULE

FORM OF POLICY

Lloyd's S.G. Policy

Be it known that   as well in   own name as for and in the name and names of all and every other person or persons to whom the same doth, may, or shall appertain in part or in all doth make assurance and cause and them, and every of them, to be insured lost or not lost, at and from   Upon all kind of goods and merchandises, and also upon the body, tackle, apparel, ordnance, munition, artillery, boat, and other furniture, of and in the good ship or vessel called the   whereof is master under God, for this present voyage or whosoever else shall go for master in the said ship, or by whatsoever other name or names the said ship, or the master thereof, is or shall be named or called; beginning the adventure upon the said goods and merchandises from the loading thereof aboard the said ship,

upon the said ship, etc.,

and so shall continue and endure, during her abode there, upon the said ship, etc.

And further, until the said ship, with all her ordnance, tackle, apparel, etc., and goods and merchandises whatsoever shall be arrived at

upon the said ship, etc., until she hath moored at anchor twenty-four hours in good safety; and upon the goods and merchandises, until the same be there discharged and safely landed. And it shall be lawful for the said ship, etc., in this voyage to proceed and sail to and touch and stay at any ports or places whatsoever without prejudice to this insurance. The said ship, etc., goods and merchandises, etc., for so much as concerns the assured by agreement between the assured and assurers in this policy, are and shall be valued at

Touching the adventures and perils which we the assurers are contented to bear and do take upon us in this voyage: they are of the seas, men of war, fire, enemies, pirates, rovers, thieves, jettisons, letters of mart and countermart, surprisals, takings at sea, arrests, restraints and detainments of all kings, princes, and people, of what nation, condition, or quality soever, barratry of the master and mariners, and of all other perils, losses, and misfortunes, that have or shall come to the hurt, detriment, or damage of the said goods and merchandises, and ship, etc., or any part thereof.

And in case of any loss or misfortune it shall be lawful to the assured, their factors, servants and assigns, to sue, labour, and travel for, in and about the defence, safeguards, and recovery of the said goods and merchandises, and ship, etc., or any part thereof without prejudice to this insurance; to the charges whereof we, the assurers, will contribute each one according to the rate and quantity of his sum herein assured.

And it is especially declared and agreed that no acts of the insurer or insured in recovering, saving, or preserving the property insured shall be considered as a waiver, or acceptance of abandonment. And it is agreed by us, the insurers, that this writing or policy of assurance shall be of as much force and effect as the surest writing of policy of assurance heretofore made in Lombard Street, or in the Royal Exchange, or elsewhere in London. And so we, the assurers, are contented, and do hereby promise and bind ourselves, each one for his own part, our heirs, executors, and goods to the assured, their executors, administrators, and assigns, for the true performance of the premises, confessing ourselves paid the consideration due unto us for this assurance by the assured, at and after the rate of

In Witness whereof we, the assurers, have subscribed our names and sums assured in London.

N.B.—Corn, fish, salt, fruit, flour, and seed are warranted free from average, unless general, or the ship be stranded—sugar, tobacco, hemp, flax, hides and skins are warranted free from average, under five pounds per cent., and all other goods, also the ship and freight, are warranted free from average, under three pounds per cent, unless general, or the ship be stranded.

RULES FOR CONSTRUCTION OF POLICY

The following are the rules referred to by this Act for the construction of a policy in the above or other like form, where the context does not otherwise require:—

1. Where the subject-matter is insured " lost or not lost," and the loss has occurred before the contract is concluded, the risk attaches unless, at such time, the assured was aware of the loss, and the insurer was not.

2. Where the subject-matter is insured " from " a particular place, the risk does not attach until the ship starts on the voyage insured.

3.—(*a*) Where a ship is insured " at and from " a particular place, and she is at that place in good safety when the contract is concluded, the risk attaches immediately.

(*b*) If she is not at that place when the contract is concluded the risk attaches as soon as she arrives there in good safety, and, unless the policy

240

otherwise provides, it is immaterial that she is covered by another policy for a specified time after arrival.

(c) Where chartered freight is insured " at and from " a particular place, and the ship is at that place in good safety when the contract is concluded the risk attaches immediately. If she be not there when the contract is concluded, the risk attaches as soon as she arrives there in good safety.

(d) Where freight, other than chartered freight, is payable without special conditions and is insured " at and from " a particular place, the risk attaches pro rata as the goods or merchandise are shipped; provided that if there be cargo in readiness which belongs to the shipowner, or which some other person has contracted with him to ship, the risk attaches as soon as the ship is ready to receive such cargo.

4. Where goods or other moveables are insured " from the loading thereof," the risk does not attach until such goods or moveables are actually on board, and the insurer is not liable for them while in transit from the shore to the ship.

5. Where the risk on goods or other moveables continues until they are " safely landed," they must be landed in the customary manner and within a reasonable time after arrival at the port of discharge, and if they are not so landed the risk ceases.

6. In the absence of any further licence or usage, the liberty to touch and stay " at any port or place whatsoever " does not authorise the ship to depart from the course of her voyage from the point of departure to the port of destination.

7. The term " perils of the seas " refers only to fortuitous accidents or casualties of the seas. It does not include the ordinary action of the winds and waves.

8. The term " pirates " includes passengers who mutiny and rioters who attack the ship from the shore.

9. The term " thieves " does not cover clandestine theft or theft committed by any one of the ship's company, whether crew or passengers.

10. The term " arrests, etc., of kings, princes, and peoples " refers to political or executive acts, and does not include a loss caused by riot or by ordinary judicial process.

11. The term " barratry " includes every wrongful act wilfully committed by the master or crew to the prejudice of the owner, or, as the case may be, the charterer.

12. The term " all other perils " includes only perils similar in kind to the perils specifically mentioned in the policy.

13. The term " average unless general " means a partial loss of the subject-matter insured other than a general average loss, and does not include " particular charges."

14. Where the ship has stranded, the insurer is liable for the excepted losses, although the loss is not attributable to the stranding, provided that when the stranding takes place the risk has attached and, if the policy be on goods, that the damaged goods are on board.

15. The term " ship " includes the hull, materials and outfit, stores and provisions for the officers and crew, and, in the case of vessels engaged in a special trade, the ordinary fittings requisite for the trade, and also, in the case of a steamship, the machinery, boilers, and coals and engine stores, if owned by the assured.

16. The term " freight " includes the profit derivable by a shipowner from the employment of his ship to carry his own goods or moveables, as well as freight payable by a third party, but does not include passage money.

17. The term " goods " means goods in the nature of merchandise, and does not include personal effects or provisions and stores for use on board.

In the absence of any usage to the contrary, deck cargo and living animals must be insured specifically, and not under the general denomination of goods.

SECOND SCHEDULE

ENACTMENTS REPEALED

Section 92

Session and Chapter.	Title or Short Title.	Extent of Repeal.
19 Geo. 2, c. 37.	An Act to regulate insurance on ships belonging to the subjects of Great Britain, and on merchandizes or effects laden thereon.	The whole Act.
28 Geo. 3, c. 56.	An Act to repeal an Act made in the twenty-fifth year of the reign of his present Majesty, intituled " An Act for regulating Insurance of Ships, and on goods, merchandizes, or effects," and for substituting other provisions for the like purpose in lieu thereof.	The whole Act as far as it relates to marine insurance.
31 & 32 Vict., c. 56.	The Policies of Marine Assurance Act. 1868.	The whole Act.

Appendix B

INSTITUTE CARGO CLAUSES.

1.	Warranted free of capture seizure and detention, and the consequences thereof or any attempt thereat, *piracy excepted*, and also from all consequences of hostilities or warlike operations, whether before or after declaration of war.	F. C. & S. clause.
2.	Warranted free of loss or damage caused by strikers locked out workmen or persons taking part in labour disturbances or riots or civil commotions.	Strikes, riots and civil commotions clause.
3.	General Average and Salvage Charges payable according to Foreign Statement or per York-Antwerp Rules if in accordance with the contract of affreightment.	G/A clause.
4.	Held covered, at a premium to be arranged, in case of deviation or change of voyage or of any omission or error in the description of the interest, vessel, or voyage.	Deviation clause.
5.	Including (subject to the terms of the Policy) all risks covered by this Policy from shippers' or manufacturers' warehouse until on board the vessel, during transhipment if any, and from the vessel whilst on quays wharves or in sheds during the ordinary course of transit until safely deposited in consignees' or other warehouse at destination named in Policy.	Warehouse to warehouse clause.
6.	Including risk of craft, raft, and/or lighter to and from the vessel. Each craft, raft, and/or lighter to be deemed a separate insurance. The Assured are not to be prejudiced by any agreement exempting lightermen from liability.	Craft, &c., clause.
7.	Including all liberties as per contract of affreightment. The Assured are not to be prejudiced by the presence of the negligence clause and/or latent defect clause in the Bills of Lading and/or Charter Party. The seaworthiness of the vessel as between the Assured and the Assurers is hereby admitted.	Bill of Lading, &c., clause.

1st August, 1912.

18600. Sold by WITHERBY & Co., Newman's Court, (74) Cornhill, London.

Appendix C

INSTITUTE CARGO CLAUSES (F.P.A.)

1. Warranted free of capture seizure and detention, and the consequences thereof or any attempt thereat, *piracy excepted*, and also from all consequences of hostilities or warlike operations, whether before or after declaration of war.

   F. C. & S. clause.

2. Warranted free of loss or damage caused by strikers locked out workmen or persons taking part in labour disturbances or riots or civil commotions.

   Strikes, riots and civil commotions clause.

3. General Average and Salvage Charges payable according to Foreign Statement or per York-Antwerp Rules if in accordance with the contract of affreightment.

   G/A clause.

4. Held covered, at a premium to be arranged, in case of deviation or change of voyage or of any omission or error in the description of the interest, vessel, or voyage.

   Deviation clause.

5. Including (subject to the terms of the Policy) all risks covered by this Policy from shippers' or manufacturers' warehouse until on board the vessel, during transhipment if any, and from the vessel whilst on quays wharves or in sheds during the ordinary course of transit until safely deposited in consignees' or other warehouse at destination named in Policy.

   Warehouse to warehouse clause.

6. Including risk of craft, raft, and/or lighter to and from the vessel. Each craft, raft, and/or lighter to be deemed a separate insurance. The Assured are not to be prejudiced by any agreement exempting lightermen from liability.

   Craft, &c., clause.

7. Including all liberties as per contract of affreightment. The Assured are not to be prejudiced by the presence of the negligence clause and/or latent defect clause in the Bills of Lading and/or Charter Party. The seaworthiness of the vessel as between the Assured and the Assurers is hereby admitted.

   Bill of Lading, &c., clause.

8. Warranted free from Particular Average unless the vessel or craft be stranded sunk or burnt, but the Assurers are to pay the insured value of any package or packages which may be totally lost in loading transhipment or discharge, also any loss of or damage to the interest insured which may reasonably be attributed to fire collision or contact of the vessel and/or craft and/or conveyance with any external substance (ice included) other than water, or to discharge of cargo at a port of distress, also to pay landing warehousing forwarding and special charges if incurred.

   F. P. A. clause.

1st August, 1912.

18601. Sold by Witherby & Co., Newman's Court (74) Cornhill, London.

Appendix D

(FOR USE ONLY WITH THE NEW MARINE POLICY FORM)

INSTITUTE CARGO CLAUSES (A)

RISKS COVERED

1   This insurance covers all risks of loss of or damage to the subject-matter insured except as provided in Clauses 4, 5, 6 and 7 below.

Risks Clause

2   This insurance covers general average and salvage charges, adjusted or determined according to the contract of affreightment and/or the governing law and practice, incurred to avoid or in connection with the avoidance of loss from any cause except those excluded in Clauses 4, 5, 6 and 7 or elsewhere in this insurance.

General Average Clause

3   This insurance is extended to indemnify the Assured against such proportion of liability under the contract of affreightment "Both to Blame Collision" Clause as is in respect of a loss recoverable hereunder. In the event of any claim by shipowners under the said Clause the Assured agree to notify the Underwriters who shall have the right, at their own cost and expense, to defend the Assured against such claim.

"Both to Blame Collision" Clause

EXCLUSIONS

4   In no case shall this insurance cover

General Exclusions Clause

   4.1   loss damage or expense attributable to wilful misconduct of the Assured

   4.2   ordinary leakage, ordinary loss in weight or volume, or ordinary wear and tear of the subject-matter insured

   4.3   loss damage or expense caused by insufficiency or unsuitability of packing or preparation of the subject-matter insured (for the purpose of this Clause 4.3 "packing" shall be deemed to include stowage in a container or liftvan but only when such stowage is carried out prior to attachment of this insurance or by the Assured or their servants)

   4.4   loss damage or expense caused by inherent vice or nature of the subject-matter insured

   4.5   loss damage or expense proximately caused by delay, even though the delay be caused by a risk insured against (except expenses payable under Clause 2 above)

   4.6   loss damage or expense arising from insolvency or financial default of the owners managers charterers or operators of the vessel

   4.7   loss damage or expense arising from the use of any weapon of war employing atomic or nuclear fission and/or fusion or other like reaction or radioactive force or matter.

5   5.1   In no case shall this insurance cover loss damage or expense arising from

Unseaworthiness and Unfitness Exclusion Clause

            unseaworthiness of vessel or craft,

            unfitness of vessel craft conveyance container or liftvan for the safe carriage of the subject-matter insured,

         where the Assured or their servants are privy to such unseaworthiness or unfitness, at the time the subject-matter insured is loaded therein.

   5.2   The Underwriters waive any breach of the implied warranties of seaworthiness of the ship and fitness of the ship to carry the subject-matter insured to destination, unless the Assured or their servants are privy to such unseaworthiness or unfitness.

6   In no case shall this insurance cover loss damage or expense caused by

War Exclusion Clause

   6.1   war civil war revolution rebellion insurrection, or civil strife arising therefrom, or any hostile act by or against a belligerent power

   6.2   capture seizure arrest restraint or detainment (piracy excepted), and the consequences thereof or any attempt thereat

   6.3   derelict mines torpedoes bombs or other derelict weapons of war.

7   In no case shall this insurance cover loss damage or expense

Strikes Exclusion Clause

   7.1   caused by strikers, locked-out workmen, or persons taking part in labour disturbances, riots or civil commotions

   7.2   resulting from strikes, lock-outs, labour disturbances, riots or civil commotions

   7.3   caused by any terrorist or any person acting from a political motive.

DURATION

8   8.1   This insurance attaches from the time the goods leave the warehouse or place of storage at the place named herein for the commencement of the transit, continues during the ordinary course of transit and terminates either

Transit Clause

   8.1.1   on delivery to the Consignees' or other final warehouse or place of storage at the destination named herein,

   8.1.2   on delivery to any other warehouse or place of storage, whether prior to or at the destination named herein, which the Assured elect to use either

   8.1.2.1   for storage other than in the ordinary course of transit or

   8.1.2.2   for allocation or distribution,

         or

   8.1.3   on the expiry of 60 days after completion of discharge overside of the goods hereby insured from the oversea vessel at the final port of discharge,

   whichever shall first occur.

   8.2   If, after discharge overside from the oversea vessel at the final port of discharge, but prior to termination of this insurance, the goods are to be forwarded to a destination other than that to which they are insured hereunder, this insurance, whilst remaining subject to termination as provided for above, shall not extend beyond the commencement of transit to such other destination.

245

INSTITUTE CARGO CLAUSES (A)

8.3   This insurance shall remain in force (subject to termination as provided for above and to the provisions of Clause 9 below) during delay beyond the control of the Assured, any deviation, forced discharge, reshipment or transhipment and during any variation of the adventure arising from the exercise of a liberty granted to shipowners or charterers under the contract of affreightment.

Termination of Contract of Carriage Clause

9   If owing to circumstances beyond the control of the Assured either the contract of carriage is terminated at a port or place other than the destination named therein or the transit is otherwise terminated before delivery of the goods as provided for in Clause 8 above, then this insurance shall also terminate *unless prompt notice is given to the Underwriters and continuation of cover is requested when the insurance shall remain in force, subject to an additional premium if required by the Underwriters,* either

    9.1   until the goods are sold and delivered at such port or place, or, unless otherwise specially agreed, until the expiry of 60 days after arrival of the goods hereby insured at such port or place, whichever shall first occur,

    or

    9.2   if the goods are forwarded within the said period of 60 days (or any agreed extension thereof) to the destination named herein or to any other destination, until terminated in accordance with the provisions of Clause 8 above.

10   Where, after attachment of this insurance, the destination is changed by the Assured, *held covered at a premium and on conditions to be arranged subject to prompt notice being given to the Underwriters.*

Change of Voyage Clause

CLAIMS

11   11.1   In order to recover under this insurance the Assured must have an insurable interest in the subject-matter insured at the time of the loss.

Insurable Interest Clause

    11.2   Subject to 11.1 above, the Assured shall be entitled to recover for insured loss occurring during the period covered by this insurance, notwithstanding that the loss occurred before the contract of insurance was concluded, unless the Assured were aware of the loss and the Underwriters were not.

12   Where, as a result of the operation of a risk covered by this insurance, the insured transit is terminated at a port or place other than that to which the subject-matter is covered under this insurance, the Underwriters will reimburse the Assured for any extra charges properly and reasonably incurred in unloading storing and forwarding the subject-matter to the destination to which it is insured hereunder.

Forwarding Charges Clause

This Clause 12, which does not apply to general average or salvage charges, shall be subject to the exclusions contained in Clauses 4, 5, 6 and 7 above, and shall not include charges arising from the fault negligence insolvency or financial default of the Assured or their servants.

13   No claim for Constructive Total Loss shall be recoverable hereunder unless the subject-matter insured is reasonably abandoned either on account of its actual total loss appearing to be unavoidable or because the cost of recovering, reconditioning and forwarding the subject-matter to the destination to which it is insured would exceed its value on arrival.

Constructive Total Loss Clause

14   14.1   If any Increased Value insurance is effected by the Assured on the cargo insured herein the agreed value of the cargo shall be deemed to be increased to the total amount insured under this insurance and all Increased Value insurances covering the loss, and liability under this insurance shall be in such proportion as the sum insured herein bears to such total amount insured.

Increased Value Clause

    In the event of claim the Assured shall provide the Underwriters with evidence of the amounts insured under all other insurances.

    14.2   **Where this insurance is on Increased Value the following clause shall apply:**
    The agreed value of the cargo shall be deemed to be equal to the total amount insured under the primary insurance and all Increased Value insurances covering the loss and effected on the cargo by the Assured, and liability under this insurance shall be in such proportion as the sum insured herein bears to such total amount insured.

    In the event of claim the Assured shall provide the Underwriters with evidence of the amounts insured under all other insurances.

BENEFIT OF INSURANCE

15   This insurance shall not inure to the benefit of the carrier or other bailee.

Not to Inure Clause

MINIMISING LOSSES

16   It is the duty of the Assured and their servants and agents in respect of loss recoverable hereunder

Duty of Assured Clause

    16.1   to take such measures as may be reasonable for the purpose of averting or minimising such loss, and

    16.2   to ensure that all rights against carriers, bailees or other third parties are properly preserved and exercised

    and the Underwriters will, in addition to any loss recoverable hereunder, reimburse the Assured for any charges properly and reasonably incurred in pursuance of these duties.

17   Measures taken by the Assured or the Underwriters with the object of saving, protecting or recovering the subject-matter insured shall not be considered as a waiver or acceptance of abandonment or otherwise prejudice the rights of either party.

Waiver Clause

AVOIDANCE OF DELAY

18   It is a condition of this insurance that the Assured shall act with reasonable despatch in all circumstances within their control.

Reasonable Despatch Clause

LAW AND PRACTICE

19   This insurance is subject to English law and practice.

English Law and Practice Clause

NOTE:— It is necessary for the Assured when they become aware of an event which is "held covered" under this insurance to give prompt notice to the Underwriters and the right to such cover is dependent upon compliance with this obligation.

Appendix E

(FOR USE ONLY WITH THE NEW MARINE POLICY FORM)

INSTITUTE CARGO CLAUSES (B)

RISKS COVERED

1 This insurance covers, except as provided in Clauses 4, 5, 6 and 7 below,

  1.1   loss of or damage to the subject-matter insured reasonably attributable to   *Risks Clause*

  1.1.1   fire or explosion

  1.1.2   vessel or craft being stranded grounded sunk or capsized

  1.1.3   overturning or derailment of land conveyance

  1.1.4   collision or contact of vessel craft or conveyance with any external object other than water

  1.1.5   discharge of cargo at a port of distress

  1.1.6   earthquake volcanic eruption or lightning,

  1.2   loss of or damage to the subject-matter insured caused by

  1.2.1   general average sacrifice

  1.2.2   jettison or washing overboard

  1.2.3   entry of sea lake or river water into vessel craft hold conveyance container liftvan or place of storage,

  1.3   total loss of any package lost overboard or dropped whilst loading on to, or unloading from, vessel or craft.

2 This insurance covers general average and salvage charges, adjusted or determined according to the contract of affreightment and/or the governing law and practice, incurred to avoid or in connection with the avoidance of loss from any cause except those excluded in Clauses 4, 5, 6 and 7 or elsewhere in this insurance.   *General Average Clause*

3 This insurance is extended to indemnify the Assured against such proportion of liability under the contract of affreightment "Both to Blame Collision" Clause as is in respect of a loss recoverable hereunder. In the event of any claim by shipowners under the said Clause the Assured agree to notify the Underwriters who shall have the right, at their own cost and expense, to defend the Assured against such claim.   *"Both to Blame Collision" Clause*

EXCLUSIONS

4 In no case shall this insurance cover   *General Exclusions Clause*

  4.1   loss damage or expense attributable to wilful misconduct of the Assured

  4.2   ordinary leakage, ordinary loss in weight or volume, or ordinary wear and tear of the subject-matter insured

  4.3   loss damage or expense caused by insufficiency or unsuitability of packing or preparation of the subject-matter insured (for the purpose of this Clause 4.3 "packing" shall be deemed to include stowage in a container or liftvan but only when such stowage is carried out prior to attachment of this insurance or by the Assured or their servants)

  4.4   loss damage or expense caused by inherent vice or nature of the subject-matter insured

  4.5   loss damage or expense proximately caused by delay, even though the delay be caused by a risk insured against (except expenses payable under Clause 2 above)

  4.6   loss damage or expense arising from insolvency or financial default of the owners managers charterers or operators of the vessel

  4.7   deliberate damage to or deliberate destruction of the subject-matter insured or any part thereof by the wrongful act of any person or persons

  4.8   loss damage or expense arising from the use of any weapon of war employing atomic or nuclear fission and/or fusion or other like reaction or radioactive force or matter.

5 5.1   In no case shall this insurance cover loss damage or expense arising from   *Unseaworthiness and Unfitness Exclusion Clause*

        unseaworthiness of vessel or craft,

        unfitness of vessel craft conveyance container or liftvan for the safe carriage of the subject-matter insured,

    where the Assured or their servants are privy to such unseaworthiness or unfitness, at the time the subject-matter insured is loaded therein.

  5.2   The Underwriters waive any breach of the implied warranties of seaworthiness of the ship and fitness of the ship to carry the subject-matter insured to destination, unless the Assured or their servants are privy to such unseaworthiness or unfitness.

6 In no case shall this insurance cover loss damage or expense caused by   *War Exclusion Clause*

  6.1   war civil war revolution rebellion insurrection, or civil strife arising therefrom, or any hostile act by or against a belligerent power

  6.2   capture seizure arrest restraint or detainment, and the consequences thereof or any attempt thereat

  6.3   derelict mines torpedoes bombs or other derelict weapons of war.

7 In no case shall this insurance cover loss damage or expense   *Strikes Exclusion Clause*

  7.1   caused by strikers, locked-out workmen, or persons taking part in labour disturbances, riots or civil commotions

  7.2   resulting from strikes, lock-outs, labour disturbances, riots or civil commotions

  7.3   caused by any terrorist or any person acting from a political motive.

DURATION

8 8.1   This insurance attaches from the time the goods leave the warehouse or place of storage at the place named herein for the commencement of the transit, continues during the ordinary course of transit and terminates either   *Transit Clause*

247

INSTITUTE CARGO CLAUSES (B)

8.1.1   on delivery to the Consignees' or other final warehouse or place of storage at the destination named herein,

8.1.2   on delivery to any other warehouse or place of storage, whether prior to or at the destination named herein, which the Assured elect to use either

8.1.2.1   for storage other than in the ordinary course of transit or

8.1.2.2   for allocation or distribution,

or

8.1.3   on the expiry of 60 days after completion of discharge overside of the goods hereby insured from the oversea vessel at the final port of discharge,

whichever shall first occur.

8.2   If, after discharge overside from the oversea vessel at the final port of discharge, but prior to termination of this insurance, the goods are to be forwarded to a destination other than that to which they are insured hereunder, this insurance, whilst remaining subject to termination as provided for above, shall not extend beyond the commencement of transit to such other destination.

8.3   This insurance shall remain in force (subject to termination as provided for above and to the provisions of Clause 9 below) during delay beyond the control of the Assured, any deviation, forced discharge, reshipment or transhipment and during any variation of the adventure arising from the exercise of a liberty granted to shipowners or charterers under the contract of affreightment.

9   If owing to circumstances beyond the control of the Assured either the contract of carriage is terminated at a port or place other than the destination named therein or the transit is otherwise terminated before delivery of the goods as provided for in Clause 8 above, then this insurance shall also terminate *unless prompt notice is given to the Underwriters and continuation of cover is requested when the insurance shall remain in force, subject to an additional premium if required by the Underwriters,* either   Termination of Contract of Carriage Clause

9.1   until the goods are sold and delivered at such port or place, or, unless otherwise specially agreed, until the expiry of 60 days after arrival of the goods hereby insured at such port or place, whichever shall first occur,

or

9.2   if the goods are forwarded within the said period of 60 days (or any agreed extension thereof) to the destination named herein or to any other destination, until terminated in accordance with the provisions of Clause 8 above.

10   Where, after attachment of this insurance, the destination is changed by the Assured, *held covered at a premium and on conditions to be arranged subject to prompt notice being given to the Underwriters.*   Change of Voyage Clause

CLAIMS

11   11.1   In order to recover under this insurance the Assured must have an insurable interest in the subject-matter insured at the time of the loss.   Insurable Interest Clause

11.2   Subject to 11.1 above, the Assured shall be entitled to recover for insured loss occurring during the period covered by this insurance, notwithstanding that the loss occurred before the contract of insurance was concluded, unless the Assured were aware of the loss and the Underwriters were not.

12   Where, as a result of the operation of a risk covered by this insurance, the insured transit is terminated at a port or place other than that to which the subject-matter is covered under this insurance, the Underwriters will reimburse the Assured for any extra charges properly and reasonably incurred in unloading storing and forwarding the subject-matter to the destination to which it is insured hereunder.   Forwarding Charges Clause

This Clause 12, which does not apply to general average or salvage charges, shall be subject to the exclusions contained in Clauses 4, 5, 6 and 7 above, and shall not include charges arising from the fault negligence insolvency or financial default of the Assured or their servants.

13   No claim for Constructive Total Loss shall be recoverable hereunder unless the subject-matter insured is reasonably abandoned either on account of its actual total loss appearing to be unavoidable or because the cost of recovering, reconditioning and forwarding the subject-matter to the destination to which it is insured would exceed its value on arrival.   Constructive Total Loss Clause

14   14.1   If any Increased Value insurance is effected by the Assured on the cargo insured herein the agreed value of the cargo shall be deemed to be increased to the total amount insured under this insurance and all Increased Value insurances covering the loss, and liability under this insurance shall be in such proportion as the sum insured herein bears to such total amount insured.   Increased Value Clause

In the event of claim the Assured shall provide the Underwriters with evidence of the amounts insured under all other insurances.

14.2   **Where this insurance is on Increased Value the following clause shall apply:**
The agreed value of the cargo shall be deemed to be equal to the total amount insured under the primary insurance and all Increased Value insurances covering the loss and effected on the cargo by the Assured, and liability under this insurance shall be in such proportion as the sum insured herein bears to such total amount insured.

In the event of claim the Assured shall provide the Underwriters with evidence of the amounts insured under all other insurances.

BENEFIT OF INSURANCE

15   This insurance shall not inure to the benefit of the carrier or other bailee.   Not to Inure Clause

MINIMISING LOSSES

16   It is the duty of the Assured and their servants and agents in respect of loss recoverable hereunder   Duty of Assured Clause

16.1   to take such measures as may be reasonable for the purpose of averting or minimising such loss, and

16.2   to ensure that all rights against carriers, bailees or other third parties are properly preserved and exercised

and the Underwriters will, in addition to any loss recoverable hereunder, reimburse the Assured for any charges properly and reasonably incurred in pursuance of these duties.

17   Measures taken by the Assured or the Underwriters with the object of saving, protecting or recovering the subject-matter insured shall not be considered as a waiver or acceptance of abandonment or otherwise prejudice the rights of either party.   Waiver Clause

AVOIDANCE OF DELAY

18   It is a condition of this insurance that the Assured shall act with reasonable despatch in all circumstances within their control.   Reasonable Despatch Clause

INSTITUTE CARGO CLAUSES (B)

LAW AND PRACTICE

19   This insurance is subject to English law and practice.

English Law
and Practice
Clause

NOTE:— It is necessary for the Assured when they become aware of an event which is "held covered" under this insurance to give prompt notice to the Underwriters and the right to such cover is dependent upon compliance with this obligation.

CL. 253.   *Sold by Witherby & Co. Ltd., London.*

Appendix F

(FOR USE ONLY WITH THE NEW MARINE POLICY FORM)

INSTITUTE CARGO CLAUSES (C)

RISKS COVERED

1   This insurance covers, except as provided in Clauses 4, 5, 6 and 7 below,   *Risks*
                                                                                                                    Clause

   1.1   loss of or damage to the subject-matter insured reasonably attributable to

   1.1.1   fire or explosion

   1.1.2   vessel or craft being stranded grounded sunk or capsized

   1.1.3   overturning or derailment of land conveyance

   1.1.4   collision or contact of vessel craft or conveyance with any external object other than water

   1.1.5   discharge of cargo at a port of distress,

   1.2   loss of or damage to the subject-matter insured caused by

   1.2.1   general average sacrifice

   1.2.2   jettison.

2   This insurance covers general average and salvage charges, adjusted or determined according to the contract of   *General*
    affreightment and/or the governing law and practice, incurred to avoid or in connection with the avoidance of   *Average*
    loss from any cause except those excluded in Clauses 4, 5, 6 and 7 or elsewhere in this insurance.   *Clause*

3   This insurance is extended to indemnify the Assured against such proportion of liability under the   *"Both to*
    contract of affreightment "Both to Blame Collision" Clause as is in respect of a loss recoverable hereunder. *Blame*
    In the event of any claim by shipowners under the said Clause the Assured agree to notify the Under-   *Collision"*
    writers who shall have the right, at their own cost and expense, to defend the Assured against such claim.   *Clause*

EXCLUSIONS

4   In no case shall this insurance cover   *General*
                                                                                                                    Exclusions
                                                                                                                    Clause

   4.1   loss damage or expense attributable to wilful misconduct of the Assured

   4.2   ordinary leakage, ordinary loss in weight or volume, or ordinary wear and tear of the subject-matter
        insured

   4.3   loss damage or expense caused by insufficiency or unsuitability of packing or preparation of the
        subject-matter insured (for the purpose of this Clause 4.3 "packing" shall be deemed to include
        stowage in a container or liftvan but only when such stowage is carried out prior to attachment of this
        insurance or by the Assured or their servants)

   4.4   loss damage or expense caused by inherent vice or nature of the subject-matter insured

   4.5   loss damage or expense proximately caused by delay, even though the delay be caused by a risk insured
        against (except expenses payable under Clause 2 above)

   4.6   loss damage or expense arising from insolvency or financial default of the owners managers charterers
        or operators of the vessel

   4.7   deliberate damage to or deliberate destruction of the subject-matter insured or any part thereof by the
        wrongful act of any person or persons

   4.8   loss damage or expense arising from the use of any weapon of war employing atomic or nuclear fission
        and/or fusion or other like reaction or radioactive force or matter.

5   5.1   In no case shall this insurance cover loss damage or expense arising from   *Unseaworthiness*
                                                                                                                            and Unfitness
        unseaworthiness of vessel or craft,   *Exclusion*
                                                                                                                            Clause
        unfitness of vessel craft conveyance container or liftvan for the safe carriage of the subject-matter
        insured,

        where the Assured or their servants are privy to such unseaworthiness or unfitness, at the time the
        subject-matter insured is loaded therein.

   5.2   The Underwriters waive any breach of the implied warranties of seaworthiness of the ship and fitness of
        the ship to carry the subject-matter insured to destination, unless the Assured or their servants are privy
        to such unseaworthiness or unfitness.

6   In no case shall this insurance cover loss damage or expense caused by   *War*
                                                                                                                    Exclusion
                                                                                                                    Clause

   6.1   war civil war revolution rebellion insurrection, or civil strife arising therefrom, or any hostile act by or
        against a belligerent power

   6.2   capture seizure arrest restraint or detainment, and the consequences thereof or any attempt thereat

   6.3   derelict mines torpedoes bombs or other derelict weapons of war.

7   In no case shall this insurance cover loss damage or expense   *Strikes*
                                                                                                                    Exclusion
                                                                                                                    Clause

   7.1   caused by strikers, locked-out workmen, or persons taking part in labour disturbances, riots or civil
        commotions

   7.2   resulting from strikes, lock-outs, labour disturbances, riots or civil commotions

   7.3   caused by any terrorist or any person acting from a political motive.

DURATION

8   8.1   This insurance attaches from the time the goods leave the warehouse or place of storage at the   *Transit*
        place named herein for the commencement of the transit, continues during the ordinary course of   *Clause*
        transit and terminates either

   8.1.1   on delivery to the Consignees' or other final warehouse or place of storage at the destination
        named herein,

   8.1.2   on delivery to any other warehouse or place of storage, whether prior to or at the destination
        named herein, which the Assured elect to use either

INSTITUTE CARGO CLAUSES (C)

8.1.2.1	for storage other than in the ordinary course of transit or	
8.1.2.2	for allocation or distribution,	
	or	
8.1.3	on the expiry of 60 days after completion of discharge overside of the goods hereby insured from the oversea vessel at the final port of discharge,	

whichever shall first occur.

8.2   If, after discharge overside from the oversea vessel at the final port of discharge, but prior to termination of this insurance, the goods are to be forwarded to a destination other than that to which they are insured hereunder, this insurance, whilst remaining subject to termination as provided for above, shall not extend beyond the commencement of transit to such other destination.

8.3   This insurance shall remain in force (subject to termination as provided for above and to the provisions of Clause 9 below) during delay beyond the control of the Assured, any deviation, forced discharge, reshipment or transhipment and during any variation of the adventure arising from the exercise of a liberty granted to shipowners or charterers under the contract of affreightment.

9   If owing to circumstances beyond the control of the Assured either the contract of carriage is terminated at a port or place other than the destination named therein or the transit is otherwise terminated before delivery of the goods as provided for in Clause 8 above, then this insurance shall also terminate *unless prompt notice is given to the Underwriters and continuation of cover is requested when the insurance shall remain in force, subject to an additional premium if required by the Underwriters,* either   *Termination of Contract of Carriage Clause*

9.1   until the goods are sold and delivered at such port or place, or, unless otherwise specially agreed, until the expiry of 60 days after arrival of the goods hereby insured at such port or place, whichever shall first occur,

     or

9.2   if the goods are forwarded within the said period of 60 days (or any agreed extension thereof) to the destination named herein or to any other destination, until terminated in accordance with the provisions of Clause 8 above.

10   Where, after attachment of this insurance, the destination is changed by the Assured, *held covered at a premium and on conditions to be arranged subject to prompt notice being given to the Underwriters.*   *Change of Voyage Clause*

CLAIMS

11   11.1   In order to recover under this insurance the Assured must have an insurable interest in the subject-matter insured at the time of the loss.   *Insurable Interest Clause*

11.2   Subject to 11.1 above, the Assured shall be entitled to recover for insured loss occurring during the period covered by this insurance, notwithstanding that the loss occurred before the contract of insurance was concluded, unless the Assured were aware of the loss and the Underwriters were not.

12   Where, as a result of the operation of a risk covered by this insurance, the insured transit is terminated at a port or place other than that to which the subject-matter is covered under this insurance, the Underwriters will reimburse the Assured for any extra charges properly and reasonably incurred in unloading storing and forwarding the subject-matter to the destination to which it is insured hereunder.   *Forwarding Charges Clause*

This Clause 12, which does not apply to general average or salvage charges, shall be subject to the exclusions contained in Clauses 4, 5, 6 and 7 above, and shall not include charges arising from the fault negligence insolvency or financial default of the Assured or their servants.

13   No claim for Constructive Total Loss shall be recoverable hereunder unless the subject-matter insured is reasonably abandoned either on account of its actual total loss appearing to be unavoidable or because the cost of recovering, reconditioning and forwarding the subject-matter to the destination to which it is insured would exceed its value on arrival.   *Constructive Total Loss Clause*

14   14.1   If any Increased Value insurance is effected by the Assured on the cargo insured herein the agreed value of the cargo shall be deemed to be increased to the total amount insured under this insurance and all Increased Value insurances covering the loss, and liability under this insurance shall be in such proportion as the sum insured herein bears to such total amount insured.   *Increased Value Clause*

In the event of claim the Assured shall provide the Underwriters with evidence of the amounts insured under all other insurances.

14.2   **Where this insurance is on Increased Value the following clause shall apply:**
The agreed value of the cargo shall be deemed to be equal to the total amount insured under the primary insurance and all Increased Value insurances covering the loss and effected on the cargo by the Assured, and liability under this insurance shall be in such proportion as the sum insured herein bears to such total amount insured.

In the event of claim the Assured shall provide the Underwriters with evidence of the amounts insured under all other insurances.

BENEFIT OF INSURANCE

15   This insurance shall not inure to the benefit of the carrier or other bailee.   *Not to Inure Clause*

MINIMISING LOSSES

16   It is the duty of the Assured and their servants and agents in respect of loss recoverable hereunder   *Duty of Assured Clause*

16.1   to take such measures as may be reasonable for the purpose of averting or minimising such loss, and

16.2   to ensure that all rights against carriers, bailees or other third parties are properly preserved and exercised

and the Underwriters will, in addition to any loss recoverable hereunder, reimburse the Assured for any charges properly and reasonably incurred in pursuance of these duties.

17   Measures taken by the Assured or the Underwriters with the object of saving, protecting or recovering the subject-matter insured shall not be considered as a waiver or acceptance of abandonment or otherwise prejudice the rights of either party.   *Waiver Clause*

AVOIDANCE OF DELAY

18   It is a condition of this insurance that the Assured shall act with reasonable despatch in all circumstances within their control.   *Reasonable Despatch Clause*

INSTITUTE CARGO CLAUSES (C)

LAW AND PRACTICE

19   This insurance is subject to English law and practice.

English Law
and Practice
Clause

NOTE:— It is necessary for the Assured when they become aware of an event which is "held covered" under this insurance to give prompt notice to the Underwriters and the right to such cover is dependent upon compliance with this obligation.

Appendix G

(FOR USE ONLY WITH THE NEW MARINE POLICY FORM)

INSTITUTE WAR CLAUSES (CARGO)

RISKS COVERED

1   This insurance covers, except as provided in Clauses 3 and 4 below, loss of or damage to the subject-matter insured caused by   *Risks Clause*

     1.1   war civil war revolution rebellion insurrection, or civil strife arising therefrom, or any hostile act by or against a belligerent power

     1.2   capture seizure arrest restraint or detainment, arising from risks covered under 1.1 above, and the consequences thereof or any attempt thereat

     1.3   derelict mines torpedoes bombs or other derelict weapons of war.

2   This insurance covers general average and salvage charges, adjusted or determined according to the contract of affreightment and/or the governing law and practice, incurred to avoid or in connection with the avoidance of loss from a risk covered under these clauses.   *General Average Clause*

EXCLUSIONS

3   In no case shall this insurance cover   *General Exclusions Clause*

     3.1   loss damage or expense attributable to wilful misconduct of the Assured

     3.2   ordinary leakage, ordinary loss in weight or volume, or ordinary wear and tear of the subject-matter insured

     3.3   loss damage or expense caused by insufficiency or unsuitability of packing or preparation of the subject-matter insured (for the purpose of this Clause 3.3 "packing" shall be deemed to include stowage in a container or liftvan but only when such stowage is carried out prior to attachment of this insurance or by the Assured or their servants)

     3.4   loss damage or expense caused by inherent vice or nature of the subject-matter insured

     3.5   loss damage or expense proximately caused by delay, even though the delay be caused by a risk insured against (except expenses payable under Clause 2 above)

     3.6   loss damage or expense arising from insolvency or financial default of the owners managers charterers or operators of the vessel

     3.7   any claim based upon loss of or frustration of the voyage or adventure

     3.8   loss damage or expense arising from any hostile use of any weapon of war employing atomic or nuclear fission and/or fusion or other like reaction or radioactive force or matter.

4   4.1   In no case shall this insurance cover loss damage or expense arising from   *Unseaworthiness and Unfitness Exclusion Clause*

         unseaworthiness of vessel or craft,

         unfitness of vessel craft conveyance container or liftvan for the safe carriage of the subject-matter insured,

         where the Assured or their servants are privy to such unseaworthiness or unfitness, at the time the subject-matter insured is loaded therein.

     4.2   The Underwriters waive any breach of the implied warranties of seaworthiness of the ship and fitness of the ship to carry the subject-matter insured to destination, unless the Assured or their servants are privy to such unseaworthiness or unfitness.

DURATION

5   5.1   This insurance   *Transit Clause*

     5.1.1   attaches only as the subject-matter insured and as to any part as that part is loaded on an oversea vessel

         and

     5.1.2   terminates, subject to 5.2 and 5.3 below, either as the subject-matter insured and as to any part as that part is discharged from an oversea vessel at the final port or place of discharge,

         or

         on expiry of 15 days counting from midnight of the day of arrival of the vessel at the final port or place of discharge,

         whichever shall first occur;

         nevertheless,

         subject to prompt notice to the Underwriters and to an additional premium, such insurance

     5.1.3   reattaches when, without having discharged the subject-matter insured at the final port or place of discharge, the vessel sails therefrom,

         and

     5.1.4   terminates, subject to 5.2 and 5.3 below, either as the subject-matter insured and as to any part as that part is thereafter discharged from the vessel at the final (or substituted) port or place of discharge,

         or

         on expiry of 15 days counting from midnight of the day of re-arrival of the vessel at the final port or place of discharge or arrival of the vessel at a substituted port or place of discharge,

         whichever shall first occur.

     5.2   If during the insured voyage the oversea vessel arrives at an intermediate port or place to discharge the subject-matter insured for on-carriage by oversea vessel or by aircraft, or the goods are discharged from the vessel at a port or place of refuge, then, subject to 5.3 below and to an additional premium if required, this insurance continues until the expiry of 15 days counting from midnight of the day of arrival of the vessel at such port or place, but thereafter reattaches as the subject-matter insured and as to any part as that part is loaded on an on-carrying oversea vessel or aircraft. During the period of 15 days the insurance remains in force after discharge only whilst the subject-matter insured and as to any part as that part is at such port or place. If the goods are on-carried within the said period of 15 days or if the insurance reattaches as provided in this Clause 5.2

INSTITUTE WAR CLAUSES (CARGO)

5.2.1 where the on-carriage is by oversea vessel this insurance continues subject to the terms of these clauses,

or

5.2.2 where the on-carriage is by aircraft, the current Institute War Clauses (Air Cargo) (excluding sendings by Post) shall be deemed to form part of this insurance and shall apply to the on-carriage by air.

5.3 If the voyage in the contract of carriage is terminated at a port or place other than the destination agreed therein, such port or place shall be deemed the final port of discharge and such insurance terminates in accordance with 5.1.2. If the subject-matter insured is subsequently reshipped to the original or any other destination, then *provided notice is given to the Underwriters before the commencement of such further transit and subject to an additional premium,* such insurance reattaches

5.3.1 in the case of the subject-matter insured having been discharged, as the subject-matter insured and as to any part as that part is loaded on the on-carrying vessel for the voyage;

5.3.2 in the case of the subject-matter not having been discharged, when the vessel sails from such deemed final port of discharge;

thereafter such insurance terminates in accordance with 5.1.4.

5.4 The insurance against the risks of mines and derelict torpedoes, floating or submerged, is extended whilst the subject-matter insured or any part thereof is on craft whilst in transit to or from the oversea vessel, but in no case beyond the expiry of 60 days after discharge from the oversea vessel unless otherwise specially agreed by the Underwriters.

5.5 *Subject to prompt notice to Underwriters, and to an additional premium if required,* this insurance shall remain in force within the provisions of these Clauses during any deviation, or any variation of the adventure arising from the exercise of a liberty granted to shipowners or charterers under the contract of affreightment.

(For the purpose of Clause 5

"arrival" shall be deemed to mean that the vessel is anchored, moored or otherwise secured at a berth or place within the Harbour Authority area. If such a berth or place is not available, arrival is deemed to have occurred when the vessel first anchors, moors or otherwise secures either at or off the intended port or place of discharge

"oversea vessel" shall be deemed to mean a vessel carrying the subject-matter from one port or place to another where such voyage involves a sea passage by that vessel)

6 Where, after attachment of this insurance, the destination is changed by the Assured, *held covered at a premium and on conditions to be arranged subject to prompt notice being given to the Underwriters.* *Change of Voyage Clause*

7 **Anything contained in this contract which is inconsistent with Clauses 3.7, 3.8 or 5 shall, to the extent of such inconsistency, be null and void.**

CLAIMS

8 8.1 In order to recover under this insurance the Assured must have an insurable interest in the subject-matter insured at the time of the loss. *Insurable Interest Clause*

8.2 Subject to 8.1 above, the Assured shall be entitled to recover for insured loss occurring during the period covered by this insurance, notwithstanding that the loss occurred before the contract of insurance was concluded, unless the Assured were aware of the loss and the Underwriters were not.

9 9.1 If any Increased Value insurance is effected by the Assured on the cargo insured herein the agreed value of the cargo shall be deemed to be increased to the total amount insured under this insurance and all Increased Value insurances covering the loss, and liability under this insurance shall be in such proportion as the sum insured herein bears to such total amount insured. *Increased Value Clause*

In the event of claim the Assured shall provide the Underwriters with evidence of the amounts insured under all other insurances.

9.2 **Where this insurance is on Increased Value the following clause shall apply:**
The agreed value of the cargo shall be deemed to be equal to the total amount insured under the primary insurance and all Increased Value insurances covering the loss and effected on the cargo by the Assured, and liability under this insurance shall be in such proportion as the sum insured herein bears to such total amount insured.

In the event of claim the Assured shall provide the Underwriters with evidence of the amounts insured under all other insurances.

BENEFIT OF INSURANCE

10 This insurance shall not inure to the benefit of the carrier or other bailee. *Not to Inure Clause*

MINIMISING LOSSES

11 It is the duty of the Assured and their servants and agents in respect of loss recoverable hereunder *Duty of Assured Clause*

11.1 to take such measures as may be reasonable for the purpose of averting or minimising such loss,

and

11.2 to ensure that all rights against carriers, bailees or other third parties are properly preserved and exercised

and the Underwriters will, in addition to any loss recoverable hereunder, reimburse the Assured for any charges properly and reasonably incurred in pursuance of these duties.

12 Measures taken by the Assured or the Underwriters with the object of saving, protecting or recovering the subject-matter insured shall not be considered as a waiver or acceptance of abandonment or otherwise prejudice the rights of either party. *Waiver Clause*

AVOIDANCE OF DELAY

13 It is a condition of this insurance that the Assured shall act with reasonable despatch in all circumstances within their control. *Reasonable Despatch Clause*

INSTITUTE WAR CLAUSES (CARGO)

LAW AND PRACTICE

14   This insurance is subject to English law and practice.

English Law
and Practice
Clause

NOTE:— It is necessary for the Assured when they become aware of an event which is "held covered" under this insurance to give prompt notice to the Underwriters and the right to such cover is dependent upon compliance with this obligation.

CL. 255. *Sold by Witherby & Co. Ltd., London.*

Appendix H

1/1/82   (FOR USE ONLY WITH THE NEW MARINE POLICY FORM)

INSTITUTE STRIKES CLAUSES (CARGO)

RISKS COVERED

1   This insurance covers, except as provided in Clauses 3 and 4 below, loss of or damage to the subject-matter insured caused by   *Risks Clause*

1.1   strikers, locked-out workmen, or persons taking part in labour disturbances, riots or civil commotions

1.2   any terrorist or any person acting from a political motive.

2   This insurance covers general average and salvage charges, adjusted or determined according to the contract of affreightment and/or the governing law and practice, incurred to avoid or in connection with the avoidance of loss from a risk covered under these clauses.   *General Average Clause*

EXCLUSIONS

3   In no case shall this insurance cover   *General Exclusions Clause*

3.1   loss damage or expense attributable to wilful misconduct of the Assured

3.2   ordinary leakage, ordinary loss in weight or volume, or ordinary wear and tear of the subject-matter insured

3.3   loss damage or expense caused by insufficiency or unsuitability of packing or preparation of the subject-matter insured (for the purpose of this Clause 3.3 "packing" shall be deemed to include stowage in a container or liftvan but only when such stowage is carried out prior to attachment of this insurance or by the Assured or their servants)

3.4   loss damage or expense caused by inherent vice or nature of the subject-matter insured

3.5   loss damage or expense proximately caused by delay, even though the delay be caused by a risk insured against (except expenses payable under Clause 2 above)

3.6   loss damage or expense arising from insolvency or financial default of the owners managers charterers or operators of the vessel

3.7   loss damage or expense arising from the absence shortage or withholding of labour of any description whatsoever resulting from any strike, lockout, labour disturbance, riot or civil commotion

3.8   any claim based upon loss of or frustration of the voyage or adventure

3.9   loss damage or expense arising from the use of any weapon of war employing atomic or nuclear fission and/or fusion or other like reaction or radioactive force or matter

3.10   loss damage or expense caused by war civil war revolution rebellion insurrection, or civil strife arising therefrom, or any hostile act by or against a belligerent power.

4   4.1   In no case shall this insurance cover loss damage or expense arising from   *Unseaworthiness and Unfitness Exclusion Clause*

unseaworthiness of vessel or craft,

unfitness of vessel craft conveyance container or liftvan for the safe carriage of the subject-matter insured,

where the Assured or their servants are privy to such unseaworthiness or unfitness, at the time the subject-matter insured is loaded therein.

4.2   The Underwriters waive any breach of the implied warranties of seaworthiness of the ship and fitness of the ship to carry the subject-matter insured to destination, unless the Assured or their servants are privy to such unseaworthiness or unfitness.

DURATION

5   5.1   This insurance attaches from the time the goods leave the warehouse or place of storage at the place named herein for the commencement of the transit, continues during the ordinary course of transit and terminates either   *Transit Clause*

5.1.1   on delivery to the Consignees' or other final warehouse or place of storage at the destination named herein,

5.1.2   on delivery to any other warehouse or place of storage, whether prior to or at the destination named herein, which the Assured elect to use either

5.1.2.1   for storage other than in the ordinary course of transit or

5.1.2.2   for allocation or distribution,

or

5.1.3   on the expiry of 60 days after completion of discharge overside of the goods hereby insured from the oversea vessel at the final port of discharge,

whichever shall first occur.

5.2   If, after discharge overside from the oversea vessel at the final port of discharge, but prior to termination of this insurance, the goods are to be forwarded to a destination other than that to which they are insured hereunder, this insurance, whilst remaining subject to termination as provided for above, shall not extend beyond the commencement of transit to such other destination.

5.3   This insurance shall remain in force (subject to termination as provided for above and to the provisions of Clause 6 below) during delay beyond the control of the Assured, any deviation, forced discharge, reshipment or transhipment and during any variation of the adventure arising from the exercise of a liberty granted to shipowners or charterers under the contract of affreightment.

256

INSTITUTE STRIKES CLAUSES (CARGO)

6 If owing to circumstances beyond the control of the Assured either the contract of carriage is terminated at a port or place other than the destination named therein or the transit is otherwise terminated before delivery of the goods as provided for in Clause 5 above, then this insurance shall also terminate *unless prompt notice is given to the Underwriters and continuation of cover is requested when the insurance shall remain in force, subject to an additional premium if required by the Underwriters,* either

Termination of Contract of Carriage Clause

   6.1   until the goods are sold and delivered at such port or place, or, unless otherwise specially agreed, until the expiry of 60 days after arrival of the goods hereby insured at such port or place, whichever shall first occur,

   or

   6.2   if the goods are forwarded within the said period of 60 days (or any agreed extension thereof) to the destination named herein or to any other destination, until terminated in accordance with the provisions of Clause 5 above.

7 Where, after attachment of this insurance, the destination is changed by the Assured, *held covered at a premium and on conditions to be arranged subject to prompt notice being given to the Underwriters.*

Change of Voyage Clause

CLAIMS

8 8.1   In order to recover under this insurance the Assured must have an insurable interest in the subject-matter insured at the time of the loss.

Insurable Interest Clause

   8.2   Subject to 8.1 above, the Assured shall be entitled to recover for insured loss occurring during the period covered by this insurance, notwithstanding that the loss occurred before the contract of insurance was concluded, unless the Assured were aware of the loss and the Underwriters were not.

9 9.1   If any Increased Value insurance is effected by the Assured on the cargo insured herein the agreed value of the cargo shall be deemed to be increased to the total amount insured under this insurance and all Increased Value insurances covering the loss, and liability under this insurance shall be in such proportion as the sum insured herein bears to such total amount insured.

Increased Value Clause

   In the event of claim the Assured shall provide the Underwriters with evidence of the amounts insured under all other insurances.

   9.2   **Where this insurance is on Increased Value the following clause shall apply:**
   The agreed value of the cargo shall be deemed to be equal to the total amount insured under the primary insurance and all Increased Value insurances covering the loss and effected on the cargo by the Assured, and liability under this insurance shall be in such proportion as the sum insured herein bears to such total amount insured.

   In the event of claim the Assured shall provide the Underwriters with evidence of the amounts insured under all other insurances.

BENEFIT OF INSURANCE

10 This insurance shall not inure to the benefit of the carrier or other bailee.

Not to Inure Clause

MINIMISING LOSSES

11 It is the duty of the Assured and their servants and agents in respect of loss recoverable hereunder

Duty of Assured Clause

   11.1   to take such measures as may be reasonable for the purpose of averting or minimising such loss, and

   11.2   to ensure that all rights against carriers, bailees or other third parties are properly preserved and exercised

   and the Underwriters will, in addition to any loss recoverable hereunder, reimburse the Assured for any charges properly and reasonably incurred in pursuance of these duties.

12 Measures taken by the Assured or the Underwriters with the object of saving, protecting or recovering the subject-matter insured shall not be considered as a waiver or acceptance of abandonment or otherwise prejudice the rights of either party.

Waiver Clause

AVOIDANCE OF DELAY

13 It is a condition of this insurance that the Assured shall act with reasonable despatch in all circumstances within their control.

Reasonable Despatch Clause

LAW AND PRACTICE

14 This insurance is subject to English law and practice.

English Law and Practice Clause

NOTE:— *It is necessary for the Assured when they become aware of an event which is "held covered" under this insurance to give prompt notice to the Underwriters and the right to such cover is dependent upon compliance with this obligation.*

Index

A

absence of labour (strikes) 206
absorption into casks 96
"Achille Lauro" 218
Additional Expenses Clauses 195, 207
air — transhipment by 158
"all consequences of hostilities" 160 *et seq.*
allocation of goods after discharge 137 *et seq.*
"all other perils" 3, 17, 22
All Risks:
    clauses 12, 16, 18
    meaning of 24
    wrongful conversion 68
    wrongful misappropriation 152
"all risks minus exceptions" approach 18
alter ego of a company 85
ambiguity in policy (war risks) 158, 192
American Cargo War Risk Reinsurance Exchange 197
American Civil War 184, 186
Anglo-Spanish Treaty, 1713 60
"any attempt thereat" 161, 164, 166, 168, 177, 186
"any hostile act by or against a belligerent power" 166, 168, 174, 177, 187, 197, 198, 202, 216, 217
apportionable part (total loss) 6
Arab-Israeli War 193
Arab War Risk Insurance Syndicate 159
"Arco Tees" 199
arrest, meaning of 188
arrest, restraint, or detainment 56, 160, 161, 168, 177, 187 *et seq.*
arrival, meaning of 143
    war risks 156
arson 88
"Asakura Maru No. 12" 199
assignment:
    of policy 30
    of interest 30
atomic weapons 26, 90, 91, 155, 201
Attestation, the 16
Average Clauses 7 *et seq.*
    W.A. Clause 10, 17
    F.P.A. Clause (1883) 7
    F.P.A. Clause (1912) 7
    F.P.A. Clause (1963) 17
"average irrespective of percentage" 11
"average unless general" 3; 4; 10